Sailing Under
John Paul Jones

Sailing Under John Paul Jones

The Memoir of Continental Navy Midshipman Nathaniel Fanning, 1778–1783

NATHANIEL FANNING

Edited by LOUIS ARTHUR NORTON

McFarland & Company, Inc., Publishers
Jefferson, North Carolina

Frontispiece: Nathaniel Fanning, circa 1800 (image from 1936 reprint of *The Log of the Bon Homme Richard* published by the Marine Historical Association, courtesy Blunt White Library, Mystic Seaport Museum).

ISBN (print) 978-1-4766-7960-0
ISBN (ebook) 978-1-4766-3754-9

LIBRARY OF CONGRESS AND BRITISH LIBRARY
CATALOGUING DATA ARE AVAILABLE

© 2020 Louis Arthur Norton. All rights reserved

No part of this book may be reproduced or transmitted in any form or by any means, electronic or mechanical, including photocopying or recording, or by any information storage and retrieval system, without permission in writing from the publisher.

Front cover artwork: *Fighting Tops, 29 May 1781,* by Charles H. Waterhouse, USMCR (Art Collection, National Museum of the Marine Corps, Triangle, Virginia)

Printed in the United States of America

*McFarland & Company, Inc., Publishers
Box 611, Jefferson, North Carolina 28640
www.mcfarlandpub.com*

To my grandchildren Sara, Jake, Sam and Caroline

The revolutionary war is a glorious Testimony in favor of Plebeian Virtu—our military and naval men are sensible of this Truth. I myself know that our Seamen who were Prisoners in England refused all the allurements that were made use of, to draw them from their allegiance to their Country—threatened with ignominious Halters, they still refused. This was not the case with the English Seamen, who, on being made Prisoners entered into the American Service and pointed out where other Prisoners could be made—and this arose from a plain cause. The Americans were all free and equal to any of their fellow citizens—the English Seamen were not so.

—Benjamin Franklin

Table of Contents

Editor's Acknowledgments	viii
Editor's Preface	1
Editor's Introduction	3
1. Catch and Release	7
2. Manifold Malevolent Captains Contentious	18
3. The Battle Between *Good Man Richard* and HBM Warship *Serapis*	25
4. Aftermath	35
5. The *Alliance* as Flagship	49
6. Taking Command of the *Ariel*	60
7. Adventures as a French Privateer	79
8. French Privateer Captain Fanning	100
9. Lieutenant in the French Navy	126
10. Aftermath of War	138
11. Reflections on French Society	149
A Brief Overview of Nathaniel Fanning's Career	155
Editor's Postscript	157
Chapter Notes	159
Bibliography	167
Index	169

Editor's Acknowledgments

This work would not have come about and been completed without many friends who have guided my maritime writings over several years. First is Jim Bradford who edited my first attempt at a maritime history biography about Joshua Barney. Also, John Hattendorf, Bill Fowler and Edward (Ted) Sloan who were especially influential teachers at Mystic Seaport's Munson Institute some years ago. Deidre Regan and Faye Kert, editors of *Sea History* and *The Northern Mariner* respectively, who between them have kindly given me over one hundred books to read and review for publication.

I also wish to thank the staff at the Naval History and Heritage Command in Washington for their assistance in helping me assemble the illustrations from their collection. These are indicated NHHC followed by a NH or NK or USN plus a catalog number.

I have been blessed with being a member of a Simsbury writer's group that read and critiqued my various literary efforts: my friends Carol Healy, Pamela Kelley, Shirley Whiddon, Christian Cruz, Beth Brody, Ames Swartzfager, and Brian Thiem. Also, Tido Holtkamp, my frequent coffee mate who expanded both my literary and seafaring horizons.

I probably should acknowledge my genes: the late, highly regarded maritime historian Arthur Jacob Marder was a cousin. Despite my best efforts and those who helped with the editing of this book deficiencies may remain and I accept responsibility for them.

Finally, my special thanks to my wonderfully patient, eagle-eyed and good-natured wife Elinor, my first draft reader and critique-offerer *par excellence*. Her steadfast support has been essential to the completion of this project.

Editor's Preface

A year after Nathaniel Fanning's death in 1805, his brother Edmund published Fanning's memoir about his life as a Continental Navy mid-shipman sailing under John Paul Jones and later as a French/American privateer officer during the last years of the American Revolutionary War. The title of the original work is *Fanning's Narrative: The Memoirs of Nathaniel Fanning 1778–1783*. Three years later, Edmund published a second edition, changing the title to *Memoirs of the Life of Captain Nathaniel Fanning*. This present edition is an attempt to make more accessible for contemporary readers an eyewitness account of events during a notable moment in American history.

Fanning describes both the heroic and shamefully narcissistic character of John Paul Jones while serving under his command. He gives an eyewitness account of Jones's most famous battle between the *Bonhomme Richard* and the *Serapis*, and analyses of the personalities and temperaments of the English commander of the *Serapis*, Captain Richard Pearson, and Jones's first lieutenant, Richard Dale. Finally, the junior officer narrates a fascinating if at times convoluted story of his service for France during

John Paul Jones bust by Jean-Antoine Houdon, once owned by Thomas Jefferson (Naval History and Heritage Command, NH 48618).

1

the years just prior to the French Revolution. The memoir is a rich primary source of his service under Jones, but Fanning admits that he was not well educated. Although at times perceptive and thought provoking, his writing can be a challenge to understand in places. Part of this can be attributed to his use of the late seventeenth century language but his occasional long rambling sentences and paragraphs add to the perplexity.

This edited memoir endeavors to straighten the literary convolutions and linguistic obscurities, using more modern language where needed, and making some minor reorganizational changes, such as breaking the work into chapters to aid the reader by compartmentalizing Fanning's "adventures," while remaining consistent with the events described. A few paragraphs are reordered so that Fanning's written thoughts are less disjointed. Finally, spelling and grammatical errors are largely corrected or explained, and factual inaccuracies concerning people, historical references, times, and places are clarified by annotations.

Editor's Introduction

A Brief Maritime History of the Revolutionary War

In July 1775, three months before the creation of the Continental Navy, the Connecticut General Assembly "Resolved that two Vessels ... be immediately fitted out, Armed and furnished, with Officers, Men, and necessary Warlike Stores, for Defence of the Sea Coasts in this Colony, under the care and direction of The Governor and Committee of Council."[1] Connecticut, Fanning's home state, was among the earliest of the rebellious American colonies to establish a navy. In order to create a maritime force, there was a need for ships, cannon and other arms. They also needed an administrative system for pay to seamen, procedures for dividing shares in prizes, a structure for obtaining and distributing supplies, facilities for fitting out vessels, rules governing discipline, and a command structure for the issuance and execution of orders. The nascent Continental Navy and the state navies of the Revolutionary era were naturally modeled after the Royal Navy. They adapted British naval regulations, rank organization, discipline, and customs that were attuned to American conditions.

The American Revolutionary War at sea consisted of sporadic actions and major engagements to smaller skirmishes, but most commonly they were individual raids and cruises to frighten and intimidate local coastal populations. In addition to the Continental Navy, American ships of war included the navies of 11 states, amphibious landing fleets operated by the Army, privateers licensed by both Congress and the states, and a fair number of maritime freebooters. Sometimes these forces were combined to engage in a single objective, but more often they competed with one another for the services of seamen because of the substantially differing maritime rewards of military service or paramilitary occupations. Also, the battle arenas for American naval activity included Lake Champlain, many vital riverine locations, the Atlantic seaboard shores, the high seas, the British Isles, and the waters of the Caribbean.

The ships that clashed upon the Atlantic Ocean waters were mostly dominated by the Americans, the French and the English mariners, each striving for dominance. In late February 1776, American captain Esek Hopkins led a squadron of seven ships in a raid of the British island, New Providence (Nassau), to obtain military supplies and munitions. In an event known as the Battle of Nassau, on March 3 and 4, Hopkins landed an amphibious assault consisting of 250 marines and sailors to first overwhelm Fort Montague then seize Fort Nassau. The Americans captured 88 cannon and 15 mortars, but the British managed to evacuate much of the gunpowder, depriving them of one essential of their mission. Three years later, in August 1779, an American naval expedition of 44 vessels manned by more than 1,000 seamen under Captain Dudley Saltonstall, including 19 transports of state militia, attacked a small enemy emplacement called Fort George at Bagaduce [Castine] on Maine's Penobscot River.[2] The lack of a unified decisive command delayed the attack for many weeks. In the meantime, a small English fleet cut off their seaward escape. The American sailors and militiamen beached and burned their ships along the Penobscot River's shores. Later, when the French Navy left the Atlantic coast, British gunboats enabled turncoat Benedict Arnold to despoil Virginia in the early months of 1781.

Nevertheless, American sailors managed to acquire a measure of glory on the seas. Privateering Yankees in swift maneuverable schooners were very successful against the heavy English frigates. Privateers were likened to the frontiersman on land, daredevils on the prowl. Freelance raiders struck rich merchantmen carrying valuable West Indian commodities bound for the continent, as well as traded goods from Québec and Hudson Bay. They also intercepted British transports and redirected their supplies to needy Continental troops. Approximately 20,000 Americans sailed as privateers and took 2000 prizes and 16,000 British prisoners. Among the boldest American Continental Navy captains were John Paul Jones, Gustavus Conyngham, and Lambert Wickes, who struck English and Scottish ports, terrorizing British waters during 1778 and 1779.[3] British insurance rates rapidly rose, mercantile houses went bankrupt, and the Admiralty was compelled to divert many warships for convoy and patrol duty—a blow to British maritime prestige. Subsequently, morale declined on the British home front.

The neutral French made these Yankee exploits possible, sending their ships to the United States and the nearby West Indies, and also opened ports to the American privateers. At L'Orient, Brest and Bordeaux they were able to obtain crews for their cruises, mainly Frenchman, to harass the British coastal waters. They were also able to take their captured prizes to these same ports where they brought substantial prices when offered for sale. When the French allied with the Americans in the summer of 1778, the Americans lost easy access to nearby European ports. At the same time, the French-American alliance enabled their naval and privateer actions to merge on the English coasts; in fact, some American captains took commissions in the French Navy.

Privateering was a double-edged sword—it both helped and harmed the rebel cause. It attracted farmers, laborers and soldiers with the allure of potential profit, draining the Army and Navy of manpower. Greed seemed to overpower privateer ship owners and their crews. Raiders attacked neutral merchant ships and even those of their French allies. Privateering and profiteering led to inflation and market speculation. As an independent force, many privateers could not survive when the French withdrew in the summer of 1782. The Continental and State Navies were insufficient in number and power to mount a blockade against the overwhelming numbers of British ships of the line.

Nathaniel Fanning sailed under John Paul Jones during his cruises on the *Bonhomme Richard*, the *Serapis*, the *Alliance* and the *Ariel*. Fanning later obtained his own command and sailed from French ports to prey upon convoys and avoid British frigates, demonstrating the guile that characterized his mentor Jones. The vivid account of Fanning's life at sea during the Revolutionary War is a riveting tale of bravery and, at times, extreme hardship.

The following is a retelling of Fanning's memoirs of 1778–1783, partly written from the remembrances recorded in his journal, and with the help of friends who helped him recollect some forgotten details. The author states that the account was not intended as a publication for a general audience. This becomes evident as some details clash with the historical record and geographical data. Fanning also recognizes his scholarly shortcomings, "never having had but barely a common education; having followed the seas for a livelihood from his early youth upwards to the present time." However, his manner of writing may suit the reader as coming from the pen of an experienced sailor. Also, it is obvious that vocabulary and writing styles have changed over 200-plus years. Fanning's narrative digresses at times, causing confusion.

It is also important to note that passage of time can distort a narrator's memory, and a memoir can be a self-serving opportunity to place oneself on a pedestal and perhaps vilify enemies. Fanning's memoir is a literary porthole—a chronicle of a junior officer's service during a portion of the Revolutionary War, under the legendary American naval hero John Paul Jones, whom Fanning considered a brave and brash tyrannical narcissist. He also relates his experiences a captain of a privateer flying a French flag, and finally his impression of the British and French courts and societies at the close of the war.

Fanning Family Biographical Information

The Fanning family immigrated to America in 1653 and took root in southern New England. Nathaniel (1755–1805) was one of seven brothers fathered by Gilbert Fanning, all of whom went to sea.[4] Nathaniel was born 31 May 1755, in Stonington, Connecticut, a small town on the state's border with Rhode Island, at the eastern entrance to Long Island Sound. He was the oldest son of Captain Gilbert Fanning and Huldah, daughter of Captain Nathan Palmer of Stonington, Connecticut. He grew up in a little settlement about two miles northeast of Stonington, called by the Indian name of Wequetequock.

Nathaniel Fanning saw naval service in various capacities during the Revolutionary War, including captain's clerk, prize-master, midshipman and lieutenant, and finally captain of his own vessels. While a privateer, he was taken as a prisoner of war in the British frigate *Andromeda*, in which vessel British general Sir William Howe, victor at the Battle of Bunker Hill, was returning to England in 1778. Accepting an appointment as a midshipman in 1779 to sail under the command of John Paul Jones, Fanning was stationed in the maintop in the battle and ultimate surrender of the *Serapis* to the *Bonhomme Richard*. He was described as "An intelligent, sensible officer who had the good fortune and merit to overcome the enemy [that was] stationed in the maintop of the *Serapis*.... It was one of Midshipman Fanning's hand grenades dropped from the maintop into the hatch of the *Serapis* that caused the terrific explosion and [led to its] final surrender."[5]

Fanning returned to the United States at the end of the war onboard the French ship *Courier de l'Europe*, arriving at New York on 19 November 1783. Shortly thereafter he married his childhood sweetheart, Elizabeth Smith, daughter of Major Oliver Smith of Stonington. Their union produced one child, Lavinia, born 11 September 1796. She married Nathan Smith of Groton, Connecticut, 6 March 1814. Lavinia died 24 December 1879, aged 83 years, the mother of 10 children.

Two of Fanning's brothers were prisoners of the British during the Revolutionary War, one dying aboard the infamous prison ship *Jersey*, the other on the notorious *Strombolo*. But a third eluded a similar fate by the intervention of his important Tory uncle Edmund Fanning, a British North American colonial administrator and military leader.

When the Revolutionary War broke out, Edmund Fanning left his home in New York and joined the British Army. The revolution deeply divided the inhabitants of colonial North America. New York was affluent and arguably a vital American port stretching back through the 17th century. Citizens who supported the crown reasoned that their loyalty would be rewarded and New York's prosperity would persist. Edmund Fanning served with distinction during the New England and southern campaigns as a British soldier. When the war ended in 1783, he, like many Tories, settled in Canada. He eventually was appointed lieutenant governor of Nova Scotia and later obtained the rank of general in the Royal Army.

1

Catch and Release

I was born in 1755 and became an adult male as my country sought independence by way of a revolution between Great Britain and her American colonies. A group of my Connecticut friends became confident that the war would prove advantageous to life in America if the rebels prevailed. As a young man I learned the potentially lucrative as well as patriotic profession of privateering by way of two short but successful expeditions against the British. When I was 23 years old I left on a third cruise out of Boston on 26 May 1778. I signed on as a prize master for the new privateer brig *Angelica* under the command of William Dennis. The vessel mounted 16 guns and carried ninety-eight men and boys and was expected to spend about six months stalking and pursuing enemy shipping. The *Angelica* only encountered one other ship, a privateer out of Salem, Massachusetts. On 31 May at around noon we discovered another distant sail, hull down [only the vessel's sail was visible above the horizon] on the southeast horizon. Our privateer was moving well under a fresh north by east following breeze when the captain ordered the helmsman to make sail for the unidentified vessel. As the captain got a better look through the ship's spyglass and we got closer, Mr. Dennis assumed that we had encountered a lightly armed Jamaican merchantman as a potential profitable prey.

The entire crew was ordered to battle stations in preparation for action. By 4 o'clock in the afternoon however, it became clear that we had inadvertently stumbled upon a well-armed English frigate. *Angelica* abruptly wore-ship thus changing course to bring the wind around to our stern and sail in a westerly direction. The frigate, in response, immediately hauled out her guns and gave chase. In three quarters of an hour the warship came alongside and commanded our little but proud Yankee ship to haul down its colors. The British vessel turned out to be the *Andromeda*, an Enterprise-class sixth-rate Royal Navy Frigate built in 1777 and mounting 28 guns. Under the command of Captain Henry Byrne, the warship was five days from Philadelphia and carried a distinguished passenger on board, Major General William Howe. The general had been the commander the British troops at the Battle of Bunker Hill, had recently resigned his post as Commander in Chief of North American Forces and was now sailing to Portsmouth, England for his latest assignment, Commander of the Defense of the British Isles.

Being out sailed, outgunned and out-manned by the *Andromeda*, we showed prudence; the ship's company surrendered and abandoned the *Angelica*. Now as prisoners, the privateer's officers and crew were conducted to the quarterdeck of the frigate where the renowned General William Howe asked us a number of pointed questions. The most significant was if we were willing to engage in his majesty's service. None of the crew gave a positive response, so the general resorted to threat and intimidation. Howe stated that we were all rebels and were acting illegally as privateers. The British government did not recognize an American letter of marque commission or document; therefore, it is likely that we would all be hanged upon the ship's arrival in Portsmouth. Meanwhile we would all suffer from confinement in a hellhole. The master-at-arms was ordered on the quarterdeck. He and his contingent searched whatever baggage the crew managed to bring with them for concealed weapons.[1] They found none, but our baggage swiftly disappeared leaving us with nothing but the clothing we wore when were brought onboard. General Howe then ordered all prisoners confined to the ship's hold.

As we assembled to descend into what appeared to be hell on the seas, we were told to stop by a group of British Jack Tars. They began to strip us almost naked and tried to humiliate us by saying, "Damn your eyes, shipmate, but you have got a damned fine coat there, fine hat, fine shoe buckles, fine jackets, and fine britches."[2] Although the Tars seemed to admire our possessions by calling each item "fine," they were derided by larding us with a derogatory oath. This was followed by, "come, come, shipmates, these fine things will only be a plague to you, as the climate is very hot where you are bound," meaning the ship's hold. Then without any further remarks, they systematically stripped us of all our apparels.

A midshipman passed by during this time, who added to the humiliating event by saying, "That is right, lads, strips the damned rebels, and give each of them a frock and some trousers. [Those] will be good enough for them to be hanged in!"[3] Each of us was issued this simple garb, quick marched along, and then shoved unceremoniously down an open hatch and into the ship's bowels. Two sentries were placed at the hatchway entrance to assure that we would stay put. Once there, we were deprived of food for twenty-four hours. Late the next day we were sent a small pittance of provisions, about two-thirds of a normal prisoner of war allowance. We complained about this outrageous treatment to Captain Bryne and General Howe, but our grievance was ignored. When they did finally give us a sort of an answer they said that we were being treated with leniency. Because we were rebels and considered pirates of the high seas, we were guilty of despicable crimes and would soon meet a hangman. We certainly did not deserve mercy. At around 9 o'clock that night the British set our *Angelical* on fire. Because the vessel still had some gunpowder in her hold, the privateer blew up and then quickly sank to a watery grave. This was unusual because the British warship abandoned a potentially valuable prize, but the primary mission of the *Andromeda* was to transport the renowned general back to English shores as quick as possible.

We American prisoners shortly began to plot a way to take over the frigate while she was underway with our surgeon as the leader. Everyone approved of his plan and we agreed to carry it out at half after eleven at night on 3 June—or die in the attempt. The surgeon attempted to become a friend to some of the British crew and found several sailors who were sympathetic with the revolutionary cause. Meanwhile the effects of the heat that had built up in the orlop [lowest] deck took its toll on us as prisoners. We all were now reduced to going stark naked when secured below. In an act of compassion, small groups of us were allowed to spend a heavily guarded hour on the gun deck, but only once a day. Below decks was rapidly developing into the inferno that General Howe assured us that it would become. The dark damp confines were putrid in the sweltering foul air. Everyone crowded around whatever served as ventilation holes so that they might catch a breath in the almost airless maritime dungeon. Also, there was no provision for washing and little in the way of sanitation. As our misery became unbearable, most of us decided it was better to be cut to pieces by cutlasses than continue suffering in that dismal pit any longer. Our surgeon noted that many British sailors were showing signs of scurvy. If he was correct, he reasoned that the sentries would be physically weakened and not be able to put up much resistance. Also, some sympathetic British sailors who had likely been pressed into service become friendly with their surgeon. They had misappropriated some cutlasses and firearms, told the surgeon where they had hidden them and that they would aid us in an uprising.

The insurrection plan was complete and now ready for execution. The surgeon had succeeded in being allowed on deck overnight by the sailors that he had befriended and were complicit in the plot. Once topside, our leader also noticed that some of the watch spent much of their time asleep at their posts, a surprising lapse of security on a British warship. This meant that our chance of surprising groggy guards had an even greater chance of success. On the evening of 3 June, our sprits became heightened as the hour of the planned insurrection neared. Then at 9 o'clock, just two and a half hours before the planned uprising, Captain Dennis's clerk whose name was Spencer decided to take a stroll on the main deck to get some night air. It is not clear just how it happened, but he suddenly sensed that something was wrong and summoned marines and other sailors to arms. A group of prisoners in the hold became confused thinking that the plan had been executed and we were in control of the frigate. They then panicked when they saw that this had not occurred and now we were in deeper trouble. The heavy hatch covers were immediately placed over the holds and held fast with heavy bars so no one could ascend to the deck. General Howe shortly became aware of the thwarted uprising and ordered that we would now be given minimal rations, only enough to sustain our lives. This meant that we were to try to survive on a half pint of water per day very little food. Everyone in the hold went from the brief euphoria the preceded our attempted rebellion into a deep almost overwhelming depression. We believed that we would likely either die of heat prostration or malnutrition or both. The thought of being hanged now seemed a very distant peril. Although we were American rebels, legally and technically we knew that we were still British subjects. His Majesty's naval surrogates were at the present guilty of cruelty and inhumanity.

In what turned out to be a strange paradox, we prisoners managed to turn our adversity into an unexpected advantage. The ship's extra water casks were harbored below our hold and laid over with a temporary deck that could be easily penetrated. With a little ingenuity, we were able to use our cups to obtain sufficient water to provide for our needs. The general's storeroom happened to be adjacent to our hold, separated by a partition of planks. We had often seen the captain's steward and the general's servants come down to draw off wine, liquor, biscuits and specially preserved meats. The bungs of each cask were corked, but only with hand or finger pressure. We reasoned that it should be easy to pry a plank or two from the partition and obtain white biscuits (probably hard tack), raisins, other dried fruit, smoked hams, and salt beef all stored in tierces (special measures).[4] It was now necessary to find a way into the officer's storeroom. On the evening of 5 June, at around ten in the evening, a Rhode Island prisoner named Howard shouted that he would not go to sleep until he had a drink of Madeira wine. He said that he was ready to risk his life and serve both himself and his mates. He would attempt to breach the partitions and enter the storeroom.

The New Englander went to work and soon managed to shift the boards back and forth as he pleased. There was just enough room for a man to crawl into the storeroom and Howard went in. Before long he found himself among an array of casks and before long found one that appeared to hold Madeira. His mates passed him a mug or two and a few empty cans. Before he handed them back through the opening and said, "My friends, as good Madeira wine as ever was drunk at the table of an Emperor."[5] I judged that he consumed about half a pint, but then passed it on to a fellow sufferer. This went on some time and before long most became merrily drunk, especially "good old" Howard. Now with a secret access to the storeroom with the judicious shifting of a few boards we were able to eat rather well. The quality was excellent and it was available in quantity. It should last for the voyage if we did not become too greedy. Now the objective became to keep the servants from being aware of our pilfering.

As prisoners, suddenly we were living rather well. We took the precaution of securing the casks, but the dried fruit, wines and meats were, in fact present in large quantities. Some sailors who had been confined to the hold had consumed a large quantity of Jamaica spirits [rum]. This was done via a hole that was bored through a bulkhead upon which rested upon a large butt of the spirit. We then managed to enter the cask through a bunghole and sipped to their hearts content through hollow quills. It was a bounty, but it could be missed before the frigate docked in Portsmouth. We kept up a pretense of suffering under the general's imposed famine. When given our pittance of provisions and water, we acted as if we were both parched and famishing.

The remainder of the voyage in the hold was still stifling and unpleasant, but since it was June, the weather at sea was moderate. *Andromeda* largely sailed with a following wind and rode the Gulf Stream. Therefore the vessel made the journey to the British Isles in good time. Finally, when the warship reached its English destination on the last day of June 1778, a "medical miracle" was noted. A significant portion of the frigate's crew had become disabled, suffering from scurvy. General Howe and Captain Byrne were astonished that their prisoners appeared well and rather hearty. One of the captain's stewards and a general's servant reported that Howe could not understand why none of those damned Yankees was sick. It appeared to him that nothing but thunder and lightning would kill them.[6]

When we had reached their anchorage, the quartermasters hauled the casks up onto the deck. He noted two things, the casks seemed too light and their Yankee captive appeared both in good health and dispositions. They concluded that the Yankees must have found their way into the general's storeroom. They complained that the prisoners had deprived "us of many a good drink of Madeira, as well as old Jamaica *stingo*"[7] Their only solace was that the "poor devils," as they called us, would likely soon be hanged after they were sentenced.

After the ship came to its anchorage the rebels were assembled on the quarterdeck. The captain said they were to be transferred to another ship, the *Princess Amelia*. He stated that there you will all be hanged unless the King decides to pardon any of you. He then said that this was unlikely "as your offences are of the blackest kind."[8] After some additional scolding, we were shunted onto several small boats that were lying alongside and rowed to a place called Hazel Hospital. Their heading took us by the notorious gallows of "Jack the Painter" that stood on a nearby point of land.[9] As they got close by, the officer in command ordered his men to ship oars. He told us that the lot of us would soon be in irons and would share the same fate as the disreputable infamous "Jack" who had set fire to the navy's dockyards in Portsmouth and destroyed a large quantity of materials intended for use of the Royal Navy.

Once we arrived at Hazel Hospital a young-looking commissioner interrogated us, but one at a time. He was interested in where we were from, where we were bound, when we were captured, what vessel captured us and finally who issued the letter of marque under which the *Angelica* sailed. This was in stark contrast to our previous treatment. There was no abusive language or overbearing threats. In fact, he stated that we were to be considered prisoners of war and treated kindly with the chance of being exchanged for British sailors if the opportunity arose. He was aware that we had been robbed of all our attire and said that in a few days we would be furnished with new clothes at the King's expense. Once this examination was finished we were marched to Forton Prison.[10] This was the place where we would be charged with the crimes of piracy and high treason.

Forton was originally built as a hospital for sick and wounded sailors during the reign of Queen Ann. It consisted of two large buildings in the center of which was a large parade ground. Junior and non-commissioned officers, sailors and marines occupied the northern building. The southern building housed officers of more senior grades. As prisoners of war, we were accommodated upon a spacious lot of about three-fourths of an acre on level ground. In its center was a large shed that was open on all sides that allowed air to circulate freely with seats for the inmate's use and several grey bleak prison buildings. An eight-foot high picket fence surrounded this large yard.

Our daily life revolved around our sleeping quarters that were on the second floor of a stone and wood barracks about two hundred feet long and perhaps forty feet in breadth. Hooks were placed on each side of the building fastened to two rows of posts placed eight feet from the sides. Our hammocks were suspended from these hooks at night, but hung in either a slack or trussed-up position by day, thus affording us sufficient room for walking or exercise. Each prisoner was given what was called a "king's rug" (a crude coverlet) and a smaller version of this blanket sewn into a bag and stuffed with straw to serve as a pillow. These were similar to that used on prison-ships. They were so full of nits and lice that the first thing that we all did in the morning's light was remove all our clothes and delouse either ourselves or our companions while sitting on crude benches. We jokingly imagined that if his Majesty's government paid us one eighth of a farthing for each louse that we killed per day, we would all be very wealthy when we were freed. But this was really not a joking matter, on several occasions prisoners suddenly became quite ill and were hospitalized. More than a few men showed what appeared to be symptoms of poisoning, diagnosed by the few surgeons who were among us. It was not long before a rumor was started insinuating that

1. Catch and Release

the jailors were purposely trying to make us ill. By elimination we thought that the likely cause was contaminated bread. Indeed, we found that the bakery had added powdered ground glass to the flour. Once again, we lost all respect for any semblance of empathy in our British jailors.

An unexpected occurrence served to keep the prisoners in line, something outside of the prison compound. A group of peasants constantly lurked about the periphery equipped with snarling tracking dogs and sizeable wooden clubs. We learned that there was a bounty of five pounds sterling for capturing an escaped American prisoner, but only half a guinea for the capture of a Frenchman. One time a sailor broke out and within a short time seventy or eighty men and their dogs beat the bushes running in every direction until they tracked down the unfortunate Yankee. The escapee was brought to what amounted to the head jailor known as "old crab" by the American prisoners. Elderly and rather ugly, the man walked with a peculiar bowlegged gait that reminded us of the movement of a crab. He was creepy, rowdy, ill-tempered and seemed to enjoy inflicting cruelty as a type of revenge. Occasionally prisoners received charitable contributions from local clergy or church groups providing some comfort, but these contributions were rare. When this source was gone, we had to fend for ourselves trying to live off one meal a day and a small beer. Our ration was three fourths of that usually allowed common prisoners of war. The overseers considered this rather generous and we were constantly reminded of this. Because of persistent cravings and hunger, this pittance was quickly consumed.

The incessant hunger led many to do disagreeable things. Men would fight over scraps left in the yard or beg for food from the peasants who lived just outside the confines of the prison. If a bone was found and still had marrow, prisoners would take a sharp stick to pry out whatever was edible. Strangely this trifle became a thing of great value, a taste of imagined liberation within what seemed like a never-ending confinement. What was puzzling to us was a surprising number of local country people came to see us on almost a daily basis. This was particularly true on Sundays, but [they] were not counted. It seemed to us that at times they could amount to over a thousand. Some would look upon us with disdain, but mostly with curiosity. Some would say tentatively, "why, Lard, neighbour, there be white people; they taulk jest as we do, by my troth; thare's a paity such good looking paple shou'd be troused up (hanged) our grat men, etc." [sic.][11]

One afternoon an officer, it was believed to be a captain, in command of about a hundred prison guards seemed determined to seek retribution for some unknown offense. He perceived that one or more American rebels had insulted him. Anyway, the officer went into the guardhouse and grabbed a hot poker from the fireplace. He then made his way to the picket fence where the some of us prisoners were drying washed shirts in the sun. He then proceeded to burn dozens of shirts. The owners of the tops had no others to put on their backs, so they ran to the officer and begged them in a civil manner, to not burn the simple clothing they had been issued. The officer ignored their appeals and continued with his malicious behavior. Seeing this, a large number of American prisoners ran to the pickets and snatch away as many shirts as they could, but were careful to not use any abusive language and further infuriate him. The officer however became enraged and ordered a sentinel to fire his musket into the crowd. The soldier obeyed his command and killed one man and wounded several others. It was estimated that there were about three hundred Americans in the yard at the time, so the captain now became concerned that a riot might ensue. He ordered all of his guards to fix bayonets, rush the prisoners and drive them into a prison building that had bars and lockable doors. This was quickly done and a possible revolt was quelled. The next day a jury was convened that met in the "old crab's" house. There were about twenty witnesses among the inhabitants of Gosport who said that the sentinel had fired the lethal shot, quickly reloaded his piece, fired again and threaten the others to shut their mouths. Still, after some deliberations, the jury announced it verdict: manslaughter.

The only positive event that followed was a Mr. David Hartley, a plain humble man and a member of the British parliament came to visit. He claimed to be a friend of the Americans and talked kindly to the prisoners. The important message that he brought was that he was certain that there would be a prisoner exchange soon, perhaps in November 1778. We prisoners had little confidence that this would happen since there had been several rumors about a prisoner exchange over many months. Still, Hartley seemed to have some credibility and in the face of the hardships that we were enduring in close overcrowded confinement, it presented a powerful ray of hope.

The distressing thought of continuing in internment caused us to attempt to do something for ourselves like digging our way out. Since the prisoners were shut down in the prison from sundown to sunrise, the nights gave us the opportunity to undermine the prison fence and escape. Digging holes produced a lot of dirt and stones that had to be disposed of in a manner which would not be noticed by the guards. This detritus was placed in canvas bags and each passed back one at a time to an old unused chimney near the center of the prison. The outside brickwork had been whitewashed. Some of the prisoners were musicians and they were given instruments to make music to sooth their fellow inmates. Sometimes while the early digging was going on, several of these fiddlers played lively tunes and other men danced as a noise distraction for the guards. The work usually began around eleven o'clock and stopped about three in the morning when the sentinel's "All's well" call was usually sounded. At this time a white paper was placed over the hole and remarkably no one seemed to notice. An alternate place to dump the diggings was under the prison's garret and again a way was found to disguise the traces of the digging. If there was too much noise and the turnkeys were alerted, they would rush into the prison compound and use threatening abusive language, but they found all the lights extinguished and the prisoners in their hammocks, their bags secured. Sometimes this incursion would be repeated several times. Usually when the evening's labor was completed and the tailings safeguarded, the diggers tried to get some rest.

Some men managed to breach the fence and, with a little money to make their way to London, about seventy-five miles away, but regrettably they were soon apprehended and severely punished. The physical punishment could be endured, but the worse was being demoted to the far end of the exchange list.[12] A better alternative was to make one's way to a nearby fishing port, steal a small boat and cross the English Channel to France.[13] During this time three hundred and thirty-eight prisoners in Forton successfully escaped and made their way to France, all over a twelve-month period.

Humane treatment by Englishmen did occur. Thomas Wren, a Unitarian minister from Portsmouth gave escapees asylum in his home.[14] This was a place to hide, receive a change of clothes, a little money and a means of safe conveyance usually to hectic London, surreptitiously to Dover and finally on to Ostend.[15] The source of money was subscriptions from Englishmen sympathetic to the American cause prior to the Declaration of Independence. This financial spring dried up as the war progressed, but the money that remained and the little that could be subscribed again was distributed to help Americans held captive. Reverend Wren was appointed as the local trustee of this charity and made it a personal undertaking to visit us in prison, usually on a weekly basis. He called us his children and collected used clothes and anything else he thought useful for our comfort or survival. Unfortunately, some prisoners behaved badly toward this kind man, accosting him and insulting him with offensive language if he did not supply them with their wants. In spite of this abuse Wren asked for their patience and assured them that he would try to find whatever they requested.

The prison mostly confined Americans, but there were also a number of Frenchmen who had been captured while serving with their Revolutionary War allies. Some who were rather scholarly amused themselves by the teaching the French language to any interested American prisoners. Most of the latter regrettably were largely illiterate, but those who used their time prudently found masters to teach reading, writing, arithmetic and navigation as well as the foreign tongue. These skills prepared the intellectually curious for opportunities that could be life-changing when freedom was granted.

According to Rev. Wren, my deliverance from captivity appeared to be close at hand. As the expected day of release approached, my desire for freedom made each day and night appear longer, but the contemplation raised my spirits. My heart leapt with joy. On 2 June 1779, the day finally arrived. That afternoon an agent's clerk appeared in the yard and announced that a large group of us were to board a cartel in the morning and would be sent to France.[16] He called out the names one by one. I was one hundred and eighteen out of the hundred and twenty to be exchanged. Being so far down on the list caused some apprehension, but hearing my name read, provided an almost inexpressible joy. The next morning at 8 o'clock we were assembled in the yard and the names read aloud again. The rest of the remaining prisoners, about four hundred and eighty, were permitted to intermingle with us. They wished us well, some asking us to deliver messages to loved ones. At 10 o'clock we were organized into a company and marched with a forty soldier escort to the Portsmouth quay and our transport. Along our way, a ragtag group of British musicians and a boisterous drummer struck up the tune *Yankee Doodle*. They continued to play until we reached the dockside. The band likely played the song to mock us, but we heard it with a sense of pride. Yet it was sad in a way; it reminded us that we left behind many poor fellows who would likely remain prisoners for several more years. It must have been crushing for those left behind seeing their comrades leave to experience the liberty they so desperately desired.[17]

During our march through Gosport, the unusual sound of the band must have roused the populace. Crowds, mostly of women, gathered on the streets. Some wished us a safe journey to our homes, a few shouted huzzas, and others cursed us calling us loathsome rebels who deserved to be hanged if they had their way. Once at the quay, we were out of range of their bellows and embarked on the cartel. On 6 June we set sail for Nantes in France. We anchored off a small town on the Loire River about thirty miles west of Nantes. Once ashore a very large throng of people came out to welcome us. We were especially moved to see friendly children who sang as they followed us: *Bon, bon, bon, cettez Boston rompez auce aux des cannon* (Here are the good Bostonians who beat the English with their great guns).[18] Once we reached the town's center, a clerk to the American agent informed us that he had been directed to provide lodgings for us at the *Hôtel d'Orléans*.

It was now about noon and a dinner was provided to us. For the first time in many months, and in some cases years, we were provided with dishes, clean napkins, a glass tumbler rather than a tin cup, a spoon, fork and prongs, the latter to lift up what we desired without using our bare hands. After we were taken to our tables, one of comrades noted that there were no knives. Because it was known that I had learned a bit of French by spending time with our fellow French captives, I was asked to request some knives. I hesitated then politely asked for *des couteaux*. A lovely looking servant girl responded, "*oui monsieur*," and she brought us a plate of small molasses cakes that are known as *gateau*. My disastrous first attempt at speaking French caused a great amount of amusement among my countrymen. Embarrassed, but not giving up, I showed her a penknife. She looked puzzled for a moment than smiled saying *Oh monsieur, ce des couteqaux que vous vouliez* (O sir, it is knives that you want). She then returned with a number of knives so that we could cut into the sumptuous of dishes that were provided. In actuality before I left Forton I was able to converse with my French prisoner friends on most subjects and it appeared that I was well understood. Once I was on French soil however, my American accent became a liability. This embarrassing episode discouraged me from using the French language for some time thereafter, but later I became rather fluent in the tongue.

On the 12th, we finally embarked for Nantes. This fairly large city of the eastern bank of the Loire River is about fourteen leagues (roughly forty-two miles) from the Nantes River's entrance to the sea. The houses of hewed stone are four or five stories tall and present a pleasing appearance when viewed from afar as we approached the municipality. Once there, we noted that the streets were very narrow and dirty, but they are mostly paved. In the town's center was the Exchange, a level piece of ground of about two acres surrounded by fairly big trees that provided ample shade. This was the central marketplace where the local merchants and nearby residents assembled to do business from noon to 2 o'clock in the afternoon. I tarried in the city until the 23rd when a windfall of money was given to the recently freed prisoners from Forton from French gentlemen. It was enough to enable us to purchase decent clothing and gave us temporary financial security. We were very grateful for the generosity and the humane treatment that was provided to us. Now that I had some funds, I set off on the 27th for the port of L'Orient.

2

Manifold Malevolent Captains Contentious

The city of L'Orient is situated about one hundred miles west southwest of Paris. It has a deep-water harbor and is the homeport of many of the king's ships of the line as well as major merchant vessels. The seaport is difficult to enter because of the many sunken shoals near its entrance. The narrowness of the channel makes ships cautious when making passages and this waterway is well protected by nearby Fort Louis. Therefore, the harbor is easy to defend. The town itself is rather small and its dwellings are not as large or impressive as those at Nantes. Its streets are laid out in a regular pattern and well paved. The port has an excellent dockyard facility along with a row of long large buildings near the quay enabling easy off or onloading. Therefore, the city is a major mercantile center and was a commercial hub for the renowned East India Company. During the previous war between England and France, the British captured many of the ships belonging to this company. This vast trading enterprise was unable to completely recover from its losses incurred during this war, thus the town went into an economic depression. The king's agents now occupy the imposing dockside warehouses. The positive news was that we Americans are now heavily engaged in free trade and found a good market for our products like tobacco and cotton. In time, the city should recover and return to prosperity.

It was here that I met the legendary John Paul Jones. The captain was looking for crew for his new ship called *Bon Homme Richard*, but I always referred to it by its Anglicized the name, *The Good Man Richard*.[1] The vessel was anchored in the harbor, but soon to be bound for America. Jones said that I could sign on as a midshipman and sail home onboard her. I went on board and, after talking to some officers, learned that the vessel would be first bound for the English Channel before transiting cross the Atlantic. This detour did not seem to present a problem, but I failed to ask about the captain's plans while sailing *The Good Man Richard* in the Channel. Since I had

2. Manifold Malevolent Captains Contentious

no other opportunity to find safe passage home, I accepted Captain Jones's offer and sailed from L'Orient on 14 August 1779.

Jones was the commodore of an American squadron with the title of Commander in Chief of all the American Ships of War in Europe evidently bestowed upon him by Benjamin Franklin in Paris. The largest ship in the squadron was *Good Man Richard* rated as carrying 40 guns: 6 eighteen pounders upon her lower gun deck, 28 twelve and nine pounders on her middle gun deck, and 6 six pounders upon her spar and quarterdecks. Her crew of officers and men approximated four hundred and fifty.[2] The frigate *Alliance* carried 36 guns consisting of twelves, nines and sixes and officers and crew numbering two hundred and ninety. Next came the frigate *Pallas* with 28 guns; the frigate *Monsieur* armed with 22 guns; the brig *Vengence* of 16 guns and finally the cutter *Cerf* of ten guns.[3] In an attempt to exercise his authority as commander and chief, he noted that the *General Mifflin*, a small American privateer mounting 16 guns, was at anchor in the Loire River. Jones directed the *Vengeance* to hail the captain of the privateer, a man named Babcock, and tell him to weigh anchor and immediately and join his squadron or be guilty of disobedience of orders.[4] Ignoring Jones, the *General Mifflin* sailed on without comment.

The first encounter of the squadron was taking a large English ship carrying silk and other valuables. Later that night Jones had a dispute with the captain of *Monsieur* who apparently asked for his ship's independence. Jones ordered all hands on the *Good Man Richard* to quarters. The captain quickly and wisely made sail and was soon out of reach of the *Good Man Richard*'s guns. We made chase but were unable to overtake her. She finally sailed out of sight. Jones, clearly exasperated, struck several junior officers over their heads with his speaking trumpet and ordered one lieutenant confined to his stateroom until released by his orders. After some time, Jones calmed down and asked the lieutenant to dine with him. The young gentleman agreed and immediately after having supper, resumed his duty station. He was one three lieutenants and a sailing master on board, but none held a commission or warrant issued from the proper office of the United States. Jones had earned a reputation of being difficult. While in command of his former warship the *Ranger*, his lieutenants that did have congressional commissions had a series of disputes with him and resigned all at the same time, but carried their commissions with them.[5]

Sailing off the east coast of Ireland, near the Dungarvan highlands, a large ship appeared to the windward. At 4 in the afternoon, Jones signaled to *Alliance* to make sail and determine the vessel's country of origin. *Alliance* got almost within cannon shot, then bore away to relay the ship's identity. The captain of the *Alliance*, Pierre Landais, a former French merchantman lieutenant, said that he could not get near enough to recognize and classify the ship, but her large upper battery indicated that she was a ship-of-the-line. Jones made a curt rude reply through his speaking trumpet calling Landais a coward, an appellation that was overheard by the crews of both ships. This was an expression of the hatred that simmered between the two captains and would erupt periodically during the cruise.[6] Unfortunately when cooperation among the Americans was needed in battle, friendly ties were essential in the quest of achieving a victory. Mutual animosity, however, was a crucial liability. The signal was raised aloft for the entire squadron to give chase. Night was rapidly coming on and the squadron had to sail quickly before their prey was out of sight. A nearby fishing boat came within shouting distance and its men hollered to us that we were, in fact, chasing an English merchantman belonging to the East-India Company.

We successfully captured her, but at 8 o'clock we encountered some trouble. There was a strong inshore current pushing us towards some rocks. Several boats were lowered and ordered to row ahead and tow the East-Indiaman away in case she came too close to the breakers. At 11 o'clock one of the boats with eleven men and a lieutenant cut away from the rest and promptly rowed on shore to a beach. Another lieutenant and a sailing-master took a cutter with twelve men to pursue the deserters. They landed not far behind the runaways, but now since the men were on sovereign Irish soil, they were taken in custody by the local constabulary. This inconvenient episode cost us twenty-two good seamen and two experienced officers.

At about midnight a severe gale sprang up that lasted almost a whole day. One of the cannons from the lower deck became loose and it nearly smashed a hole in our ship's bulwark before we were able to secure the gun. Some seams started to leak in the captured vessel and we had to keep four pumps working full time to keep the vessel afloat. This was not surprising because she had been in the king's service for sixty years. When launched she was a ship-of-the–line mounting 64 guns. At the end of her naval service she was condemned at Brest as being unseaworthy. The East India Company purchased her and refitted the vessel. She made two voyages to the Indies

Pierre Landais (Naval History and Heritage Command, NH 204, Saint Memin Collection).

2. Manifold Malevolent Captains Contentious 21

and then was condemned for a second time to become a fleet of hulks belonging to the King of France. Somehow she had put to sea once again and, during the gale off Ireland, she began to come apart at many joints. This was a useless seizure, yet Jones, in later years, would refer with pride to his capture of an English sixty-four, but never giving details.

The weather finally turned favorable allowing us to make way for the Lewis Islands north of Scotland, the appointed place for our squadron's next rendezvous. This was accomplished on 20 August. In the intervening time we had captured 11 vessels. Some were valuable enough for us to put a prize crew and master onboard and have them sailed to L'Orient; the other captured English ships that had been sailing between Ireland and Denmark were less important and were simply sunk. On 22 August we saw a ship in toward shore of us and gave chase, then we noticed three more in the northwest quarter. We gained upon the first of them and discovered that she was an English mail ship mounting 22 guns, employed in His Majesty's Service. Her route was between Leith, Scotland and Quebec and on this passage was carrying cables, cordage and military stores for the British garrisons in Canada. She offered no resistance and, when ordered, hauled down her colors. The three sails that we spied earlier were *Alliance* with her prize of an English warship mounting 24 guns laden with similar goods that our prize carried, plus the *Pallas*. The next morning *Vengeance* joined us, but she had not seen *Cerf* or any other tenders. Our squadron now stood among the Orkney Islands after taking two prizes and sent them for a port in France. Cruising off the windswept islands for several days, we found good hunting and were able to burn and sink sixteen small sailing vessels. We then rounded the northeastern part of Scotland and took seven colliers and torched them. Soon we approached Edinburgh castle and sailed off the landmark for several days.

On 10 September Jones had a dispute with another of his lieutenants and ordered him below to confinement in his cabin. As the officer descended the ladder, the captain kicked him on his breaches several times. In half an hour Jones had his servant invite him to dine with him, which the lieutenant did. This surprising behavioral pattern was a common occurrence with Jones. He could be highly incensed for one instant, then ready to reconcile for the next.[7]

Later that evening a signal was flown instructing all of the squadron's captains and lieutenants to assemble onboard the *Good Man Richard*. He informed them of his plan to move all the ships up to Leith on the Firth of Forth.[8] We were to fly English colors and the officers were to wear British naval uniforms that he would provide.[9] We might then sail pass Edinburgh castle unnoticed and continue to anchor off Leith. There we would set out spring lines on our cables and present an array of broadsides to the citizens. Although Leith was a large wealthy city, it likely was unprepared with fortifications to protect it from an invading foe. Further, Jones said that once the

Americans were safely at anchor an officer was to be sent to the city bearing a flag of truce. Once there, he was to demand that the city give the officer one hundred thousand pounds sterling within half an hour and then be transported to the commodore's ship.[10] If obtaining such a large sum on such short notice was not possible, any deficiency in making up our demand could be paid in silver plate (sterling silver in bars or silver household goods). If they refused to comply within the allotted time, the town would be fired upon and set afire with red-hot shot. Once the conflagration was started they would immediately set sail. There was obvious opposition to the plan. We were unfamiliar with the waters near Leith, its currents, channels, and hidden shoals made the passage dangerous. The wind might not co-operate for voyaging in both directions. The garrison at Edinburgh was always fully manned and, even if we were not challenged on our way to the township, they might warn the people at Leith of a suspicious armada sailing toward the town. Assuming that we were successful in obtaining the desired booty, escaping back to sea and passing the castle once again would be a formidable task. The land-based garrison was fortified with earthen and stonewalls and had 20 forty-eight pounders. We would have to sail within point-blank range of their much larger guns and our own were incapable of producing much damage in returning fire. Although in retrospect the plan seemed too dangerous, Jones was extremely artful in his presentation. After some discussion, the plan was unanimously agreed to.

The officers were then supplied with English Navy uniforms, each in accord with their rank onboard their American ship. We then formed a line and made a favorable run up to the Firth of Forth before a following wind. Shortly thereafter the commodore's ship was signaled to heave to. Unfortunately, the tide was against us and we were obliged to temporarily halt our planned incursion. In the meantime, the English governor at Leith, Sir John Anstruther who owned a mansion on the north shore of the Firth of Forth, mistakenly assumed that we were an English squadron, led by a similar appearing vessel HMS *Romney*. He sent a cutter with an officer and small crew to our ship and requested the name of the squadron's commander, the names of the accompanying ships, whether they required any assistance or provisions—and if we intended to dock at Leith or any other intentions. The officer then said that the governor requested him to ask if we could spare a barrel or two of gunpowder. The fort at Leith had shot, but was almost out of this vital explosive. He also added that we should be aware that several American privateers that had taken several English vessels were known to be cruising the coast. He was concerned that they might come up the river, attack at night and try to destroy the town. The officer went on to say that many of the town's citizens were apprehensive, believing that this event was quite possible. Jones was pleased about obtaining this intelligence and very amused about the request for powder. He then asked the officer to give Sir John his compliments, provided the officer with fictitious names for his ships that corresponded to names of British naval vessels of the same size and number of guns of his squadron. The captains of each of the American ships were aware of the English ship that they were assigned to temporarily emulate. As the officer had asked, Jones gave him a barrel of powder likely to counteract any suspicion.[11]

As I previously related, we were waiting for the tide to change direction when a series of incidents thwarted Jones's plans to plunder Leith. First the wind suddenly shifted to the southwest away from the favorable northeast where it had consistently helped our approach. At about the same time a prize brig that we had captured and largely manned by impressed English sailors ran aground. The whole crew disembarked to the nearby shore and scattered into the bushes and forest. As soon as this was discovered, several boats were launched and armed parties were dispatched to apprehend the runaways. It was assumed that deserters would try to make their way to the castle and tell them who we really were and inform them about our plans. This took up precious time and was unsuccessful. A decision was made to abandon both the search and the stranded brig and get underway so that our squadron could safely escape to the sea. Evidently our original identity ruse had still worked. Not a single shot was fired from shore, even though we were quite vulnerable to their guns for several hours.

On 11 September, we resumed our aggressive ways and took two prizes. Prize masters and crews were ordered to sail them to Dunkirk. We next headed for the Yorkshire town of Scarborough located on the North Sea. While sailing near there our squadron only encountered small coasters or pilot boats. We had no use for them, but they did supply us with fresh water and provisions. On 22 September we discovered an English convoy escorted by two sloops of war.[12] The largest of these vessels signaled the fleet about our presence and ordered them to disperse to save themselves. The two sloops of war and an armed merchantman then made sail for us. Jones decided to ignore them and ordered his squadron to crowd on as much canvas as they could and pursue the now unprotected fleet. Before long *Alliance* caught up with two of the English ships and they struck their colors. We had just put our second lieutenant in a tender with twenty armed men to take possession of these vessels when a lookout shouted down to the deck that there was another fleet under sail to the east of us. The weather was clearing about this time and we were able to count thirty-seven vessels just emerging from a blanket of coastal fog. They appeared to be bound for land. Jones took out his spyglass and peered at them for a few minutes. He then said to his officers who stood nearby on the quarterdeck, "that this is the very best fleet which I have been so long cruising for."[13] He immediately directed the squadron to abandon the pursuit of the small fleet of thirteen sail that we almost had in our possession.

Instead he ordered the squadron to sail after the larger fleet that lay east of us. Demonstrating impatience or possibly greed, he left the tender commanded by one of our best officers and manned by twenty of our best men behind. Its orders were to follow us, but fend for itself. The ships of the squadron set as much sail as we could to chase the enemy with the wind varying between the south and west. At half-past 6 o'clock we got close enough to distinguish that two members of the fleet were ships of war, one a frigate and the other a sloop of war. These two vessels now perceived us as the enemy and, by our maneuvering, that our intent was to attack them. They now stood off to engage us to protect their convoy. Meanwhile several merchant ships made their way toward land hoping to find a harbor, but none was nearer than Scarborough.

At 7 o'clock Jones signaled both the *Alliance* and *Pallas*. Shortly thereafter, he hailed Captain Landais and ordered him to engage the larger of the two ships together with the *Good Man Richard*. As soon as *Alliance* fired its initial broadside, if the opportunity presented itself, her crew should be prepared to board the enemy vessel. Landais agreed and, as the word of the battle plan spread, the officers and crew responded with a traditional three cheers. They were primed and ready. Next Jones ordered *Pallas* to fight the smaller vessel that at the time was the nearest to us.

The breeze was from the south southwest at about six knots. As we closed in on our target that had hove to, she drew up her courses and displayed St. George's colors.[14,15] We, in turn, drew up into an order of battle and displayed the American striped flag. The large vessel then signaled her consort to put up as much sail as she could and endeavor to escape to the leeward. *Pallas* decided to give chase and the *Alliance* likewise quit her station and ran to the leeward, an action against Jones's orders. With the *Vengeance* well to our stern, we were now left alone to contend with a ship that was far superior to us in arms.

I had been given command of the main top some time ago. I was ordered down to the quarterdeck along with the captains of the fore and mizzen tops. The latter young midshipmen, not quite seventeen, and I received our orders straight from Jones in person. We were to direct fire at enemy tops and silence them using muskets, blunderbusses, swivels, and cohorns (small mortars). It was of particular importance to direct our fire into the nearest tops that were opposite us. Silencing these top-platforms was crucial because a favorite British tactic was to fire down upon the enemy's quarterdeck and kill or disrupt those in command of the opposing ship. With our orders understood, we drew up a double ration of grog and climbed aloft back to our stations. By the time we were ready to commence firing, our opponent hauled down the St. George ensign and hoisted a red flag with the union jack in its canton that the captain carefully nailed to the flagstaff.[16] The previously unknown antagonist turned out to be His Britannic Majesty's 44-gun warship *Serapis* under the command of Captain Richard Pearson.[17]

3

The Battle Between *Good Man Richard* and HBM Warship *Serapis*

Before I relate an account of the action, I shall describe details of each of vessel's armament and crews. Although some of these data were described earlier, particular facts are repeated so that one can assess which side had the advantage during this long bloody battle. Since sailing from L'Orient *Good Man Richard* had lost several of her officers and men to man prizes back to France. Others had deserted during the hapless Leith adventure. One lieutenant and twenty men were on board the small tender that Jones sailed away from earlier—rather heedlessly.[1] I wish to review I begin with the arms available to *Good Man Richard:*

6 eighteen pounders upon the lower gun deck;
14 twelve pounders upon the middle gun deck;
14 nine pounders upon the middle gun deck;
2 six pounders upon the quarterdeck;
2 six pounders upon the spar deck (1 in each gangway);
2 six pounders upon her forecastle.

It should be noted that there were a number of men on board who had been captured while taking their vessels as prizes. Seven or eight chose to fight with us, but others declined. Accounting for all the additions and subtractions, *Good Man Richard*'s fighting crew did not exceed three hundred eighty men and boys. About three hundred of these were Americans with the rest an assortment of English, French, Scotch, Irish, Portuguese and Maltese sailors.

The *Serapis* officially rated as a 44, but at the beginning of this battle she mounted 50 guns:

20 eighteen pounders upon the lower gun deck;
20 nine pounders upon the upper deck;

6 six pounders upon the quarterdeck;
4 six pounders upon her forecastle.

The British warship carried a company of 305 officers and men and 15 Lascars (East-Indian).

Prior to the battle, *Good Man Richard*'s crew and officers were assigned to stations as follows:

In the maintop fifteen marines, and four sailors and myself. (20).
In the foretop one midshipman, ten marines, and three sailors, (14).
In the mizzen-top one midshipman, six marines, and two sailors, (9).
A French volunteer colonel manned the poop with twenty French marines. (21).[2]
On the quarterdeck, the commodore, an Irish lieutenant colonel-volunteer, three midshipmen acting as aid-de-camps to the commodore, the purser, a number of sailors and marines.
The sailing-master was occasionally on the quarterdeck, the ship's gangways, forecastle and poop.
One of the master's mates had charge of the six 18 pounders on the lower gun-deck, where there were also stationed ten men to each of these guns.
The first lieutenant, Richard Dale, was stationed upon the second or middle gun-deck, with the gunner and the other master's mate; because we were left at this time with only one lieutenant on board, these last two were to act has lieutenants as the situation required. Mr. Dale had a sufficient number of men stationed with him for managing the guns plus other arms such as cutlasses, boarding axes and boarding pikes.
The boatswain's station was on the forecastle where he had the command of the forecastle men and guns mount there.
The carpenter was not assigned to any particular part on the ship, but was merely told to do his duty as he saw the need for it.
The rest of the petty officers and crew were placed in different parts of the ship.

I shall now give my account of this famous battle fought on the night of 22 September 1779, between the American ship *Good Man Richard* commanded by John Paul Jones and the English ship of war *Serapis*, commanded by Captain Richard Parsons off Flamborough Head on the Yorkshire coast by the North Sea, just south of Scarborough.

The two vessels nearly came within hailing distance of each other when Captain Jones ordered the yards of *Good Man Richard* slung with chains and our courses hauled to. At about the same time, *Serapis* tacked and now bore down to attack us. Just after eight in the evening a large moon majestically rose above the horizon, the clouds parted and the ocean's surface became extremely calm. An almost other worldly silvery luminosity lit the scene. Suddenly the enemy ship hailed us with an almost unintelligible hoarse and bombastic: "What ship is this?" Our ship responded, "Come a little nearer, and I will tell you."[3]

The next question came in a condescending manner, "What are you laden with?"

This was answered in a similarly contemptuous, "Round, grape, and double headed-shot."[4]

The British reply was from a discharge of *Serapis*'s upper and quarterdeck guns into us. They did not fire from lower deck guns, perhaps thinking that they could overpower us with the use of fewer weapons. However, we returned fire and what would be a lengthy battle had begun.

When we opened fire coming from three of our starboard forward deck guns first call and most of the men who were stationed by them were killed. When Jones became aware of the unfortunate circumstance, he gave orders to hold fire of the other three 18-pounders on that deck as well as the men who were assigned to discharge their guns on the lower decks. This was an indication that we were overmatched. At the same time, she had maneuvered to a position under our stern, putting us in a disadvantage that we could not prevent. They commenced to rake us with broadsides and showers of musketry from above. Several of her 18-pound shots passed completely through our ship producing mayhem among our crew. Our ensign-staff was shot away early on during the firefight and our thirteen-striped flag had fallen into the sea.

Since the wind was very light and our ship was short on officers and crew, *Serapis* easily out-sailed us. This advantage became obvious to the enemy and was improved upon by keeping to our stern and raking us for and aft. Our French colonel who was stationed upon the poop deck found that almost all of his men have been slain. He had little choice other than to quit that station and take those few men who had survived to fight from quarterdeck. The enemy's position under our stern infuriated Jones, but there was little that he could do as our men fell by scores in all parts of the ship. Meanwhile our sailors in the tops kept an incessant and well-directed fire into the enemy's tops. Being well executed and apparently effective, it was, at the moment, the only positive aspect of the battle from our standpoint.

At this point Jones issued orders to extricate us from the scene of bloody carnage. It appeared that if the battle lasted for a half hour, it was probable that the enemy would have slain nearly all our officers and men and we would have been compelled to yield to a superior force. At this critical juncture Captain Jones ordered the sailing master, a Yankee named Stacy, to bring us around.⁵ As *Serapis* passed across our bow, our helm was turned so that the wind was to our stern. The main and mizzen topsails that were braced suddenly swelled from a fresh breeze. *Good Man Richard* quickly shot ahead crossing the enemy ship's bow. We become entangled with her mizzen shroud and the vang on her starboard side.⁶ Jones became excited and cried out, "Well-done, my brave lad's, we have got her now; throw on board the grappling-irons, and standby for boarding."⁷ This was quickly done, but the enemy soon cutaway the lines which were fixed to the grappling irons. More were thrown onboard, and enemy repeated the defensive act but many hooks held on. The grappling irons, in time, allowed our crew to haul the enemy's ship to a position snuggly along our side. Her jib-stay was cut away aloft which then fell on our poop deck. This was where Jones and Stacy were stationed and they attempted to fasten the enemy's jib-stay to our mizzenmast. Frustrated, Mr. Stacy started to curse, but Jones admonished the sailing master saying, "It was no time for swearing now, you may by the next moment be in eternity; but let us do our duty."⁸

The wind ceased to blow and strong current now pushed the ships that were now locked together toward Scarborough. Captain Pearson realized that he could not easily extricate *Serapis* from us so let go one of his anchors. His strategy was to try to cut us adrift and let the current take us toward shore, out of their reach, but giving them time to reorder. Meanwhile forty minutes had passed since the action had started. The small arms fire from the tops had continued without an interruption. Our muskets, blunderbusses, swivels, cohorns and pistols succeeded in silencing their top men except for one sailor in the enemy's foretop. He would peep out behind head of the foremast and fire into our tops. As soon as I saw where the fellow was hiding, I ordered a marine to hold his fire and wait until he could get his gun sights directly on him. Shortly thereafter he shot the prowling sailor with his musket. The British top man fell from aloft and onto the forecastle deck below.

Both ships remained tethered together positioned with the head of each locked next to the opponent's stern. This meant that the heaviest cannon that both vessels carried amidships could not be used because it was impossible get to their muzzles to sponge and then reload them. Therefore, both adversaries had to resort to hand to hand combat and board each other. The boarding party *Serapis* fought its way to the forward part of our quarterdeck. In a counter attack several were killed and the remainder driven back to their own ship. Our men quickly followed the retreating sailors, but were killed. A succession of attacks and counter-attacks followed resulting in many additional lives being lost on both sides.

The *Serapis*'s anchor was holding fast to the ocean bottom, ten to twelve fathoms beneath us. The two vessels, intertwined in kind of a clinch, were about a league [three nautical miles] east by south of Flamborough Head.

3. Battle Between Good Man Richard *and* Serapis

By means of the bright moonlight we could discern the enemy's fleet now close to shore, but our own squadron was nowhere in sight with one minor exception. The brig *Vengeance* and the small tender that had been left behind with one officer and twenty men were about half a league astern of us, but neither seemed to take the risk to come to our assistance. I did not know how much time had elapsed since the battle had begun, but my best guess it was just under fifty minutes. At sea, we depend upon the turning of a sand glass or our chronometer, but there was no time for that. Since we had silenced the enemy's tops, we now directed our fire down upon our opponent's decks and forecastle. This operation proved quite successful and in about twenty-five minutes the decks were clear of men. There were men still below however and they kept up a constant fire from four of their bow guns on their starboard side. These were two eighteen-pounders on the lower deck and two nine-pounders on her upper gun deck, but under cover of the forecastle. These four guns were able to produce a great deal of damage to us. Her larboard [port] cannon, however, were of no use because of the position of the two ships.

About this time several shot-damaged sails that had hung limply over the quarterdeck of *Serapis* caught fire. The fire quickly climbed into her rigging and, since both vessels were entangled, it spread to our vessel endangering both ships of burning. The firing stopped until the two contending parties could extinguish the blaze. Once accomplished, the destructive gunfire resumed. By this time, our top men had taken possession of the enemy's tops since their yards were lodged within ours. We then transferred some of our men with assorted harassing and troublesome weapons to their fore and main tops. These included stinkpots, flasks of combustible material and hand grenades that we threw among those few enemy sailors who appeared below. The battle now reached its third hour and we took control of the *Serapis*'s top, a location that commanded quarterdeck, the upper gun deck and the forecastle. We promptly became confident that the enemy could not hold out much longer and she would strike her colors to us, then an unexpected incident occurred.

Rumors had begun to be circulated among the crew stationed between decks that Captain Jones and all his principle officers had been killed; that the gunners were now in command of *Good Man Richard*; and that the ship had four or five feet of water in the hold and was in danger of sinking. Those crewmen therefore asked a gunner, the ship's carpenter and the master-at-arms to go on deck and plead with the enemy for quarters in the hope of saving all our lives. The three men mounted the quarterdeck and displayed a crudely fashioned white truce flag. They then bellowed as loud as they could, "Quarters, quarters, for God's sake, Quarters! Our ship is sinking!"[9] They then moved to the poop doubtlessly with the intent of hauling down our colors. When I heard this in the top, I was deceived into thinking that the sounds had originated from the enemy ship. I told my men that enemy had struck and was begging for quarters. Meanwhile the three addled American seamen on the poop deck found that our ensign along with our ensign-staff was gone. They quickly returned to the quarterdeck and once again pled loudly for quarters. Suddenly an even louder voice was heard. It was our commodore who shouted, "Quarters! What damn rascals are them? Shoot them—kill them!"[10] Jones was on the forecastle, having just discharged his pistols when this trio appeared on the quarterdeck. The carpenter and the master-at-arms, hearing Jones's voice quickly disappeared below, but the gunner was a little slower. Jones then threw both pistols at the lagging sailor and struck him on the head. He either fractured the man's skull with the weapon or the sailor broke his skull when he fell down the gangway ladder to the deck below. Anyway, that is where the seaman remained, prostrate until the battle ended.[11]

Both ships continued to shoot at each other at point blank range and then another fire broke out on board *Serapis* and *Good Man Richard*. This conflagration once again climbed the rigging of both ships and set our maintop ablaze. My men were alarmed. Through enormous exertion they overcame extraordinary difficulty being so high above the deck and attempted to extinguish the fire. The water that we had with us in a tub was largely for hydrating the men. We threw it on the flames with little to no result. Next, we took off our coats and jackets, threw them onto the fire and then stomped upon the clothing to smoother the flames. Since the crews of both vessels were once again busily labored at fighting the inferno, the canon and musket fire temporarily ceased.

Once the fires were almost miraculously put out, the enemy demanded to know if we had in fact struck because of the three men that had pleaded for quarters earlier. They asked us to haul down our pennant as a surrender gesture, but noticed that our flagstaff was missing.

Jones replied, "Ay, ay, we'll do that when we can fight no longer, but we shall see yours come down the first; for you must know that Yankees do not haul down their colors till they are fairly beaten."[12]

The combat now resumed, but this time with even greater ferocity if possible. This continued for a few minutes when the cry of fire was heard for the third time from both ships. All hands were employed in extinguishing it and once again they were successful. Then the battle was renewed with what seemed like the highest level of violence. Muskets and smaller guns blazed away; hand grenades and stinkpots filled the air. It was becoming almost impossible to fight on deck, therefore men grabbed pikes and boarding axes and attacked each other hand to hand through the ship's gun-ports that were rather large. The cannon that had usually been run through the ports had become useless because they were muzzle loaded. There was insufficient room to properly operate them.

3. Battle Between Good Man Richard and Serapis

The *Serapis*'s greater weight of shot did a great deal of damage wounding or killing most of the members of the *Good Man Richard*'s gun crews, thereby diminishing much of our ship's firepower. In addition, the *Good Man Richard*'s hull was breached in several places and her rudder was badly damaged. The moon had risen high overhead in the night's sky and brilliantly illuminated the battle scene. *Alliance* finally sailed into the fray. She rounded the stern of the *Good Man Richard* and the bow of the *Serapis*. *Alliance* cut loose a well-directed broadside of grapeshot. It did hit both ships, but most of its damage was done to our vessel. Some of us onboard the *Good Man Richard* believed that she was an English man-of-war had joined the fray. The *Alliance* then changed course, returned to the two stricken ships and fired another grapeshot broadside into the bow of the *Good Man Richard*, wounding many Americans still left on deck and those in the rigging. The brightness of the moon that night made it quite easy to distinguish between the two vessels. The *Good Man Richard* was painted all black while the *Serapis* had yellow sides. Still, at the exact time of the attack, the moon had retreated behind a dense cloud, however, the impression was that our ship was being intentionally attacked. Landais ordered yet another grapeshot broadside to be indiscriminately fired.[13] The *Alliance* kept her position that caused a great deal of havoc onboard our vessel as she repeatedly shot at us. In desperation Jones ordered the commodore's identity signal, three lighted lanterns arranged in horizontal line, hoisted about fifteen feet aloft in the fore, main and mizzen shrouds on the larboard side. The intent was that the *Alliance* would identify us a friend rather the foe and not fire again presumably in error. This had the desired effect and she ceased her fire.[14]

At thirty-five minutes after midnight, one of my men tossed a single hand grenade from the maintop with the intention of hitting a group of English sailors who were huddled together on the enemy's gun deck.[15] The grenade struck the combing of the nearby upper hatchway, rebounded and fell between their decks. It detonated and, in doing so, ignited a quantity of loose powder that had been scattered about the enemy's cannon. This produced a huge explosion within a confined space and killed or wounded about twenty of the enemy. The enemy now pled for quarters much to the dismay of Captain Pearson. Only a small amount of time passed before the captain of *Serapis* gave the order to one of his crew to ascend to the quarterdeck and haul down the British flag. Neither this sailor nor any of his comrades moved to obey the command. They told their captain that they were afraid to expose themselves on deck because of the musket fire our riflemen had continuously wreaked on them. Pearson then took it upon himself to ascend to the quarterdeck and haul down the ensign that he had nailed to the flagstaff at the beginning of the battle. This was the very flag that he had sworn to his principle officers that he would never strike to whom they called that "infamous pirate" John Paul Jones.

Relinquished sword (from John Frost, *The Book of the Navy Comprising a General History of the American Marine; and Particular Accounts of All the Celebrated Naval Battles from the Declaration of Independence to the Present Time*, New York: D. Appleton and Company, 1842, p. 230).

Now that the enemy's flag had been struck, Jones ordered Richard Dale, his first lieutenant, to select the number of crewmen to take possession of the prize. This was immediately done. Regrettably several of our men were killed by the English onboard the *Serapis* after she had struck to us. They meekly apologized afterwards saying the men who were in breach honor among combatants were not aware that their ship had struck her colors. This ended the memorable battle that had continued for more than four hours under moonlight. The officers of the *Serapis* headed by Captain Pearson came onboard our ship. He inquired for Captain Jones to whom he was introduced by Mr. Mease our purser.[16] After meeting, Pearson presented his sword and said, "It is with great reluctance that I am now obligated to resign you this, for it is painful to me, more particularly at this time, when compelled to deliver up my sword to a man who may be said to fight with a halter around his neck!" Jones accepted his sword and replied, "Sir you have fought like a hero, and I make no doubt but your sovereign will regard you in a most ample manner for it."[17] Captain Pearson then asked Jones what country supplied most of the

3. Battle Between Good Man Richard and Serapis

American boarder with British ensign (from John Frost, *The Book of the Navy Comprising a General History of the American Marine; and Particular Accounts of All the Celebrated Naval Battles from the Declaration of Independence to the Present Time*, New York: D. Appleton and Company, 1842, p. 46).

crew. Jones answered Americans. Very well said the English Captain, "It has been *diamond cut diamond* with us."[18] Shortly thereafter Captain Pearson's officers surrendered their side arms to Lieutenant Dale. A brief conversation followed during which the defeated English Captain noted that the American had fought equally as bravely as his own men. The two captains then withdrew to Jones's cabin and drank a glass or two of wine together.[19]

4

Aftermath

When the sun rose the next morning, the American ensign flew from both the *Good Man Richard* and the vanquished *Serapis*. Both ships, now wrecks, were promptly separated from each other. The three masts of the *Serapis* were largely unsupported and soon fell overboard with all her sails, tops, yards and rigging. They made a dreadful noise when they plunged in a jumble into the sea. Early in the action our guns had heavily damaged them. The main mast was shot through about a foot above the gangway, the fore mast just below the foretop and the mizzenmast roughly ten feet above the quarterdeck. Several eighteen-pound shots had gone through our mainmast and most of the shrouds that supported the formerly stout timber had to be cut or shot away. Only the stoppers that had been fixed on them by the quartermaster kept them standing. Since we were stationed on the maintop above them, we were quite concerned as the battle progressed and were relieved when ordered down to the quarterdeck as soon as the enemy struck.

We now realized to our dismay that we had two more enemies to conquer that would take a great deal of brawn and ingenuity to overcome, fire and water. Our pumps had been working without a stop for about two hours, but the water in the hold was rapidly rising. *Good Man Richard*'s hull had been damaged below the waterline. Several shots ruptured the integrity of our bottom and it seemed impossible to stop the ensuing massive leak. It seemed unlikely that we could halt the flow; therefore, we were endangered of sinking. Meanwhile small isolated fires made their way into inflammable portions of the ship such as rotten wood, pitch tar and oakum. In many cases the more water that was tossed on the ubiquitous fires, the more furiously they would burn, analogous to throwing water on a kettle of pitch, tar or turpentine when on fire. The fires were now progressing toward the pine boards that made up the bulkhead protecting the powder magazine. It became obvious that putting out the fire was as unlikely as was freeing the ship of leaked in water. Either the ship would burn to the water's edge and then sink or simply sink first. Jones ordered a distress signal to be sent aloft and *Alliance*, *Vengeance* and *Pallas* responded by sending their boats to assist us. Once they reached us, he ordered the crew to remove the powder from our magazines and said that no one was to quit until it was all gunpowder was safely stored on the boats by our side. Our English prisoners were frightened by this as many of us were because the fire had advanced all around the powder room. Everyone expected to be blown asunder at any moment. Jones however said that he did not intend to abandon his ship until every cask of powder had been removed. As a result, the English officers and men volunteered to assist us in moving the gunpowder. This sped up the process and, when accomplished, Jones asked the English prisoners to embark on these boats and board the *Serapis*. He also left orders that all American and British wounded were to be put onboard *Alliance, Vengeance* and *Pallas* before abandoning the *Good Man Richard*.

In some battles odd events take place and this one had to do with an enemy officer. A British first lieutenant whose name was Stanhope had clambered down one of the *Serapis*'s stern ladders and remained in the water during the combat. Once there, he hung on with only his head above water while the action took place above him. An American officer noticed that when the British officers surrendered on our quarterdeck, one was completely wet. He was then questioned about how his clothes became so sodden. He said that just before *Serapis* struck, he attempted sound [test the depth] of her pump-well to see how much water she had in her, slipped and subsequently fell into it. Several enemy petty officers disputed his story and related how he cowardly hid during the mêlée. Stanhope, who normally would be treated with deference as an officer, was placed in confinement with the *Serapis*'s ordinary sailors—a humiliating experience.[1]

The *Pallis* had captured the consort of the *Serapis*, the 22-gun *Countess of Scarborough*, after a brisk action that lasted only a half hour.[2] Now the two ships joined the squadron. *Serapis* had suffered hull damage during the action and was thought to be sinking. Therefore, crews from the entire squadron and some able-bodied prisoners manned the chain pumps and kept them constantly going. The pump handles were double manned and the work was so taxing that the men were often relieved. It was estimated that the two machines could lift a ton of water a minute when operating at full capacity and speed. Therefore, about two hundred forty tons of water was sucked out of *Serapis* in four hours until the carpenters were successful in stopping up shot holes, etc.

Meanwhile on the *Good Man Richard*, we were busily employed getting out the wounded and embarking them on board the boats that belonged to our squadron. Suddenly an alarm was sounded. About fifty English prisoners found their way out of confinement and took possession of our ship and attempted to run her in ashore. They had control of the quarterdeck, spar deck, and forecastle, and had the ship before the wind with her braces squared,

4. Aftermath

steering directly for land, the wind being about east. Another battle arose, but since we had the arms needed for close combat, we soon overpowered the escaping prisoners even though they outnumbered us. We again became masters of the ship however two captives were killed, some others were wounded and thirteen were driven overboard. Several managed to take possession of one of our boats that was tied up alongside our ship and made their escape to land.[3] The rest of these desperate English sailors were ordered into the boats and transported on board the *Pallis.*

I now took full view of the mangled carcasses of the slain onboard our ship, especially between decks, the bloody scene was enough to appall the stoutest heart. To see the dead laying in heaps—to hear the groans of the wounded and the dying—the entrails of the dead scattered promiscuously around. The blood (*American too*) *over one's shoes,* was enough to move pity from the most hardened and *callous breast.* And although my spirit was somehow dampened at this shocking sight, yet when I came to reflect we were *conquerors,* and over those who wish to bind America in chains of everlasting slavery, my spirits revived and I thought perhaps that some faithful historian in some future period would enroll me among the heroes and deliverers of my country. Pardon me gentle reader, for this involuntary digression, let this be my excuse that I felt the spirit which infused courage into my breast on the night and during the battle which I have just given you a faithful description of, even while my pen was tracing the dreadful conflict.

Two of our prizes that we now had were King's ships. Before their capture, they were part of a thirty-vessel convoy fleet from the Baltic Sea to Scarborough, England. Although they were in sight during the battle and still seen by us the morning after near land, our squadron made no attempts to capture any of them. The reason was that the dire condition of the wrecked *Serapis* required the utmost exertion of our entire squadron if we hoped to save this potentially valuable ship.[4] It is likely, however, that had the captain of the *Alliance* obeyed the orders given to him before the commencement of the action by Jones, the whole of the enemy's fleet would have fallen into our hands as Captain Pearson, the English commander, acknowledged after the sea battle. But after the long and hard-fought battle ended, it was not thought prudent to dispatch the squadron to capture any of the vulnerable English merchant ships.

Having now executed the orders left us by Captain Jones, we thought of leaving the *Good Man Richard* to the mercy of the winds and waves. The wind is now blowing a fresh gale from the northeast, so I went down into the gunroom with some others, to see the lieutenant's and other officer's trunks that were to be taken out and put into the boats. Oh God! What havoc! Not a piece of them could be found as large as a continental dollar! We found several shirts, coats, etc., but they were so pierced and shredded by a variety of shot, they were of no value. The breach from cannonballs that our ship had endured was made through and through our ship's quarter and gunroom. I believe that if the ship could have been placed upon the land and buried to her lower gun deck, a man might have been able to drive a coach and six horses through one side of the breach and emerge out the other. The splinters and pieces of our shattered ship were scattered about and were laid in heaps. Perhaps twenty carpenters at work on wood and timbers as many as five days of constant labor would not have made such a pile. Upon the whole, I think this battle, and every circumstance attending it minutely considered, may be ranked with propriety, the most-bloody, hardest fought, greatest scene of carnage on both sides, ever fought between two ships of war of any nation under heaven.[5]

During the action, the enemy threw roughly a hundred 18-pound powder cartridges into our gunroom with the view of blowing up our ship. If they had been successful, both ships as well as the officers and crews were destined for the same fate. Our ship lay so near to that of the enemy the inevitable result would have been that we all would have gone into eternity together. The officers of our ships lost all their clothing in this action except what they were wearing. For my own part, the coat that I had on my back was partly singed when our main top caught fire and my face was blackened with burned powder. We who were still on board the *Good Man Richard* thought it was necessary to abandon her. She would serve as a coffin for many of my brave countrymen who fought and died in this bed of honor while they were struggling for our liberty. It was painful for me to forever quit this ship where onboard so much bravery had been displayed during this battle. Necessity and self-preservation required that it be done and accomplished promptly since her lower hold was nearly full of water.

We accordingly embarked onboard a small tender, and soon thereafter reach the *Serapis*. Captain Jones ordered me not to board of her, take three hands with me and return to the *Good Man Richard*. He said that he had left sundry valuable papers in his cabin, naming or described the place, and asked me to get them, even at the risk of my life. The captain also warned me not to tarry. After having received such direct orders, I knew it would be in vain to protest. I therefore made sail in our little tender upon my little bark, but worried about the result. The wind then blew a fresh gale, and a pretty rough sea arose. I sailed a relatively straight course for *Good Man Richard*, which was than about a mile from the *Serapis* and tried not to run any risk. Arriving alongside and under the now silent guns of the *Good Men Richard*, we found that she was lying nearly headed into the wind with the top sails aback and the water running in and out of her lower deck ports. We dashed along under her stern where we became becalmed. I now ordered the oars to be got out as I found by her lack of motion that she was nearly underwater and at the point

4. Aftermath

of sinking. This shocked me and I had my men pull on their oars with all their might. Finding our situation very dangerous, we got off about four rods from her when she heavily pitched into the sea, heavy rolled over and disappeared almost instantaneously.[6] The ocean suction occasioned by this event together with the agitation of the waters was so great that for a minute or two we were concerned that we might join her underwater. As a consequence of the ocean's turbulence we shipped a great deal of water over the bow of our little tender. If we had not had a deck, we might have met the same fate of the *Good Man Richard*.

As the *Alliance*, *Vengeance* and *Pallas* rejoined Jones, they likely heard a few choice remarks about what had transpired during the battle. From the bloodstained deck of the *Serapis*, the survivors of both the American and British vessels watched the waves engulf the *Good Man Richard* from a safe distance. It was noted in the captain's log that on 25 September the sea claimed the mortally wounded hulk of the once proud *Good Man Richard* (*Bonhomme Richard*).

The *Bonhomme Richard* (center) and *Serapis* (right) tethered together by grappling lines, rendering their midship guns useless, while sailors on deck engage in hand-to-hand combat. *Alliance* (left) joins the battle, firing grapeshot toward *Serapis'* bow (Naval History and Heritage Command, USN 902430).

Editor's Summary of Battle

Jones ordered the British ensign hauled down, the American colors hoisted in their stead and then the *Bonhomme Richard*'s starboard battery opened fire. *Serapis* quickly responded with a retaliatory broadside and the battle commenced. On the first or second American broadside two of *Bonhomme Richard*'s 18-pounders blew up killing or wounding many in the gun crews. This also disabled the entire battery of 18-pounders and nearly blew a hole in the ship. Therefore, at the beginning of the battle, Jones has lost his heaviest artillery amounting to about one fifth of his firepower.

After the exchange of several more broadsides, Jones recognized that the British ship vastly overpowered his own, therefore he decided that his best option was to attempt boarding his foe. Jones backed the *Bonhomme Richard*'s fore and main topsails, slowing the ship, then fell off the wind. This enabled him to drop astern of *Serapis*. Shifting his helm to port, Jones brought *Bonhomme Richard* down directly upon *Serapis*' stern and then attempted to grapple the enemy so that the crew could board. The attempt failed. *Serapis* surged ahead then swung to starboard so that she would come across *Bonhomme Richard*'s bow and be in a prime position to rake her.

Unfortunately for the *Serapis* the winds were too light and she could not generate sufficient way on to clear *Bonhomme Richard*. As the British ship tried to cross the American's bow, *Bonhomme Richard*'s bowsprit became entangled in *Serapis*' mizzen mast rigging. It was at this time that British Captain Pearson called to Jones and enquired if his ship has struck. Jones replied, "I have not yet begun to fight" or something close to that effect. *Bonhomme Richard* then backed her topsails, bringing as much wind as was available onto the fore side of the sails, and the ship backed down. With the two ships now entangled, *Serapis* turned to port, again and now assumed a generally westerly course. *Bonhomme Richard* followed suit.

Serapis adapted to her new course more quickly than the *Bonhomme Richard*'s and ended ahead of the American ship. Because of the light winds, Captain Pearson apparently felt his ship did not have enough way to successfully tack in front of Jones and bring his superior broadside into action. Therefore, he backed *Serapis*' topsails thus slowing her down. *Bonhomme Richard*, with only a minimum of steerageway, advanced on *Serapis*. The American's sails then blanketed or blocked *Serapis*' wind.

Because her sails were not able to draw, the British ship lost her maneuverability. With *Bonhomme Richard* now off *Serapis*' port bow, Jones put the helm over and fell off the wind in his own an attempt to cross the enemy's bow thus putting *Bonhomme Richard* in a raking position. This was also unsuccessful. Her sails free to draw, *Serapis* again moved ahead and two ships locked together. *Serapis*' bow was in *Bonhomme Richard*'s starboard quarter and the British ship's jib boom plunged through the American's mizzen rigging. A forestay from the *Serapis* had parted and the rubble laid across the *Bonhomme Richard*'s poop deck and Jones scrambled up the ladder to the poop deck and fastened the line to the mizzenmast.

About a half hour into the battle, *Serapis* once again tried to cross the bow of *Bonhomme Richard* but, blanketed by the American's sails, *Serapis* lost momen-

4. Aftermath

tum. Jones saw an opportunity to board and placed his ship's bow into the British ship's side. A boarding party was ordered to cross the rails but was beaten back. The two vessels separated once again.

The wind, acting on both ships, began to pivot them, but *Bonhomme Richard* more so than *Serapis*. In a short time *Bonhomme Richard* slowly ended up alongside the enemy. A fluke of *Serapis'* starboard anchor hooked onto *Bonhomme Richard*'s quarterdeck bulwarks. Grappling irons were thrown and now the two ships were locked together in a deadly embrace. Jones, perhaps by intent or accident, had the enemy where he wanted him. Positioned hull to hull, *Serapis* was unable to use its superior firepower, speed, and experience. *Bonhomme Richard* carried a large contingent of marines who were stationed in the fighting tops along with sailor marksman. Their mission was to clear *Serapis'* tops of men then turn their muskets on the British officers and then anyone else on deck. Pearson tried to order the lines of the grappling hooks cut and these irons cast off, but the British sailors were gunned down by the musketry marksmanship of marines and sailors. In a desperate attempt to break the grip of the American ship, Captain Pearson ordered an anchor dropped with the hope that a sudden stop might jolt the two ships apart.

It was now about an hour into the battle. The wind and tide gradually swung the ships, now held by *Serapis'* anchor, in a 180-degree turn. For the next two hours the two ships will be locked and continued to fight. *Serapis* using her superior firepower pounded the hull of the American ship in an attempt to sink her. American marksmen, however, kept the British weather decks clear of sailors. At one point, flaming wads from the guns set fire to the sails and rigging of both ships, and fighting came to a halt in order to fight the fires.

While Jones and Pearson battled, the *Pallas* had taken on the much smaller *Countess of Scarborough*, the other British escort, keeping her from lending a hand to *Serapis*. Early in this stage of the battle, *Alliance* entered the fray and fired indiscriminately, raking *Bonhomme Richard* and killing several sailors. *Alliance* then dropped down briefly to observe the engagement between *Pallas* and the *Countess*, before she beat to windward, away from the action. About 9:30, *Alliance*'s commanding officer, Pierre Landais, once again joined the action, but hardly in support of commodore Jones. *Alliance* crossed the bow of *Serapis* and stern of *Bonhomme Richard*, and fired into both ships, but mainly into the American ship. Landais then turned down wind, wore-ship enabling him to cross the bow of *Bonhomme Richard* and stern of *Serapis*. Another broadside slashed into *Bonhomme Richard* killing several men and a petty officer on the forecastle.

The culmination of the battle came about 10 o'clock. Marine William Hamilton carried a basket of hand grenades and a slow-match aloft onto the *Bonhomme Richard*'s main yard and began lighting and dropping grenades onto the decks of the British ship below. One of the grenades bounced through an open hatch onto *Serapis'* gun-deck and exploded. Spilled gunpowder and cartridge bags that had littered the deck set off a chain reaction of explosives down the length of the deck causing devastation. Twenty men were killed and many others badly burned.

Pearson was on the verge of striking the colors of his ship when he heard three of *Bonhomme Richard*'s sailors shouting and asking for quarter. One of the men, the carpenter who had inspected the ship for damage, sank to his chin in the water that was rising in the ship's hold. Unable to find an officer, he found a gunner's mate and the master-at-arms. They headed aft, and not finding the captain and hearing that he was dead, decided to call for quarter. Jones, who was very much alive and not about to surrender, pulled his pistol from his sash or holster and tried to shoot one of them. Apparently having previously fired the pistol, he hurled the weapon at the gunner's mate and knocking him out. Pearson, however, had heard the call for quarter and asked Jones if he wished to surrender. Jones responded that he had no such thought and was determined to make Pearson strike. The British captain was not yet ready to concede the battle and ordered his boarders to attack *Bonhomme Richard*. The American sailors firmly resisted the attack and the British sailors were forced to retreat back to the relative safety of *Serapis*.

Meanwhile, Jones ordered his three remaining nine-pounders on *Bonhomme Richard*'s quarterdeck to batter away at *Serapis*' mainmast, gradually shattering it with double-headed shot. Just before 10:30, Pearson had only four of eighteen-pounders still firing and the mainmast of *Serapis* was on the verge of falling overboard. Pearson realized that the end was in sight and called for quarter. Jones told Pearson that if he intended to strike, he must haul down his ensign. At the beginning of the battle Pearson had nailed the ensign to the flagstaff. Now he personally tore it down from its staff and laid it upon the poop deck.

Lieutenant Richard Dale, *Bonhomme Richard*'s first lieutenant, swung on board *Serapis*, followed by a boarding party led by a midshipman. Securing the *Serapis*, Dale escorted Captain Pearson back to *Bonhomme Richard* that was floating wreckage and introduced him to Commodore Jones. About the time Pearson arrived on board *Bonhomme Richard*, *Serapis*' mainmast went over the side and took the mizzen topmast with it. Following custom, Pearson presented his sword to Jones, and Jones commented upon how he and his men had fought bravely. Jones then invited the defeated captain to his badly damaged cabin and, as was the custom among officers and gentlemen, they shared some wine.

Throughout the night and the next day, *Bonhomme Richard*'s crew worked to save the ship, but the water continued to rise overwhelming the pumps before it could be discharged overboard. Fortunately for Jones, the next day was dark and foggy, effectively hiding his efforts to repair the ships. He ordered the wounded of both sides transferred to other vessels of the squadron. Jones returned to *Bonhomme Richard* about 7:00 the following morning and decided that his old battered ship could not be saved. At 7:30 he transferred his commodore's flag to *Serapis* and gave the order to abandon *Bonhomme Richard*. On September 25, at 11:00, the battered American ship slipped beneath the waves.

We now attempted to get onboard the *Serapis*, but the wind and weather that assisted in the *Good Man Richard*'s demise made this a difficult passage. Suddenly it became very foggy and consequently we lost sight of the *Serapis* and the rest of the squadron. The wind increased, in the seas ran high. We were obliged to balance the mainsail upon our tender and heave to. By this time, she shipped so much water onboard we had great difficulty keeping her

4. Aftermath

from sinking. We continued to be tossed about for about thirty hours, part of that time at the mercy of the wind and waves. In the end, the wind began to abate and the sea became relatively smooth. During this time, we had no food onboard and only a quart of fresh water. Soon thereafter we arrived alongside the *Serapis* with light hearts and very hungry stomachs and were received with a hearty welcome and a great deal of happiness. This was especially true of Captain Jones who had assumed that we were lost.

When the nasty weather abated every officer and man on board the *Serapis*, excepting the sick the wounded, were employed to erect jury masts and then rig them. We received three spare topmasts and other spars from the *Alliance* for this purpose. Landais's ship had several of the kind we needed, but they were also badly damaged and even pierced through with shot holes in places making them unfit for our needs.

The roll of ship's officers and crew was called at the direction of the commodore. We then learned that we had lost one hundred sixty-five officers, men and boys killed, and one hundred thirty-seven wounded and missing in the recent battle. Of the wounded, nearly one hundred were thrown overboard from the vessels in the squadron where they have been brought after the action. With regard to so many of the wounded dying, it was probably due to the lack of skill of the surgeons available to perform amputations on them.[7] Looking back on this heartbreak, we only had one surgeon in the squadron who really knew his job, and that was a Doctor Brooks, a Virginian. This unfortunate man was obliged to work as a bloody butcher from the commencement of the battle until toward just night of the following day. The greater part of the wounded had their legs or arms shot away. Where their bones were badly fractured, the surgeons were forced to perform an amputation operation. Some of these poor fellows underwent this painful surgery done by unskilled surgeons other than by Doctor Brooks. Because they had been put onboard different vessels of our squadron, it was nearly impossible for the doctor to give the patients the attention that their medical cases required. In addition, the gale winds that succeeded the action made it practicable for him to visit the other wounded. It turned out that those injured men onboard the *Serapis* were fortunate. The gunner's mate who had suffered a skull fracture either from Jones' pistol blow or his subsequent tumble into the hold was found among the wounded and recovering well. Because of this sailor's act of cowardice by begging for quarters of the enemy during the action, the man was sent to do duty as a common sailor. The demotion was a relatively lenient punishment for his misconduct.

The *Serapis* was not only dismasted in the fight, quarter rails, rigging, nettings, and the like were completely leveled with her quarterdeck. Her bowsprit was made useless by our cannon balls as was her boats. Several of her cannon were in a similar situation having been dismounted in the fray. The slaughter among her officers and men was not so great as onboard the *Good Man Richard*. By her muster roll, it appeared that the *Serapis* lost in the action one hundred thirty-seven of her crew killed including officers and about seventy-six wounded. This included nearly twenty who were blown up at the closing event of the action by a hand grenade and powder explosion. Not one recovered, but they lingered along for three days. They were burned so badly that the flesh of several of them dropped off from their bones and they died in great pain. During the battle, there were perhaps about fifteen hundred people upon the land at Flamborough Head or near it. They watched the scene of human carnage in the moonlight and some of whom I have seen since said that the tops the nearest ship to land, which was the *Good Man Richard*, appeared to these spectators to be in a constant blaze of fire after the first action.

On 26 September, four days after the battle, the *Serapis* was in condition to sail. Accordingly, we crowded on all the sails we could and steered for the coast of Holland in the company of our squadron. The next day an English 64-gun vessel and three frigates, which had been dispatched by the British government to capture us, arrived upon the very spot where the action had been fought. They learned from fishermen in a local small boat that our squadron was last seen sailing towards Holland and they directed their course to chase after us.

With the *Serapis* as our temporary flagship, our squadron arrived off the Texel bar on 3 October. Captain Jones dispatched our first lieutenant in the barge with a letter to the Dutch admiral who commanded several Dutch men-of-war at anchor in the Texel Roads. The American commodore requested permission for the squadron to enter Texel and shelter in the roads. At this time Holland was not at war with England, thus the lieutenant returned with an absolute refusal from the Dutch admiral alleging that his government would not approve of such a politically sensitive measure. By this time the English squadron that had been pursuing us was now in sight. Our ship however was not in any condition to go into battle because we lacked men on board needed to fire its guns. Also, we were crammed full with wounded men between decks. These unfortunate seamen would be a hindrance if we had to manage the heaviest cannon we had on board in a firefight. No time was to be lost so Captain Jones acted quickly. He once again dispatched the lieutenant with a letter to the Dutch admiral that described, in blunt terms the danger that awaited his squadron and closed this message in feisty language stating that if the admiral refused to grant his request for the second time, he must bear the consequences. Jones went on to say that if he did not receive permission he would nevertheless make sail and enter Texel and place himself under the personal protection of the Dutch admiral. This strategy had the desired effect. The American lieutenant returned on board with the favorable answer and pilots were then sent and received onboard our

4. Aftermath

ships. With the English a little more than a long cannon shot away, the signal was made for the squadron to enter the Texel Roads. Arriving among the Dutch ships, our squadron came to anchor in about eight fathoms of water. Before our ship could furl her sails the Dutch admiral sent his barge commanded by an officer to compliment Captain Jones on his safe arrival. He also asked Jones to come onboard his flagship the *Amsterdam*. As soon as the commodore was seated in the admiral's barge, the crews of the vessels of our squadron gave Jones three cheers. On his return to the *Serapis* we fired a salute the Dutch admiral with our canon and the Dutch flagship returned the salute. This ceremony must have been very galling to the English onboard their fleet. They must have heard every gun because they were not more than four miles from us lying off the bar. Soon after our arrival we obtained authorization to land our sick and wounded men upon an island in the bay from the Stadholder. About a fortnight after our arrival in the Texel, Captain Pearson, along with his officers, were paroled at The Helder by permission of the Prince of Orange.[8,9]

Not long after this, Captain Landais who had commanded the *Alliance*, was suspended from his command by the American minister at Paris, Benjamin Franklin. This was done as a consequence of Captain Jones's complaint to Mr. Franklin of Landais's cowardice and bad conduct sent before we arrived in Holland. Landais was ordered to travel Paris to answer to the charges. Before he set out, however, Landais sent commander of the *Pallas*, Captain Cottineau, a written challenge to a duel.[10] Cottineau agreed to accept the encounter and they went on shore at The Helder, prepared for a swordfight with their seconds. Landais was the victor by seriously wounding Cottineau.

Shortly after this incident, Landais sent another written challenge, this time to Captain Jones. Perhaps thinking it was foolish to expose himself to single combatant who had the reputation of being a master of the small sword, he declined to accept the encounter. Instead, he answered the challenge by ordering Landais to be arrested. When Landais heard of this, he eluded the men who were charged to apprehend him and immediately left for Paris.

The captain of the *Serapis*, when taken had a large amount of silver plate and other articles in his cabin. According to the rules of war, these objects belonged to the captors. Instead of taking the advantage of this, Captain Jones had all the articles belonging to Captain Pearson packed into trunks and sent them with his lieutenant on shore at The Helder with his compliments to Captain Pearson together with directions to accept them as coming from the American captain. The first lieutenant went on shore, delivered Captain Jones's message, but returned with the trunks together with a verbal answer from the condescending English captain stating that he would not receive the articles in question delivered to him from the hands of a rebel officer. Once again, by the victor's conventions of war Jones was entitled to keep them. Pearson, at the time, intimated that he would receive the articles from the hands of Captain Cotteneau who held a naval commission issued by the French king, a recognized nation. Cotteneau was immediately sent for and was directed by Captain Jones to carry these articles as well as his sword and pistols on shore and give them to Captain Pearson. Cotteneau performed this task and returned back to Captain Jones. He commented that the Captain Pearson graciously receive the articles, but did not condescend to return any thanks or compliments to Jones.[11] In my opinion, that showed a lack of respect, courtesy and good breeding. All the English prisoners onboard the squadron, some five hundred thirty-seven, were landed by special permission of the Dutch government on an island maintained by the American agent then residing in Amsterdam. About the same time, the English minister residing at The Hague, Sir Joseph Yorke, made serious complaints to the Prince of Orange and the Dutch government about our being in a Dutch port. They had unlawfully allowed His Britannic Majesty's rebel subjects to take refuge in Texel with prizes that were His Majesty's ships-of-war. The Dutch admiral had permitted this to transpire and protected the rebels. If left to complete their mission, His Majesty's ships which had been dispatched from England to capture these rebel vessels would have surely taken every one of them. Soon thereafter the Dutch admiral treated the American commodore with a cool reserve. They did not visit each other as usual after this.

Captain Jones now set off for Amsterdam and was well received. He was treated with every mark of deference and this was enormously annoying to the English minister. He had the gall to insist that the Dutch government turn over the two English ships of war and all the English prisoners that had been in our possession. He demanded this with an unqualified answer. The Dutch government was not intimidated and wished for additional time to consider this important issue. The English minister said that he was unwilling to allow more than three days to pass before the Dutch government provided an answer. The Dutch thought this was too short a time and the British minister threatened to leave The Hague and sail for England.

While in Amsterdam, Captain Jones was venerated as a conqueror as though he had been in the Dutch naval service and they were at war with England. This so delighted Jones that his narcissism was soon displayed. In his self-importance he entered the Dutch Parliament's Statehouse, mounted the balcony, and flaunted himself in front of the populace and people of distinction walking below. Not long after this, boats were requisitioned at the government's expense and the English officers, together with all the English prisoners captured by our little squadron, were embarked on cartels and sent to England. Whether an equal number of American prisoners were to be exchanged I do not know, but Captain Jones assured us that this was the case.

The crews on board our vessels at this time were ailing and we had lost

4. Aftermath

the service of a number of men. We now began to repair the *Separis* and had employed a number of Dutch carpenters, who, together with our own, were busily at work. We then received orders from the commodore at Amsterdam to Mr. Deal that we were to replace the jury-masts and should receive by the next day three new masts to replace those that our ship had lost. Accordingly, carpenters and sailors immediately set to work to get ready to step the new masts in place when they appeared. The next day counter orders arrived from the commodore. The jury-masts were again set in place and rigged as before and preparations were made for sailing at a moment's warning. The crews of the different ships in our squadron assisted us in this confusing business. The next day fresh orders were received from the headquarters at Amsterdam. We were to unrig the jury-masts again and make ready to receive new masts. Orders and counter-orders in like manner and form were received on board the *Serapis* every day for about 10 days in succession which kept all hands constantly at work night and day. At last we received our new masts alongside and stepped them in their places, got our topmast on end, our yards athwart and rigged, provisions on board, and were ready for sea by 16 November. At about 10 o'clock at night on that date, the commodore arrived onboard from Amsterdam and gave immediate orders to the officers and crew of the *Serapis* to vacate her and board the frigate *Alliance*. In addition, his orders were to leave the former English warship about midnight as silently as possible. Captain Cottineau of the *Pallas*, with a set of officers and crew, occupied our place is on board the *Serapis*. The next morning French colors were displayed onboard and on the flagstaff. At the same time a French captain and crew took possession of the *Countess of Scarborough*. All this, it seems, was done under detailed advice received from the French ambassador at The Hague together with the American agent at Amsterdam. This was done to obstruct the intentions of the Dutch government who were about to deliver these prizes into the hands of English. There were repeated complaints made to the Dutch government, accompanied with threats by the English minister, regarding these two English ships that were taken by his Majesty's rebellious subjects. The Dutch government was placed in a diplomatic bind and was being coerced to deliver the two prizes in question up to the English. This became known to the French minister and the American agent. They therefore sent orders to abandon the two English ships and place each under a French captain, officers and crew. This maneuver completely thwarted the English minister and hindered the ostensible intent of the Dutch government.

The French minister now claimed both prizes in the name the French King and stated that his Christian Majesty's subjects had captured the ships. If they were to deliver the vessels to the English, they must be reasonable after such a breach of faith on their part. If not, he would immediately leave The Hague without ceremony and return to the French court. The English fleet was still lying off the Texel bar to receive the *Serapis* and the *Countess in Scarborough* as the English minister communicated to the English commander that the Dutch government had agreed to deliver on a certain date. The awaiting British fleet however was driven some distance northward by a violent gale. Soon thereafter the two prize ships took advantage of the English squadron's absence from their patrol off the bar and put to sea. The two prize vessels arrived safely at L'Orient, France together with the rest of the squadron except for the frigate *Alliance*.

5

The *Alliance* as Flagship

When Jones took command of the *Alliance* we had a set of officers and crew that belonged to the both the *Good Man Richard* and Landais's former ship. The entire number of officers and men on board of that ship, including boys was four hundred twenty-seven and nearly all were Americans. We now felt that we were able to take any 44-gun ship in the British Navy and Captain Jones took great pains to impress this idea upon the minds of his officers and crew.

A well-written journal kept by a midshipman who belonged to the *Serapis* and who was killed in the late action was found onboard the vessel. This journal recounts that he had been in America and was onboard when Lord Dunsmore ravaged the southern states during our Revolutionary War.[1] I must confess that chilled my blood and my mind was struck with horror while reading some of the pages of this journal. He went into numerous exploits that he had performed against the rebels in America. It seems by his own story that he murdered many decrepit old men and women. I first thought that I would have this unusual journal published to show my countrymen and countrywomen an example of British inhumanity. But on reflection, this young Englishman might still have a living aged father and mother and perhaps siblings. This publicity might damage their feelings notwithstanding the enormities of which this young man had been guilty. His family likely possessed tender feelings of compassion and benevolence toward him. Besides, the young midshipman might have been prompted to commit these horrible deeds by examples set to him by his superior officers. In addition, what finally persuaded me not to make this detailed journal public was the old adage about never speaking ill of the dead.

We were ready for sailing, but the British squadron that had pursued us blockaded the entrance of the port of Texel, obliging us to remain inside the roads. Using the anchorage time, the *Alliance* was unrigged, her yards and topmasts were taken down by Captain Jones's orders. The tops were also lowered down and placed upon the deck. The carpenters were directed to make new larger ones so as to hold more men. Since the recent battle, Captain Jones observed that having several men stationed in the tops of the ship of war gave him a great advantage. At the same time our main and fore yards were reduced in size as well as in length. Prior to this, those yards were nearly as large and as broad as an English 74-gun warship.

Two of our volunteer midshipmen asked Captain Jones permission to leave the Continental Naval Service. Captain Jones consented and gave us midshipmen, including me, a certificate indicating that we had served honorably as follows:

> *To the honorable President of Congress of United States of America:*
> These certify, that the bearer having served under my command in the capacity of midshipmen on board the *Good Man Richard*, ship of war belonging to United States, until she was lost in the action with the *Serapis*, an English ship-of-war of superior force; and since on board on the last mentioned ship and *Alliance* frigate, his bravery and good conduct on board first mentioned ship and while he has been in the service, will, I hope, recommend him to the notice of Congress, and his country, and believing as I do, that he will in a higher station, make a meritorious and deserving sea officer, I subscribe myself to these presents. (Signed) J. P. Jones
>
> *Done on board of the United States frigate Alliance this 10th day of December 1779.*

It must be acknowledged that Captain Jones treated his midshipmen with a great deal of respect in some instances and in others with a degree of cruelty. I will mention examples of both and leave the reader to judge whether my assertions are correct. It was a constant practice of Jones to invite midshipmen to eat with him almost daily. There were six of us; four were rated and carried upon the ships books, the other two were acting midshipmen. The latter duo received no pay for their services. When we went to have dinner with him we were required to appear in his quarters wearing our best clothes, otherwise we were sure not to receive a favorable reception. He usually conversed with his midshipmen as freely as he did with his lieutenants, the sailing master and the purser. When it came to doing our duty however, he was all business. When at sea in the daytime, he would have one midshipman aloft as a lookout. This could be upon the main top gallant yard, the main top gallant cross trees, the fore top gallant yard or fore top gallant cross trees. Sometimes when one of us was sent to the top gallant yard and Jones thought the midshipman was not as attentive as he should be, he would let the fore top gallant halyards loose and the poor midshipmen on the yard would suddenly fall. He would feel himself lucky if this shocking action did not severely injure him. Another dangerous duty that Jones required of his midshipmen was whenever all hands were called to reef the topsails or to shake out a reef, one of us was expected to be at each yardarm to pass the earrings. Whenever this happened all hands were called to reef or let out the reefs of all

5. The Alliance *as Flagship*   51

the topsails. If this order was given when a number of us were asleep in our berths, it was quite amusing to see the pitiable midshipmen scramble. Some would climb aloft without anything on except their shirt and perhaps a pair of under-drawers for all to see while getting on to the yardarms. There were many times that I had to ascend aloft in this predicament. I assume this will suffice for how Jones treated this class of junior officers.

At this time the Dutch had one 64-gun ship at anchor in the Texel and that vessel hoisted the Dutch admiral's flag. In addition, there were several 50-gun ships and frigates. On the morning of 17 December, the Dutch admiral sent his barge with an officer on board to us. He told Captain Jones that the admiral had orders not to allow an American flagged ship in the Texel roads. This lieutenant was commanded by him to request that Jones get underway immediately and stand off to sea. If not, he would incur the admiral's greatest displeasure. Captain Jones received this message without appearing offended. He treated the officer politely and, in dismissing him, told the lieutenant to inform the admiral that as soon as the wind was fair, he intended to go to sea. At this time, the *Alliance* was the only American ship in Texel that flew the stars and stripes.

The English squadron was still cruising in sight of us almost every day, but at some distance away. Regardless of this threat, Jones did not like being shut up in port. The active and enterprising genius that possessed his heart could not tolerate this situation. The Dutch admiral continued to torment him with impertinent messages and it became customary for him to send his barges every day with a Dutch officer onboard commanding us to depart. Sometimes this order came accompanied by threats and at other times with more decent words. This maritime melodrama continued over the course of several days while the wind remained contrary for sailing out of the anchorage. At last Jones became tired of the repetitious treatment and he sent word in an exasperated manner to the Dutch admiral saying he resented being imposed upon. He also said that although the Admiral had the honor of commanding a 64-gun ship, if he were at sea with the *Alliance*, the admiral would not dare insult him there. After this exchange, the admiral sent no more barges or anyone to board us until the day we sailed from Texel. The admiral did, however, send some men to assist us in getting underway and a pilot to help work us over the bar. Our departure took place on the 28th day of December about 10 in the morning. By noon we had cleared the bar and discerned two ships in the distance that appeared to be directly before us. They came up to us nearly within the gunshot range, then tacked, and hoisted English colors, but stood away from us. One of the ships was a 28 and the other a 30-gun frigate. At the same time all hands were called to quarters on board our ship. My station as usual was in the maintop. It was my opinion, that if these two English ships of war had decided to engage us, we would have given them a good Yankee beating and the night of 22 September would have been recreated. It appeared by their maneuvering however, that they were afraid of us. We did not change our course because the wind was favorable for the Straits of Dover, the place where we had set our course. The two English ships of war kept inside of us and we were called down and then back to quarters several times during the night. They kept on dogging us. Sometimes they would shorten sails and drop astern of us and other times would make sail as if it was their intention to come alongside and engage us in battle. It seemed that as soon as they saw we were prepared to meet them, they would back off and keep out of gunshot range. On 1 January 1780, we were abreast of Goodwin Sands and saw several English men-of-war lying near them.[2] Our thirteen striped flag flew on a flagstaff over our stern, a long streaming coachwhip pennant aloft, and an American Jack set forward. This was perhaps the first American colors some of them had ever seen. I believed that those Englishmen thought we were pretty saucy fellows.

At 2 P.M. the two frigates that had chased us from the Texel bar appeared to be making preparation to attack us. Captain Jones directed those in charge of our great guns not to fire upon the enemy until they were within pistol-shot. As soon as they had come within long gunshot range, they immediately tacked-ship and sailed away from us. They tacked once again

Battle flag saved from *BonHomme Richard* (Naval History and Heritage Command, NH 115316).

and stood away for some time. We now sailed very quietly along the English shore that was about two leagues distant on our starboard side. We had a leading breeze from the northeast. With American colors waving in the brisk wind and all our sails set we gave the appearance of defiance to old England's wooden walls. We Yankees now had enough spirit and resolve to batter some of them to pieces if they would but give us a fair contest. At this juncture we were abreast of the east end of the Isle of Wight and could plainly see English men-of-war lying at anchor at Spithead. The two frigates that had so often threatened to give us battle now appeared to be determined to finally confront us. Accordingly, the larger ship, that of their commodore, hoisted his broad pendant by way of giving us a challenge and made several other signals that we could not understand. Both ships hauled up their courses, handed their topgallant sails and slung their yards. It now looked as if battle preparations were in earnest. Onboard our ship, we were ready in high spirits with every officer, man and boy at his station. We had shortened sail for the enemy to come alongside of us and, indeed, the enemy now got within musket shot. Everyone expected that action would commence in one or two minutes more, but nothing took place. All at once they dropped their courses, trimmed their sails and abruptly took to their seafarer's heels to run away. We presumed that the enemy was frightened by our fordable and warlike appearance. The *Alliance* made sail so as to do battle with the cowards and was fast gaining on them when we found that we were being chased by a ship-of-the-line. She likely had discovered that we were an enemy vessel when we slipped her cables at Spithead. We also then realized that the signals that the larger of the two English frigates made earlier was to acknowledge that they were not a match for the lone American frigate, but they were confident of being able to capture us with the assistance one of their line-of-battle ships.

After this incident becomes public knowledge, I hope there will be no more boasts from the British such as that one Englishman being able to beat two Yankees; or that one frigate of 36-guns, officered and manned with full-blooded Englishman could easily capture two American frigates in consort, each of 36-guns and officered and manned with full-blooded Yankees. These and similar braggadocio expressions were quite frequently received from them when I was their prisoner both at sea and onshore.[3]

The English ship-of-the-line by this time found that we were out sailing her. She took in some sails and hauled on the wind towards the English shore where we soon lost sight of her. We cruised several days between Ushant and the Land's End of England during which time we only met neutral ships and small vessels. Afterwards we changed course and steered for Cape Finisterre.

There is one event that I had forgot to mention as we laid at anchor at the Texel. We had captured several prizes during our cruise on the *Good Man Richard*. Because of this, Captain Jones's officers and crew requested small advances in the money that they thought the prizes might generate. This was a real necessity for those who had lost all or almost all their clothing during the late action. The officers and men repeatedly petitioned Captain Jones about their needs that had become urgent with the severely cold weather setting in. It appeared to us to be unconscionable to go to sea almost bereft of appropriate attire. To quell the general discontent, he informed us that a few days before we sailed from Texel, a large sum of money had been sent onboard our ship from the American agent in Amsterdam. It was to be distributed among the officers, men and boys now belonging to the ship or those who had belonged to the *Good Man Richard*. When it came to be divided however, the officers received only about five ducats a piece without having any regard to rank. The sailors, marines, and boys received one ducat each [roughly half a guinea]. We were all quite disappointed, particularly the sailors. Some of them flew into a rage as soon as they had received their piddling ducat. In fury they threw the coins from the ship as far as they could into the sea. I do not know who was to blame. Neither do I know how much money had been sent on board our ship at this time. However, Captain Jones's officers said that he had taken the greatest part of this money for himself.

In a few days after this affair, we set our course for Cape Finisterre and made landfall. On the third day after our arrival we took two prizes that were laden with powder, lead, and other valuables. We manned the vessels and sent them back to the United States as prizes. After cruising here several days longer, we needed fresh water and provisions so we put into Coruna, Spain. While we lay in that port a number of the Spaniards came onboard to examine our ship, among whom were some Spanish gentlemen. When they came up on our quarterdeck, some took pains to let us know they were of members of a noble order by showing us their fingernails that were remarkably long and clean. This was their way of indicating that they expected a great deal of attention paid to them while they remained onboard.

This Spanish port was a remarkably good one for large ships. The harbor is large and vessels may ride at anchor here with safety. The town is rather large and the buildings are mostly made of white hewn stone. The dwelling houses are three to five stories high and the land that encompasses the harbor is also very high. We stayed at Coruna for about two weeks, received provisions and other needed necessities and then Captain Jones ordered the frigate to get underway. Many sailors however refused declaring that they would not do their duty, nor go to sea again unless they received part of the wages due to them or at least some part of their prize money. The men insisted that the funds ought to have been paid to them as Captain Jones had promised before we left Texel a long time ago. In response he stated that he intended to go directly to L'Orient in France where, soon after our arrival, they should have the prize money paid to them. Contrary to his promise, however, he cruised several weeks at sea without attempting to get into that port. Jones now tried all sorts of persuasion in order to get the sailors to do their various duties, but to no avail. They remained inflexible and adhered to their determination of not going to sea again without pay. He then urged his officers to prevail upon the sailors to perform their jobs. They succeeded by making additional promises to persuade them to get the ship underway. Jones declared once again, in the presence of his officers and crew, pledging his word and honor, that as soon as they were clear of land, he would sail directly to L'Orient. He also noted that the wind was favorable to steer for that port and said we should arrive there as soon as possible. The ship now got underway and *Alliance* sailed out of the port for the sea.

We had gotten a few miles from the land when Jones had his officers convened in the great cabin. After a short and pertinent harangue, he told them he now intended to cruise at sea about twenty days before he should proceed to the L'Orient. With the kind of contemptuous smile to which he seemed addicted he said, "Gentlemen, you cannot conceive what an additional honor it will be to us all, if in the cruising a few days we should have the good luck to fall in with an English frigate [with] our force and carry her in with us." And added, "This would crown our former victories and our names, in consequence thereof would be handed down to the latest posterity, by some faithful historian of our country."[4] We told him we did not object to cruising a few days longer, but once again pointed out that the neither the crew nor the officers had sufficient clothes for ourselves and that he was well aware of our shortage of wearing apparel since the late action. It was the winter season and we were in no condition to remain up on deck and do our duty. We guaranteed him that we could not think of cruising any longer in our present difficult circumstances in an appeal to his sense of compassion. One of Captain Jones's lieutenants added that he felt that his crew was in a state bordering upon mutiny. He went on to say that he believed we should not hazard our own lives by such an undertaking. "Well then," said Jones, "I mean to cruise as long as I please. I do not want your advice, neither did I send to you to comply with your denial, but only by way of paying you a compliment, which is more than you deserve, by your opposition. Therefore, you know my mind. Go to your duty each one of you and let me hear no more grumbling."[5] He said this in a rage, stamped this foot and commanded us to get out of his sight. We obeyed these commands and the *Alliance* continued to cruise seventeen days longer. We saw an English frigate and it came so near to us that we could plainly see she was a 32-gun ship. Our crew however swore that they would not fight, although I believed that if we had been united we might have taken her with ease. Captain Jones then realized that he was in a dangerous situation. He ordered our courses dropped and we ran from her and made all the sail we could. All this time the captain appeared agitated, biting his lips often and walking the quarterdeck constantly muttering to himself. Night set in and we lost sight of the frigate that was chasing us. Three days thereafter, we arrived safely in the port of the L'Orient and dropped our anchor where we found the *Serapis* with several of our prizes. It was now February and soon after going ashore we received instructions from Mr. Franklin, the American minister in Paris, to get the *Alliance* ready for sea again as quickly as possible so that we could carry public dispatches [mail] to America.

During this last cruise in the *Alliance;* Captain Jones's officers who had belonged to the *Good Man Richard* and Captain Landais's officers had heated words and squabbles with each other in the wardroom. It became clear that we had two disparate sets of officers onboard the *Alliance* who often displayed divided loyalties. The quarrels were frequent among them and they would sometimes challenge one another, all on account of the cowardice of Captain Landais during the late battle. Those officers who had served under Landais maintained that he was a brave man and certainly as courageous as Captain Jones. Jones's officers however quite strenuously maintained the opposite view. Therefore, during this last cruise our wardroom exhibited a great deal of bickering and discord among our officers.

Those of us who had been the crew of the *Good Man Richard* until she was lost now contacted a Mr. Morylan, the local American agent who was responsible for fitting the *Alliance* out from L'Orient prior to her last cruises. That is to say we made applications to him for our prize money, but he declared that he had nothing to do with that sort of affair. Instead Mr. Morylan said that we had to apply to the Board of War in America to receive our earned funds. Because of this a number of Americans, in time, became beggars in a foreign country. This was especially true of those who lost their legs and arms fighting gloriously under the American banners. Sometime afterwards several who returned to America made application to the Board of War in Philadelphia. In an exasperating typical bureaucratic excuse, the Honorable Board declared that the *Good Man Richard* was not originally fitted by order of Congress or any of their ministers. It was their opinion that she was a French privateer.[6] We were never able to learn whether that ship belonged to the French or Americans, but we knew at the time that we had fought onboard the *Good Man Richard* under the American colors, that our prizes were sold in France and the moneys arising from the sales had long since been collected. We also learned that the greater part of this money was in the hands of a Monsieur Chaumont living in the city of Paris.

Meanwhile a great many alterations and renovations were now being made in almost every part of the ship by the *Alliance*'s carpenters. It was our opinion that this would entail a considerable and unnecessary expense to the United States. Captain Jones, however, was now so comfortable with his command over her, he was pleased to have everything altered

5. The Alliance as Flagship

onboard to please his fantasy. I presume that the cost was only as a secondary consideration. The refurbished *Alliance* was ready for sea by the middle of June 1780 and we only waited for a favorable wind in order to proceed for America.

We had heard that Captain Landais's ship had recently arrived in L'Orient, but the captain was going about the port city incognito. In time he publicly came forward as a leading character upon the stage to enact the following dramatic role: On 23 June at 2 o'clock in the afternoon, Captain Jones's officers were below at dinner while Jones was on shore dining with the military commandant of L'Orient. Landais's officers at this time were all assembled on the quarterdeck. We became aware of their presence when we heard three loud huzzas coming from above. The sudden commotion surprised us and we climbed the ladder to the quarterdeck as fast as our legs could carry us. We then saw Landais walking forward and aft waving a paper in his hand. The yards above him were all manned with his former crewmen. Upon seeing the first group of us, he instructed Mr. Diggs, his former first lieutenant, to assemble all Captain Jones's officers on deck because he had something to say to them. When we all answered to the hastily ordered muster, Landais holding his commission in his hand, addressed the assembly in nearly the following words: "Here you see, gentlemen, the commission that the Congress had given me for this frigate and you see I now command her and that there is no man in France who has a right to take this commission from me. Therefore gentlemen, all you who do not acknowledge me to be captain of this ship you must directly go to shore taking your baggage and everything which belongs to you."[7] Accordingly, there was no other alternative left us but to obey these orders. All the offices who had served onboard the *Good Man Richard* under Captain Jones were forced to leave the *Alliance* except for one or two who chose to remain onboard. Landais, however, forbad any of the combined crew of *The Good Man Richard* and *Alliance* from quitting her. In about three quarters of an hour after this the *Alliance*, with the assistance of part of the crew of several men-of-war that had been lying in the harbor, made sail. The ship passed the citadel without molestation and came to anchor under the Isle of Groaix off L'Orient. No gunshots were heard from any of the French fortifications.

Jones was on shore when this remarkable event took place and did not hear about the takeover incident until the *Alliance* was safely at anchor. I suspected that the man was dreadfully enraged when he first heard what had taken place. The captain's passion knew no bounds. In the first outburst of his anger, he acted more like a mad man than a conqueror. However, when he realized that he was out-maneuvered by Landais, he started to calm down—perhaps trying to contemplate a counter move. The French commandant, at whose table he was sitting when he heard this news, offered him all the assistance in his power. Jones appeared to think that he had some hope of getting the *Alliance* into his possession again. He therefore left the commandant, contacted a French general and commandeered a large row galley that was tied up at the quay. This vessel mounted two 18-pounders forward and one aft, was rowed with sixteen oars and was capable of being rigged with lateen sails. He was also provided with about three hundred French troops for this expedition some stationed onboard the row galley and the rest onboard other smaller boats. Jones flattered himself by thinking that this force was capable of retaking the *Alliance*. He believed that Captain Landais, his officers and crew would offer little to no resistance. He also expected all the officers who had served under him to join and lend their assistance in this Quixote-like undertaking. To his misfortune, they all declined having anything to do with this affair except for one of his lieutenants. Jones refused to embark with the troops, which in my opinion he should have done. In time everything was in readiness and the little squadron moved out of the harbor flying American and French colors. They now proceeded toward the Isle of Groaix where the *Alliance* was anchored. The officer of the deck on watch onboard the *Alliance* sent a message to the commander of the expedition that said, "If they came within the reach of his cannon [about a mile] he would sink them."[8] The little fleet rested upon their oars a few minutes, then backed away and returned to port after setting out on this senseless mission. Upon seeing their return without taking the *Alliance*, Jones became so infuriated that he could hardly contain himself. He swore bitterly, stamped his feet, uttered all sorts of profanities and seemed frantic with rage. Three French ships-of-the-line were lying in the harbor at this time. Jones, with the help of the commandant, endeavored to prevail upon the French admiral to send out one or two of the ships to force the *Alliance* to return to port. The admiral however told Captain Jones that he, as a king's naval officer, would not interfere in the quarrel between him and Landais. He assured Jones that the departure of either of the ships under his command was more than his commission allowed, especially on the mission that Jones had in mind. In fact, this French admiral, the commander of the citadel commonly called Fort Louis, and Landais were all collaborators. Landais had been to the harbor fortification many times as well as being a frequent visitor onboard the French admiral's ship. Both the fort and the admiral's ship were two of the places where the plot was conceived to take the *Alliance* out of Jones's hands. The plan had been brought to completion and ultimately to great success.

In a day or two after this transaction, Arthur Lee the United States Envoy to the French royal government in Paris and the public mail set sail for America onboard the frigate *Alliance*. On the ship's passage however, Captain Landais and his first lieutenant were confined to their quarters by the other ship's officers. These two ranking commanders had refused to fight an English

5. The Alliance as Flagship

32–gun frigate that at various times challenged them to do battle. Arriving in Boston, Captain Landais and his first lieutenant were tried by a court composed of naval officers in United States Continental Naval Service. The two men were demoted, discharged and sentenced never being capable of serving as officers in the navy again.[9]

Captain Jones was now left to wander about without a ship to command and sail home to the United States. He took a trip to Paris to try his luck and to spend our money then in the hands of Mr. Chaumont. While there, he was praised and highly flattered by the king and queen. The king presented him with an elegant gold hilted sword set in diamonds valued at about 100 guineas in recognition of his bravery onboard the *Good Man Richard*. While he was in Paris, Her Majesty Queen Marie Antoinette invited him to sit with her in her own royal box at the performance of a play at one of the renowned local theaters. At that time, she presented him with a present, an elegant nosegay. These events caused a great deal of indignation among the King's naval officers who were then stationed at Paris in his service.

6

Taking Command of the *Ariel*

About middle of July, Captain Jones returned from Paris to L'Orient with the expressed purpose of obtaining command of the ship of war called *Ariel*. She was rated as a 20-gun ship, but she mounted 24 guns, six and nine-pounders. The French had recently captured this ship from the English. She was now to be renovated in L'Orient's dockyard and the carpenters and seamen worked hard to get her ready for sea. Jones' influence was so great and highly regarded, they called him "King of Brittany."[1] In spite of the Landais harangue, the inhabitants of L'Orient appeared to think that Jones deserved the honorary title.

On 7 October 1780, we set sail from this now familiar French port for the United States in the *Ariel*. We were the leading ship of a convoy of fourteen American vessels among which were three letters of marque. We luckily were underway before a strong wind blowing from the East Southeast. The wind suddenly shifted into the west-southwest later that evening forcing us to take in our topgallant sails and close reef our courses. We transited in this sail configuration as long as the ship could tolerate it. As darkness approached it became stormy and we lost sight of the fleet that we were accompanying. The vessel had to carry these shortened sails in order to weather the Penmark, a long range of sunken rocks about a league or three miles from land that we judged to be to our lee. By midnight we took in our courses because the wind blew so violently. Flying even a single sail might blow us ashore. The ship now became endangered in the rough sea and listed heavily, nearly upon its beam-ends. Our pumps were worked constantly and furiously just to keep us afloat. Some French soldiers who were stationed onboard helped crank them. Frightened by their situation, they suddenly let go of the siphon's handles, crossed themselves and started to pray. Our officers drove them back to the cranks and threaten them with death if they quit their duty again or did not work the apparatus with all their strength. For the time being this produced the desired result, but one of our chain pumps became fouled and refused

6. Taking Command of the Ariel

to deliver water. During this time Jones concentrated on the ship's position rather than on the storm and its effects in the ship. He took it upon himself to sound the ocean depth with our deep-sea lead and determined that we were rapidly being driven into shoal waters. It would not be long before we would collide with the rocks off Penmark unless we did something to prevent it. Because of the extreme emergency, Jones and his senior officers conferred on the quarterdeck. They decided that the best option was to cut away our foremast and cast out a sheet anchor. The anchor was thrown almost immediately and the cutting of the stout mast took more time, but it was accomplished. We sounded the bottom once again and recorded that the water's depth was thirty-five fathoms. The cable of the sheet anchor was spliced a number of times to add length. When it was thrust overboard to the leeward, the ship was brought to a halt and it rode with its head into the wind. The sea started to produce mountainous waves. We had less than three hundred fathoms of cable played out when the ship shuddered as it was brought to her anchor. She labored hard, rolled deeply and then suddenly came up. This untoward maneuver sprung our mainmast just below our gun deck and was in great danger of being ripped out. Orders were given to cut away the mainmast above the quarterdeck and this was quickly carried out. When our largest mast fell over the side to our leeward, it carried the head of the mizzenmast with it. By this time our pumps were all working again and freed the ship of water, but when the masts toppled over, the motion was so quick and violent, most of the crew fell on the decks and were forced to grab hold of anything that they could reach to keep them from being swept overboard. The chain pumps that had been choked were cleaned worked well. In spite of the gale our anchor and cables also held on and we now thought that our lives might be spared, even though the gale did not abate until the morning of the 9th.

By noon the wind abated enough so that we could erect jury-rigged masts and attach whatever spars and sails we could muster. By four in the afternoon the breeze had moderated. As it blew from the west-southwest, the sea became much smoother. We hauled on the cable until it was short and, with great exertion, tried to wrestle the anchor onboard. This took a long time to weigh in, but we were successful. We soon set sail for L'Orient and made it safely to the harbor once again. The many French friends that we had made appeared very happy to see us. They feared that we had been lost in the violent gale. It had produced a great deal of damage among the ships at anchor in the harbor of L'Orient and those tied up alongside the quays.

Before we set sail from this port on the *Ariel*, a number of American gentlemen had come onboard our vessel to arrange passage for the United States. Some of them were with us during the recent ferocious gale. Among them was a young gentleman by the name of Sullivan, a nephew of an American general.[2] At this time he was serving as a lieutenant in Count Dillon's

French army brigade stationed in the garrison at Fort Louis near L'Orient. When he first contacted us after arriving in Paris, he showed Captain Jones's officers letters of recommendation from several important French politicians and very prominent officers in the American army. He also had a letter from Benjamin Franklin to Captain Jones in which the minister asked Jones to take young Sullivan onboard, treat him with kindness and allow him to make passage on the *Ariel*. Regrettably Captain Jones tried to exploit the young man and abused him while he was onboard. I was an eyewitness to Jones's conduct toward this young gentleman and shall relate the events as I saw them.

When the *Ariel* had come to anchor in L'Orient after the storm, the passengers who had arranged to sail with us were ready to go ashore. Their trunks were placed onboard the boats tied alongside the ship. Young Sullivan was among them and also made preparation to go on shore. At this time Captain Jones politely asked him to stay onboard for two or three days to keep an eye on his marines and make sure that they did their duty properly. At that time the ship's regular captain of the marines was confined to a sickbed. Jones told the American but now French army lieutenant that he would save the expense of living on shore if he stayed onboard our ship. This seemed like a reasonable invitation, so the young man consented. He then told Jones that if he remained onboard for the time that the captain requested, he wished to go ashore thereafter until the ship was ready to sail for America. Jones said he was considered a passenger and was free to do as he pleased. After four days on the confines of the *Ariel*, Sullivan decided to go ashore. However, Jones urged him to remain a few days longer because the captain of marines had not completely recovered. This request was also consented to. After this extended time had expired, Jones made a third request asking the young man to remain onboard much longer. At this repeated request Sullivan lost patience. He abruptly told Jones, in no uncertain terms, that he was unaccustomed to such treatment. Since he was not under any obligation to the captain, Sullivan asked to have his baggage removed from the ship and go on ashore on the very next boat that came alongside. Infuriated, Jones called the lieutenant a "rascal," withdrew his sword from its scabbard and rushed at Sullivan shouting that he intended to run him through. Sullivan, without retreating or appearing intimidated calmly replied, "You are on board of your own ship, Captain Jones, therefore I know the consequence of making at this time any resistance; but sir, remember what I have the honor to say to you; if I have the good luck to see you on shore, depend upon it, I will make you repent of this unheard of insult and cruelty."[3] Jones did not reply, but as Sullivan prepared to descend to a boat to go ashore, the captain directed his first lieutenant to have the Army officer passenger taken below and confined in the ship's crew quarters. He then ordered his master at arms to immediately put "the rascal" in irons, hands and feet. A few days thereafter one or more of Jones's officers requested that Mr. Sullivan's hands be removed from the irons. The captain reluctantly consented.

Sometime thereafter the officers in Count Dillon's brigade learned of unseemly treatment given to their brother officer by Captain Jones. One of the brigade's colonels, a mentor and friend of Mr. Sullivan, boarded our ship and immediately asked if what he had heard about the lieutenant was true. Perhaps Jones started to think that his ill treatment of Sullivan might have gotten out of hand. He assumed that the colonel was a courageous man and if he found that the treatment of Sullivan was as bad as he heard ashore, he might assault the American captain. Consequently, Jones decided to employ a little distraction by inviting the colonel into his cabin, offering him a glass or two of wine, and suggesting that the French colonel dine with him. The army officer consented, but after a long chat the colonel requested to speak to Sullivan. Jones tried to change the subject and told the colonel that any story of Sullivan being put in irons or being harmed was false. The colonel then inquired why he had not seen him on shore since the *Ariel* had returned back to this port. Jones replied that Sullivan had become sick and was confined to his cabin. The colonel then asked to see him. Jones said that he was getting dressed and that he asked his servant to tell him to report to the captain's cabin when he was properly dressed. This seemed to satisfy the colonel for the moment and they both entered into conversation about the battle between the *Serapis* and *Good Man Richard*. This was the very distraction that Jones had hoped would draw the colonel's attention away from the Sullivan issue. There were countless details that could be discussed and examined until dinner was served. This sidetracked the colonel from his primary mission for a time and Jones now discovered that the Frenchman was a lover of good wine. Therefore, the captain made sure that his guest was amply supplied with the best he had onboard. After an hour or two of wine and engaging conversation, the utterly charmed colonel bade goodbye without following up on Sullivan's disappearance.

A few days later Jones by chance met the colonel on shore. The French officer once again raised the issue about Sullivan's mistreatment, why he had not allowed him to come ashore or permit him to have visitors onboard the *Ariel*. Bystanders heard him say, "If you do not liberate him shortly, and give him leave to come on shore, I shall myself take the matter up and learn you better manners."[4] This threat appeared to daunt Jones and he promised the colonel that Sullivan would be given his liberty. Accordingly, when Jones returned onboard he directed his first Lieutenant to release the young man from irons, allow him to come forward, but to inform him that he was impressed and was to serve as a common seaman on the *Ariel*. Sullivan's baggage was sent forward to the forecastle and he was told he would take his mess with the boatswain's mates—if they were willing. Unknown to Jones, however, the midshipmen provided comfortable lodging for Sullivan in one of the ship's staterooms and allowed him to take meals in the officer's mess.

The next time Jones met the colonel on shore, the army officer threatened to run his sword through him for not allowing Sullivan to come ashore as he had promised. He insisted that Jones immediately return to his ship and order Sullivan to come on shore. The colonel said that he would be waiting for the lieutenant's appearance and also added that if Jones refused his request, the American would greatly regret his snub. Jones promised to comply. When he returned to the *Ariel* Jones ordered me to man the jolly boat and take Sullivan and his baggage ashore. Prior to his release, however, Jones instructed me to break Sullivan's sword into pieces. The lieutenant was put ashore where the colonel was awaiting him and then they walked together in deep conversation; one would suppose discussing measures to severely punish to Jones. Lieutenant Sullivan had an explosive temperament coupled with unremitting courage. Shortly after landing, Sullivan purchased a new sword and a stout hickory cane. With those two implements in hand, he proceeded to Jones's private lodgings on shore. The lieutenant burst into the captain's room. Sullivan's confrontation of Jones started with reminding him of the abusive and brutal treatment he had endured on the *Ariel* under the captain's orders. He also reminded him that that he promised to seek satisfaction and punish him when he was released. Without ceremony or a second being present, Sullivan issued Jones a challenge to a duel and commanded Jones to step outside so that they could settle their business in an honorable way with their swords. He said that if the captain refused, he would beat Jones with his cane. Upon issuing the latter threat, Sullivan with an enraged expression on his visage lifted his cane aloft over the captain's head. He remained in this intimidating position until Jones made a response. The captain had been sitting at his desk writing when his antagonist had entered the room. Jones had put his pen in his mouth when Sullivan started to make his challenge and kept it there throughout the diatribe. Now he casually placed his pen on the desk, rose from his chair and coldly looked his adversary in the eye. He said that he declined to fight the lieutenant and asked him to leave his lodgings immediately or he would call the guard to take this madman and likely assassin into custody. Because of this rejoinder, Sullivan became even more infuriated and repeatedly struck Jones. The captain cried out for help as the savage blows left him bloodied. When the beating ended, the *Good Man Richard*'s hero slumped into his chair in pain, abject humiliation and finally into reflection. Once Jones had regained a degree of composure, he lodged a formal complaint to L'Orient's French military commandant against his assailant, but Lieutenant Sullivan had managed to disappear.

Word about the confrontation and beating quickly spread about the town and this set off a hue and cry. The police, military guards and other law

6. Taking Command of the Ariel

enforcement units looked all over the city and even broke into private dwellings to find Sullivan. They raucously scoured the countryside and all public roads in an attempt to capture the runaway and bring him into their custody.

In reality all the apparent fuss was a ruse. Sullivan was under the protection of his fellow officers at the Fort Louis garrison at the mouth of the harbor, about six miles away. Had Sullivan been arrested, his punishment might well have been severe since the civil and national laws for this type of offense mandated a twelve years prison sentence and a heavy fine. Since the lieutenant had resided in France for a long time, he was aware of the potential legal consequences of his crime. However, he wisely escaped finding protection among his French military comrades. Upon learning about the circumstances that precipitated his offence, few people in L'Orient and those on shipboard were sorry that Jones had suffered such a drubbing. It became obvious to most people that the search for Sullivan was never as earnest as it appeared. Jones's popularity was waning in many quarters. In spite of this, the commandant and several of the king's officers remained friendly toward him. This may have been in response to instructions from the king himself; at least that was what inhabitants of L'Orient seemed to believe. Never the less, these officials rendered Jones all assistance that was asked of them and was in their power to provide.

Soon after the Sullivan affair had subsided, the captain of the marines caned Jones in front of local L'Orient residents for not accepting a challenge that he had issued to him. Jones, now doubly disgraced by these beatings, rarely went ashore. When he did so, it was mostly at night.

Meanwhile the *Ariel* was nearly ready to return to sea. Several petty officers asked Jones for their share of prize money before they embarked. They said that they were unprepared to make the journey because they lacked adequate winter clothes and had no cash to buy them. This appeared to be a reasonable request and consistent with meeting his crew's needs. Jones however became predictably angered and had several of the men imprisoned in L'Orient for what he called their "impertinence."

About 10 December we made an unusual preparation for our departure. A large number of the most prominent residents of L'Orient were invited onboard the *Ariel* for a special occasion. Among the guests were a prince, three admirals and some ladies of the highest social station. Each received a written invitation from Captain Jones in which he requested they come onboard the next day and join him for dinner at 3 o'clock in the afternoon. He also mentioned that in the evening he would exhibit a sham sea-fight that would partly depict his battle with the *Serapis*, particularly what he deemed was the extraordinary action that took place on the tops. For this quasi-recreation, all the boats belonging to our ship were busily employed with their respective crews from ten of the morning of the preceding day until about midnight. These small vessels were used to bring the guests onboard and ferry the articles that Jones wished to use for his theatrical scenes. Jones seemed unconcerned about the money that was to be expended or the additional labor of his crew for this event. All pains were taken to make the hastily cobbled theater sets appear magnificent to the audience. The quarterdeck of our ship was covered with an elegant carpet. Overhead was suspended an elegant awning whose edges were cut in scallops and decorated with silk roses and other ornaments. At the sides were thin canvases lined with pink colored silk fabric that reached down to the quarterdeck. On the walls of this set were hung French paintings and mirrors. One or more renowned French artist had painted the images. In my opinion, some of these were quite indecent, especially for the eyes of a virtuous Frenchwoman. In these days they were a part of French etiquette for such occasions. I would estimate the dinner place settings that were used to be worth several thousand guineas. French cooks and waiters or servants were brought from shore to assist in the extravaganza. For the nearly 20 hours that preceded the serving of dinner we nearly choked from the smell of garlic, onions and other odiferous vegetables. A well-known French lady reputed to be an excellent culinary connoisseur as well as an interior decorator was asked to come onboard before the scheduled dinner. The evening prior to the day the invited company was to dine, Captain Jones greeted her when she came onboard and quickly turned on his charm. He then asked the lady if she would be so kind as to supervise the approaching feast. She consented.

The following day the guests were ushered onboard with a thirteen-gun salute. The ship was bedecked in the American thirteen stripes as well as the colors of all the nations friendly to the United States. Captain Jones and his officers were dressed in their best uniforms, neatly displaying impeccable military comportment. We midshipmen were instructed by the captain to conduct ourselves with propriety and tacitly obey the lady supervising the ceremony. At quarter before three in the afternoon three of the ship's boats were dispatched ashore to bring the company onboard. The crewmembers who had official uniforms were now smartly dressed in blue broadcloth and wore either American or French cockades in their hats. Jones received the guests as they boarded and conducted them to their seats on the quarterdeck with great civility and professional naval courtesy. [The prince was distinguished from the rest of the guests by a brilliant star that he wore on his left breast.]

Dinner was served at half past three in the afternoon. The company did not rise from their table until the sun had set. Jones was well aware that the latter part of this event would be under a full moon, so just at moonrise, the captain ordered his first lieutenant to call all hands to their battle stations. This was his way of approximating the atmosphere during the actual battle. I mounted the main top, the place where I had commanded and served under

6. Taking Command of the Ariel

Jones for these many months. Before we climbed aloft, we had previously placed a large supply of ammunition, blunderbusses, muskets, cohorns, hand grenades, etc., on the tops platform. A single blank canon shot was fired from the forecastle as the signal to commence the sham battle. The deafening cacophony of discharging weapons began shortly after eight o'clock and lasted roughly an hour and a quarter without an intermission. There was the roar of the great cannon, the hammer-like pounding of swivels, sharp reports of small arms detonating and the crackling, hissing and popping of grenades, stink pots, and powder flasks as they fell into the water alongside the *Ariel*. This was a spectacle like no other heard or seen in L'Orient. Finally, some of the ladies became frightened and Jones ordered the firing to cease. If not for this occurrence the sham fight might have continued even longer.

Now that the fighting had stopped and the smoke began to clear, a band that the commandant had ordered onboard provided music and paraded on the close confines of the quarterdeck. At around midnight, the company took their leave and the boats sent them safely ashore with the same order as when they came onboard. Several midshipmen were given the added assignment of assisting them to the safety of their lodgings because of the lateness of the hour.

For several days thereafter the conversation in the taverns, coffee houses and private dwelling of L'Orient was about Captain Jones's feast and mock battle. I believed that this diner and demonstration must have cost Jones as well as the United States a vast sum of money. There was a considerable amount of powder burned and alcohol drunk. The estimated cost of the whole affair came to 3,027 crowns, 6 shillings and 8 pence in Massachusetts' currency according to the American agent's clerk.[5] Whether Captain Jones charged the whole or part of the lavish event to the United States is unknown.

An order soon arrived from Paris, signed by Mr. Franklin, directing Captain Jones to set free the petty officers that belonged to *Ariel* and whom he had constrained in prison. Their offense was demanding their share of prize money, an extremely reasonable request in the light of the expense of the recent Jones shipboard extravaganza. Jones relented, obeyed the order and the young men resumed their respective stations onboard. The *Ariel* was now ready for sea except she needed additional men to complete or complement her crew. Jones and his officers endeavored to recruit the men he deemed essential, but were unsuccessful. The captain then contacted his friend the commandant and asked him to sanction the impressment of local citizens into service as seamen. The commandant absolutely refused to grant him permission to do this. However, he quietly said that he would not interfere as long as he only pressed Americans residing in the port of L'Orient or its immediate vicinity. Jones persuaded the commanding officer of the French Marine Department to help him in his quest. Several American letters of marque were then at anchor in the port. Their crewmen who were found ashore were forced to board the *Ariel*. Against their will and much to the consternation of the American privateer captains then in L'Orient these men became temporary Continental Navy sailors. Some of the officers and men were disgusted and disapproved of this illegal deed—but they were determined to sail to America. Once there, they would be done with Jones. I, however decided to quit the captain then and there. I had the right to do so because I had never signed the ship's articles. Fortunately, I had obtained a certificate from Jones entitling me to my share of the ship's prize money, so I would not be destitute.

On 15 December 1780 the *Ariel* sailed for America for a second voyage, this time with a smaller convoy of ships. I remained in L'Orient and made daily trips to the office of a Monseigneur Moylan to obtain my back-wages and prize money. After many fruitless claim submissions, I was given twenty-eight crowns, a small part of my wages for serving onboard the *Good Man Richard, Serapis, Alliance* and *Ariel* during perilous times. This nevertheless was just about adequate to pay for my food and lodging. Because I had spent a fair amount of time in L'Orient, I had made numerous French friends, among them was a merchant named Bellimont who was interested in investing in a privateer that was being made ready to sail at the not too distant port of Morlaix. He asked me if I would be willing to take command of the vessel, and if so, proceed to Morlaix's dockyard. I was grateful, but declined the offer. I had expected to obtain a similar command based from L'Orient.

[*At this point Nathaniel Fanning's Memoir digresses to relate his view of the "enterprising, celebrated and eccentric character" John Paul Jones plus Captains Richard Pearson and Richard Dale.*]

Biographical Sketch of the Life and Character of John Paul Jones, Esq.

John Paul Jones was born in Selkirk, Scotland the seat of the county by that name on 23 September 1747. This date was a written entry in a book titled: *The way to be happy in her miserable world*. It was among the books Captain Jones had with him when he commanded the *Good Man Richard*, but was lost in the aftermath of the *Serapis* battle.[6] Part of the time while I served onboard that ship, I functioned as Jones's secretary copying his dispatches to Congress and help pen his letters, etc. When I worked in his cabin, he generously allowed me to have free access to his books. This is where I found the information recorded. This version of his birth agreed with what he repeatedly said to several gentlemen. He also said that he never attended to any regular school in his life. An old maiden aunt, part of in father's fam-

6. Taking Command of the Ariel

ily, taught him his letters and to read a little when he was very young. His name at the time was John Paul. He said that when he turned twenty-two he added the name Jones to it. From some documents that I saw it appears that this was the surname of his mother before she was married to his father. The education he obtained after the age of nine was from reading a great many books. He was an avid reader and claimed that he doggedly studied day and night. When he was nine years old he left his family and set out to seek his fortune. He had no other clothes than those on his back and no money. Soon after this, he arrived at Leith and signed onboard an English ship as cabin boy. The ship engaged in the coal trade and was known by the English as a *collier*. Jones worked in this difficult and unglamorous dirty business for a number of years. He rose to the rank of mate when he turned seventeen and became a captain at age nineteen. His maritime skills rapidly increased and by the time he was twenty-four, he was given command of an English merchant ship that sailed between England and the West Indies. There is no record of how many voyages he made plying this trade route, but the ship's carpenter was drowned during the last voyage he made to the islands. Several of the vessel's crew stated that while the ship was anchored in the West Indies, the carpenter had been found guilty of some unspecified misdemeanor. Jones decided that he would punished him, but in a very peculiar way. Jones ordered an old broken pot placed upon the forecastle and then put a small quantity of gunpowder into it. Once this was done he instructed the carpenter to sit upon it without his breeches. He then directed the cook to alight the powder. The explosion that followed frightened the carpenter and likely hurt him. In response he jumped overboard and subsequently drowned.

When he returned to Hull, England with his ship, Jones was arrested by the local officers of justice, charged with the murder of his carpenter. Although he was indicted, the incident never went to trial. Jones found an unspecified means of escaping from jail and made his way to the United States of America. Once there he was engaged to sail on the Continental ship-of-war

John Paul Jones engraving by Henri Toussaint, 1906 (from *John Paul Jones Commemoration*).

Alfred in a squadron under the command of Esek Hopkins. Afterwards a fleet of United States vessels sailed on an expedition to New Providence.[7] "I once noted in one of his letters to the President of Congress, which I was copying, that he boasted that with his own hands he hoisted the first American flag that ever floated over the stern of the vessel of war belonging to United States."[8]

After Jones returned from New Providence with the American squadron, he evidently impressed some of his superior officers. They obtained a temporary commission for him and gave him command of a small sloop mounting 12 guns in the service of United States. After a cruise in the sloop was completed, he was granted a Continental Navy Commission from Congress and given command a new ship of war called the *Ranger* mounting 18 carriage guns [six-pounders]. The ship's company consisted of one hundred fifty-eight officers and men. The *Ranger* sailed from the United States for the coast of England and cruised off its shores for some time. On day while sailing off Whitehaven, Jones sent a landing party commanded by his first lieutenant ashore. Their mission was to abduct the Count of Selkirk, but unharmed. Once he was in their custody, they were to carry him back to the *Ranger* and then they were to sail to France with the Count as a hostage. The officer who commanded this party landed without opposition and they proceeded to the residence of the Count. Their planning was poor; they did not find him at home because he was in London at the time serving as a Member of Parliament. Perhaps frustrated the landing party plundered the house of its silver plate plus other valuable articles, retreated to their boats and arrived safely onboard their ship. They immediately made sail and landed at Brest, France. When this ungentlemanly affair reached Paris, the French Court expressed its displeasure and protested about the affair to the American minister. The minister in turn ordered the misbegotten articles landed at Brest and had them returned in an English cartel ship that had been at anchor in the harbor. Jones consented to the order, but it is not known whether it was with his approval.

Later the *Ranger* sailed off Waterford or the Lough of Belfast in Ireland. While the vessel was in sight of the port several fishing boats came alongside. One of the fishermen informed Jones that there was an English ship-of-war lying in that port. He was sure that it was a king's ship but had no further information about its armament or how many men she carried. Jones thought this an opportunity for him to test his naval skills and those of his ship's company that was nearly made up of full-blooded Yankees. With this in mind he sent a small boat into the harbor with a written challenge to the captain of the sloop of war *Drake* that mounted 22-guns of the same caliber as those onboard the *Ranger*. The message to the English captain said that he wished to meet him outside the harbor and exchange a few broadsides with the *Drake*.[9] This challenge was well written and politely worded, but rather terse in its nature. The English vessel was quickly made ready and besides her usual compliment of men a number of Irish noblemen embarked as well. Before long the English ship weighed anchor and spread her canvas to meet the American ship. The inhabitants of the port gave the British vessel three cheers and wished the captain and his crew success. It seemed that the prayers of thousands in and around Waterford accompanied these brave and dauntless English and Irishmen. It was thought that they would easily be victorious over these audacious rebels who dared to insult his majesty's loyal subjects in their home waters. The two ships met and fought fiercely for about an hour and a quarter. In the end the *Drake* yielded to the superior skill and bravery of the Americans and was forced to strike her colors.

When the two ships first met, those on board the *Ranger* declared that the English ship was nearly twice as large as the Continental Navy vessel. Indeed, she had nearly twice as many men including volunteers. The *Drake* made several unproductive attempts to board the *Ranger*, but their lack of success was largely due to the pains Jones had taken to instruct his top-men how to act during the upcoming *mêlée*. He also commanded his lieutenants in charge of the cannon to see that the guns were loaded with grape in double-headed charges. They were to take careful aim before firing and only discharge one cannon at a time. Jones also cautioned them about the necessity to stay cool and deliberate, not be too hasty. He said that with courage, steadiness and perseverance, they should give a good account of themselves against this British warship and in a short time. In contrast, the English ship maneuvered badly in relation to her adversary and fired her cannon broadsides all at the same time. The physical reaction of this massive discharge of firepower caused her to heel over, thus exposing the defenseless hull between the wind and water to her opponent. Jones's tactic took advantage of this vulnerability. The result was that the *Drake* was damaged below the waterline and began to leak. This impairment quickly shortened the action. Her crew scampered about in confusion among a great many wounded and gruesomely slaughtered British sailors. The *Drake* lost one hundred and five men killed and seventy-two wounded. The casualty tally on the *Ranger* was about a dozen killed and nine wounded.[10] The triumphant American warship and her prize sailed to France soon thereafter.

Sometime later they arrived in France. Captain Jones had some serious misunderstanding with his lieutenants and, after an ugly squabble, Jones left the *Ranger*. Some said that the American minister in Paris removed him from the ship but others say he left on his own accord. I do not know which account is the truth. The only thing that I know for certain is Jones was appointed commander of the *Good Man Richard* after he quit the *Ranger*. His behavior while on board this vessel is documented in the previous part of this memoir.

While Jones was aboard the *Ranger* he wrote a letter to the Countess of Selkirk that I copied by his direction. Ever since that time I have been sorry that I did not preserve a copy so that I could insert it here. The letter appeared in several English gazettes and was said by some to be well written. The document was evidence that Jones was to be well versed in the English Language and displayed an abundance of wit and humor. The captain states that his object in landing a party of men from the *Ranger* was to take the Count, her husband, as a prisoner, and carry him to France. Once there he was to be detained until the British government consented to a general exchange of American prisoners then detained in England. The Count was esteemed in England and Captain Jones, who was quite aware of this, had no doubt that if his project succeeded the British ministry would be forced into negotiations and likely consent to his demands.

In his letter Jones disavowed having any knowledge of the countess's house being plundered and her silver plate and other valuables being taken by his landing party. He said that he only became aware of the robbery some weeks later after arriving in France. The moment he became aware of the theft, he was among the first to consent that it should be returned. Jones begged that lady's pardon for presuming to write to her and also for the trouble and pain the plundering of her house must have caused her. He hoped that she would not blame any of this unfortunate pilfering-business on him. In this same letter, he went on to declare in severe terms what he considered the malice of the British ministry for waging war against the people of the United States. He condemned them in the following lines:

"For they, 'twas they unsheathed the ruthless blade
'And Heaven shall mark the havoc it has made!'"[11]

There was a wealth of poetry in the letter, but this is all that I am able to remember. The captain closed by saying that he hoped the Countess, after what had happened, would not withdraw her kind and friendly assistance so long experienced to his family.[12]

Jones had a sexual encounter with the wife of the American agent at L'Orient that was consistent with the captain's penchant for lovely ladies. One afternoon the American agent came onboard to conduct some business with the ship's purser. During this time Jones went ashore and told his officers that once this official was on our vessel, no boat was to leave for shore. Also, they must not allow anyone to come along side during his absence. The agent became agitated at about 8 o'clock in the evening and requested to the officer on watch have a boat bring him ashore. The Lieutenant replied that he had orders that no one was to leave the ship until Jones returned. The agent understandably suspected that there was a secret tryst between Jones and his wife and became enraged. The agent had been wary of Jones. At one time he had surprised the captain with his wife in a "very loving posture."[13] The agent was a man of about sixty and considered by many to be homely, but he had wealth

6. Taking Command of the Ariel

and a notable position in society. His wife was merely seventeen, quite attractive and given to coquetry. She was also fond of the theater and was known to accompany any gentleman who would be so polite as to offer her a ticket.

The agent was detained onboard for the entire night while the captain lingered on shore with the lady in question. The officers onboard the ship suspected what was about and plied the agent with so much wine that he fell quietly and drunkenly asleep in a cabin. This lascivious meeting soon became public in L'Orient.

Another time Jones sailed on a short cruise, but carried a woman with him who was married and the mother of two small children. The French husband who was left behind and did not appear to regret the loss of his mate for the time that she was gone. When the captain returned to port, he sent the lady back to her husband with a sum of money to present to him as a gesture of consolation for her absence.

After defeating of the *Serapis* in the now famous sea battle, while Jones visited Paris he was invited to dine with the Count de Vergennes, the French Minister of Foreign Affairs. The dinner guests consisted of noblemen and other prominent French families of the city. In time the conversation turned to Jones's courageousness as the victorious captain during his recent sea battle. One of the invitees noted that the King of England had recently knighted Captain Pearson. Now that his former adversary had this celebrated title, he asked Jones if he would ever dare to meet him again. Jones replied that if he ever had the good fortune of meeting him again at sea with a force equal to his, he was confident that he would beat him so badly that they would likely make him a Lord. This undoubtedly both pleased and amused the assembled company. After this, hardly a day did not pass without an invitation to dine with members of Paris's high society.

While at L'Orient one evening Jones had a "rendezvous" with a lady of pleasure. During the intermission of a theater performance they were attending, the captain suggested that he and the lady "retire" to a convenient place. During this carnal sojourn Jones misplaced his expensive gold watch. Shortly thereafter one of his midshipmen, also with another lady of pleasure, retired to the same location. The midshipman found the distinctive timepiece in the room and decided to temporarily keep it. Shortly thereafter he showed the watch to me, then we both realized what our captain was up to. We went to a park near the playhouse and devised a scheme regarding what we might do with it. We took it to a well-known tavern that the captain frequented. We pawned it to the master of the tavern for a dozen bottles of his best Bordeaux wine. On our way back to the ship we met two of our brother officers and we told them what we had done. We then asked them to join us in having a very good evening—at our gallant officer's expense.

The captain was pleased to be able to recover his cherished watch and paid the tavern owner for the dozen bottles of wine to receive it back. I believe thereafter that Jones never mentioned to anybody about how he happened to lose it. When the story became publicly known, it produced a great deal of mirth to the people in the town as well as those on board our ship. The crew used to mention it while at the capstan bars as they labored to heave the anchor onboard the ship, an amusing distraction from repetitive tedious work.

The English said that Captain Jones fought with a noose around his neck, an allusion to his having been indicted for murder. They suggested that if he should fall into their hands as a prisoner of war, he would not be considered as a POW, but would be hanged immediately. They also said that Jones never truly fought, nor would he fight because he was perpetually drunk. The English generally believed that he had a severe alcohol problem and called him a pot-valiant [courageous because of being drunk]. I personally despise such mean, unctuous and dastardly words used to undermine a man's well-earned reputation. The English uttered similar unjust derision against General George Washington.

About three years after the battle between *Good Man Richard* and the *Serapis* I was visiting London and happened to enter a print shop. There I saw a print depicting Captain Jones that named him among the world's greatest pirates. In another print shop and in a nearby coffee house, I saw his likeness that was nearly larger-than-life. He was represented carrying twelve pistols secured in a sash around his waistline, six on each side. Three men were shown kneeling before him. In the same picture one appeared to be shot dead having fallen at the feet of Jones while he held a pistol in each hand aimed at the other two men. This alluded to the men of the *Good Man Richard* who cried out quarters during the late battle.

As to the report of Jones being pot-valiant, I declare that it is absolutely not true. While I sailed with him, I spent a long time in his cabin. I can attest that I never saw him drink any kind of whiskey or similar spirit. On the contrary, his constant drink was water, lemonade or lime-juice with a little bit of sugar to make it more palatable. It is true, however, that while we were at sea in a good weather he made his custom to drink three glasses of wine immediately after the tablecloth was removed.

On the passage from L'Orient to Philadelphia in the *Ariel*, Jones encountered an English 32-gun frigate not far from Bermuda. This vessel was far better armed than the ship under his command. As evening approached the English frigate changed course and sailed directly for him. Jones realized that his little ship was no match for her. In time the English war ship came alongside and hailed the American ship. The ship's officer asked the ship's identity and who was in command. At that time Jones had acquired an accurate list of all English ships-of-war that were then cruising upon the North American Coast and in the West Indies. Captain Jones directed one of his lieutenants to

6. Taking Command of the Ariel

answer that it was one of His Majesty's ships of roughly *Ariel*'s size and that Jones knew to be cruising in that general latitude. He also had the lieutenant mention the captain's name as well.

Physically Captain Jones was about five feet six inches tall with a well-proportioned body and rounded shoulders. His face could take on a fierce adversarial appearance and he was fond of presenting himself with a studied military bearing. Jones was an excellent seaman and, according to my judgment, knew naval tactics as well as almost any man of his age. That said, it must be mentioned that his moral character was colored with some unfortunate qualities. For example, his conduct in relation to the treatment of young Lieutenant Sullivan was condemnable to a high degree, but at the same time his courage and daring as a naval commander cannot be doubted.

When Jones wanted to be, he was skilled in the use of language and flattery thus making him persuasive to the occasional obstinate seamen. He excelled in this capacity as much as any man with which I was acquainted. I have seen him walk upon the docks of L'Orient for hours with a single seaman in order to persuade him to sign the ships articles that he commanded and was often successful. When he pressed American seamen into service in that port, however, he was quite unpopular and was condemned by all except for a few of his officers who were instructed to execute his orders. I am happy to say that I had no hand in this impressment business. After these incidents his pride and vanity while he visited Paris and Amsterdam were generally criticized. This certainly gave great offense to many persons whom he had befriended earlier. Yet, many lauded Jones's conduct toward Captain Pearson as his conqueror. His enemies, the English, even applauded his action toward one of their nation who was Jones's prisoner. It was the custom and rule of war that he had the right to keep all the defeated commander's effects. While at Texel he selflessly ordered these belongings sent to Captain Pearson by way of the French Navy Captain Cotteneau from whom Pearson felt he could honorably accept.

I shall mention one more event and then close with circumstances that occurred near the place and at the time of his death. This incident was verbally told to me by an officer who was present well after it happened.

While Jones was on his first cruise in the *Good Man Richard* in the company of the frigate *Alliance*, they fell afoul of each other. The *Good Man Richard* carried away the mizzenmast of the *Alliance* and the *Alliance* carried away the head of the *Good Man Richard*. With heavy sea running at the time, both ships were in danger of going down. At the time the two commanders were below and they blamed the incident on their own officers who were conning the ships. The first lieutenant whom Jones had put in charge was a chap named Robinson. Jones considered him at fault and ordered him confined below for not properly doing his duty. Soon after both ships arrived safely at L'Orient Jones directed a court-martial to be convened to try Mr. Robinson and the court sat onboard the *Good Man Richard*. When all the witnesses testified for and against Mr. Robinson, they members of the court gave their unanimous opinion that the lieutenant should be dismissed from the service.

Jones, however, refused to accept the verdict. He said it was in his power to have dismissed him without calling the court-martial together, alleging that it was his duty as commanding officer to add something more to this sentence. He then asked that they declare him incapable of ever serving again in the Navy of United States in the character of an officer. After some discussion the court-martial board agreed, added this to the court's sentence and read it to Mr. Robinson in their presence. Robinson was sent ashore after this was concluded without money and destitute of friends, although he had at the time money due to him for his services.[14]

On or about the year 1792, Captain Jones led a party of American gentleman to Paris where the French constituent assembly was sitting in order to congratulate them and all Americans on their recent revolution. In doing so, Jones made a very stirring speech to the assembly and its president. The president, in turn, made a short but courteous reply.

It was the last public act Jones did of which I have any knowledge. Very soon thereafter he died in great poverty in the city of Paris as was reported in the Paris gazettes.[15] When this news reached the public constituent assembly, one of the members rose and made a motion that a committee of their body should be chosen to attend Captain Jones's funeral. This was objected to by some of the members because Jones was not of the Roman Catholic faith, the state's national faith at the time. This objection failed to prevail; the motion was then put to a vote and carried. A distinguished committee was accordingly chosen and it attended the American commodore's funeral.

It ought to have been mentioned in the foregoing biographical sketch that after leaving the American naval service, John Paul Jones was commissioned in the Russian Naval Service for about eighteen months and fulfilled his station with the rank of admiral. Because of rumors of mysterious sexual intrigues plus other nefarious cabals concocted by a number of English officers then in the same service, his old enemies succeeded in convincing those in the Royal Palace that his merits were less savory than they appeared. This ultimately led to Admiral John Paul Jones dismissal from the navy of Empress Catherine the Great.

A Short Sketch of the Character of Captain Pearson

Richard Pearson was born to poor parents in the County of Cornwall, England on or about the year 1729. He lived with them in relative poverty

6. Taking Command of the Ariel

until he was about 14 years of age. At that time, he left his parents and set out for the seaport of Portsmouth. There he met several sailors who persuaded him to go onboard an English warship. He had managed to receive a rudimentary education before he left his parents. His superiors noticed that the boy had a great deal of native intelligence and he quickly acquired some knowledge of seamanship. Before long Pearson was appointed captain of the mizzen-top then became a forecastle man. The young man performed remarkably well in these duty stations and was noticed by all. The ship's captain decided to promote him to the rank of midshipmen. From this lowly appointed British Navy position, Pearson rose rapidly. A few years thereafter he was given command of a sloop of war.

Sir Richard Pearson, captain, Royal Navy (Naval History and Heritage Command, NH 51764).

During the war between the English and French, before the beginning of the American Revolution, he was recognized for achieving many acts of valor. I know nothing further of him until after his epic battle with Captain Jones. In this action everyone would conclude that Pearson showed courage and that his conduct during the battle would have done honor to any experienced commander. It is his conduct toward Jones, however, that appeared reprehensible to me on several occasions. The British captain displayed a haughtiness and arrogance that some say was typical of the conduct of many British naval commanders, especially during the contest between Great Britain and the rebellious United Colonies. King George III knighted Captain Pearson, but the merchants of Scarborough also honored him by presenting him with a service of silver plate, part of which represented that town in miniature. This was the city from which most of the fleet in his convoy came from at the time he encountered Jones. The local citizens appreciated his naval skill and bravery. The silver service was given him as a token of their gratitude and esteem for carrying out his duty and safely delivering almost the entire fleet under his care at the commencement of the battle. The gift was estimated at being worth about five hundred guineas.

A Short Sketch of the Character of Richard Dale, Esq.

John Paul Jones's first Lieutenant, when he commanded the *Good Man Richard*, a ship of 40 guns until she was lost; the *Serapis* of 50 guns; the *Alliance* of 36 guns and the *Ariel* of 24 guns; ships of war in the service of United States

Richard Dale, Esq., if my memory serves me right, was born in the state of Maryland.[16] When he was quite young he took a liking to the sea which has been his favorite element ever since. During the American Revolution he fought in several naval battles for his country and earned well-deserved accolades from his fellow Americans.

Because of his conduct, bravery, and perseverance in the noteworthy battle between the *Good Man Richard* and the *Serapis*, he earned applause and glory. While in the service of the United States Navy he had been conspicuous in his merits and gallantry up on all occasions. In my opinion this entitled Mr. Dale to be enrolled among the liberators of our country.

While I sailed with the first lieutenant, he was beloved by his brother officers and the ship's crew. He was a clever good-natured sea officer and was always diligent in his duty. This gained him the approval of his superiors. Mr. Dale engaged in conversation with all ranks of people. He was polite in his manners and a good companion. Finally, Mr. Dale displayed none of that haughty, overbearing, domineering spirit towards their inferiors, especially those who unfortunately were of low rank; a trait so frequently seen among officers of similar rank onboard English warships.

Richard Dale (Naval History and Heritage Command, NH 51764).

7

Adventures as a French Privateer

I shall now pursue the history of my journal taking up the threads of it where I left off.[1]

On 20 December, having obtained several letters of recommendation regarding my abilities as a seaman and some cash from the French gentleman with whom I had frequent contact, I thought it worthwhile to mention the generosity of the French people to strangers. They are generally honest and charitable regardless of the contrary opinion often published in the English gazettes.

I had obtained a passport, so I set off for Morlaix where I safely arrived on 23 December. I delivered my letters of recommendation to the people who were pleased to see me. They soon gave me the command of the lugsail privateer *Count de Guichen* that mounted fourteen carriage guns, all three-pounders.[2] The privateer was ready for sea. Her principal officers resided at the port and held commissions from the king and letters of marque. They said, however, that their orders from the Minister of Marine prohibited them from granting or delivering any official French commissions to foreigners. Therefore, the command of the privateer was given to French Navy Lieutenant [Nicholas] Anthon from Morlaix, a gentleman, a good seaman and appearing to be fearless. I was designated as the second captain of the privateer and Captain Anthon largely gave me command of the privateer during the cruise because he did not speak English. I pretty much did as I pleased onboard the ship, ordering the making or taking in the sail, chasing vessels, positioning and commanding the crew in times of action, and deciding when to board an enemy vessel, etc. Most of the ship's officers and crew nevertheless where Yankees or Bostonian's as the French then called all Yankees. The French, especially their ladies, seemed remarkably fond of Americans to the point of adoration.

Morlaix is situated between two commanding mountains. The city is divided into two parts by a narrow river that empties into the English Channel located about five miles from the town. Ships as large as three hundred tons can tie-up in safety alongside its quays mostly sheltered from the winds. These piers are built of large square stones fastened together in such a way as to become one solid rock. When a vessel is tied to a quay it often is resting on a gravel bottom at low tide. This is a very great convenience especially for graving or scrubbing their bottoms free of seaweed. The entrance to the port of Morlaix is protected by a castle built upon an outcropping of rocks situated above the harbor's entrance. This fortification has two tiers of large cannon and, in war times, the military base houses about sixty officers and men.

On 23 March 1781 we departed Morlaix in the privateer and arrived off the coast of Ireland. On the 27th we took four prizes which we ransomed and detained a man as a hostage out of each of them. On the 27th at daybreak we observed several other vessels toward the shore of us. Since the sea was quite calm, I launched a small boat and embarked with an officer and about a dozen armed sailors. At 7 A.M. we re-boarded the *Count de Guichen* with ransom bills amounting to upwards of twelve hundred guineas and five hostages to assure that we received payment of that sum. Upon our return the French captain greeted us on deck as he had just awakened having been on watch the better part of the preceding night. He was pleased when I told him of our successful enterprise, but was disturbed about not telling him about our departure. By noon we had ventured close to land where we discovered a large ship to the west of us toward the port of Cork, Ireland. It appeared to be a frigate flying an English ensign, pendant and a jack under an impressive cloud of sail. It was not long before she was abreast of us, but still some distance away. We studied her through our spyglass and determined that she carried one tier of guns, twelve on each side.

After observing her awhile we decided that she was probably an English letter of marque likely commanded by a British overconfident fellow. She passed by at some distance and seemed to take no notice of us perhaps assuming that we were a small fishing boat. We made sail after her and when we came within a mile or two from her stern she came about. The English vessel surprised us by firing a broadside of twelve cannon at us, all her guns on her port side. The distance was so great, none of the shot reached more than half way to us. This indicated cowardice on the part of her captain. I conferred with Captain Anthon and we agreed that the ship was likely ours for the taking. As we approached nearer to the vessel, her appearance became more formidable. A number of men with muskets could be seen upon the quarterdeck and her crew was larger than we expected. She tacked and came about again then fired another broadside at us. We now prepared to board her knowing that this tactic usually succeeded when facing an English warship or letter of marque, especially when the enemy has a greater strength than the attacker. When we sailed within cannon shot of her, she hauled up her

7. Adventures as a French Privateer

courses, handed in her topgallant sails and appeared to be taking measures for a determined resistance. We then displayed the French ensign and also hoisted an American pennant aloft showing our two nationalities. This last gesture was personal. I wanted to let the Englishmen know that they were also about to fight the Yankees. A drummer was stationed at the head of our foremast and supported himself with one foot on the ratlines of the fore-shrouds and the other on the foreyard. A young fifer was positioned nearby. The wind was blowing at about four knots. When we got close enough for them to hear the drum and fife, the two boys started to play Yankee Doodle and continued to perform throughout the action.

The English ship fired a number of broadsides at us, but without causing injury and doing little damage. Meanwhile we edged close and came within pistol-shot of her. When the *Count de Guichen* came under her stern, we poured our broadside into her. This discharge raked her fore and aft and made a confounding racket in the cabin among the crockery. This single broadside succeeded in driving all the Englishmen off the quarterdeck and they descended onto the main deck. We now attempted to board the enemy, but our privateer was moving so swiftly we darted by her and were not able to set our grappling hooks on her bulwarks. We passed her forefoot, wore-ship and then gave her another broadside. At the same time one of the enemy's shot managed to cut away our jib halyards and the slings of our foreyard. The heavy yard toppled to the deck and knocked over our drummer. When the enemy saw that their cannonball had silenced us, they erupted into three cheers. After firing their musketry into us and yet another broadside, they crowded on all their sails and tried to leave the battle scene. We, however, had no intention of losing our quarry in this way. We soon cut away the debris on the deck, made all needed repairs and quickly gave chase. The wind began to subside, but being faster that the English vessel we soon gained upon her. When the enemy became aware of this, they once again took in their light sails, hauled up their courses and prepared for renewed action. We reloaded our guns to deliver two broadsides and readied our crew for boarding. I went forward, hailed them with a speaking trumpet and commanded them to haul down their colors. They did not reply, so I gave a prearranged signal to Captain Anthon. He then ordered the privateer to run under the enemy's stern once again gave the Englishman another broadside. I prepared a boarding party and intended to command it once we were close enough to hurl the grapples. We would then make the ships fast and cross over the rails. As we ran under her stern, our cannon shot into her cabin. Our privateer luffed up to stop under her lee and I crouched to get ready to board. At the same instant the enemy bellowed out asking for quarters and lowered the British ensign.

The entire conflict lasted about an hour and some of the fighting had become quite severe. The vessel did indeed prove to be an English letter of marque, four hundred tons burthen and carrying twelve long six-ponders two shot ranged carronades that fired eighteen-pound shot, ten cohorns, twelve brass swivels and fifty-fifty five men plus twenty-six male passengers and seven ladies. Her homeport was Bristol and she was bound for the West Indies largely laden with dry goods. The invoice of her cargo said its value amounted to thirty thousand pounds sterling.

I quickly came onboard after she struck and asked for the captain who came forward and delivered his sword to me. A British Army major and a captain also surrendered their swords to me. The last two were bound for the West Indies to rejoin the regiment to which they belonged. The ladies also crowded around me and offered their purses, but I refused to accept them. One lady was wringing her hands mournful of the loss of her husband who was killed in the action. A cannon shot had passed through his body. The gentlemen passengers crowded all around and taunted me saying that I had slain one of his majesty's colonels. Their protests drew little sympathy from me. I openly communicated my attitude by saying I hoped that all of his majesty's colonels were dead. I was uneasy about expressing this uncharitable and unchristian-like response. I then got down to business securing the prisoners and sent them onboard the privateer. I immersed myself in my duty to absolve my tactless outburst as well as a sense of guilt. I certainly pitied the lady whose husband was killed and later personally apologized to her for the harshness of some of my comments. I did not ask for forgiveness from anyone else. There was a perhaps perverse sense of honor regarding the sometimes-appalling outcome of any battle.

The English vessel lost an army lieutenant colonel, a master's mate, one boatswain's mate, four seamen and one boy killed plus eleven men and boys wounded. No one was killed on our privateer, but five were slightly wounded. This prize ship was very well provided with a variety of weapons and warfare stores. She carried both more and heavier guns than we had onboard our privateer. We were at quite a disadvantage at the time and did not realize it. The defeated quarry's guns were now hoisted on our deck and became our possession.

I requested to be given command of the prize, but Captain Anthon did not consent. All her officers, male passengers, ladies with their servants, and the crew except for three and one master's mate who was left to help sail the prize vessel were placed onboard the privateer. The ladies remained onboard the ship with their servants at their request.

We put a prize master onboard the captured ship together with thirteen able seamen and ordered them to sail with all possible speed to either Brest or Morlaix. Our privateer was to escort her as best we could, until we reached the safety of one of those ports.

We kept up with our valuable prize until we came within sight of Ushant near the entrance of Brest. At that point a violent gale from the northeast sprung up that separated us. (We later learned that the English recaptured her shortly thereafter.) Our privateer started to leak. This forced us to heave all our cannon overboard except for four to lighten our load. Two days later we limped in distress into the port of Brest. Once safely there, laid her ashore [careened the vessel] to have the major leak repaired and clean her bottom.

I feel that the port of Brest is one of the best seaports for ships of war in the world especially one lying upon the Atlantic Ocean not far from the British Channel. The Land's End of England is located north and a little westerly from the city. Ships-of-the-line of all sizes together with sloops of war lay at their respective moorings in the seventy fathoms of low tide water found in the harbor. This French haven is surrounded by a relatively high landmass that offers protection from storms and is easily fortified. Each ship of war possesses her own numbered and named storage magazine ashore. This is where her sails, rigging, etc., are deposited and when they have occasion to do major overhauling and refitting they are sure to find an ample supply of any article that might be needed. This is a great convenience and I do not believe that the British offer a similar one.

While I was there, I went to see the slaves who were confined in Brest. They were mostly employed by the government to work on the docks and different parts of town. The place where they were confined was exceptionally well-built. It had a great many dingy quarters where the slaves were all chained at night, fifty or sixty together in a group. They were restrained by a stout chain that led to an enormous ringbolt affixed to the floor in the center of the room. The men had a little straw to lie upon and were arranged feet to feet thus forming a large circle. Extending through each room's stout iron bound door was a cannon loaded with round or grape shot. The gun was ready and primed with a match device in a tub by its side. The guards had orders to fire the cannon into them upon the least noise coming for the captives. The slaves, however, sometimes purposely produced a commotion to provoke their persecutors to send them into the next more peaceful world choosing to die a sudden death at the mouth of a cannon rather than continue in their wretched state of bondage.

There were some wealthy men among them, merchants whose only crime was carrying on what was considered an illicit trade and usually from different parts of the kingdom. Many of the slaves had very respectable families, but they were condemned to servitude for a very considerable part of their lives. Unfortunately, the families of the slaves were subjected to scorn by a multitude of citizens because the heads of the households were now upon the lowest tier of society. Human nature can be distressing.

I am now pained as I relate the brutal facts that underlie a nation that calls itself civilized. The indigenous people of America would have winced, felt ashamed and stood incredulous at such actions against these deprived people guilty of minor crimes, but given an excessive punishment. I cannot turn away from the injustice I saw any more than I can turn away from a poor beggar asking for money to buy a piece of bread. In many ways this situation sheds light upon the hypocrisy of a civilized society built upon the enslavement of people, a structure fabricated on the dehumanization of particular group of human beings.

Some of these merchants were sentenced for three, four and some for six years according to the nature of their crimes. They were obliged to work hard and submit their backs to the sting of the lash during servitude just as those who have been found guilty of robbery, murder, rape, etc. Those responsible of the more serious crimes were for the most part slaves for life. An officer of the admiralty informed me that the number of men serving in this deplorable situation exceeded six thousand. Each was obliged to wear chains or drag them while at their duty station and they were tethered together, two by two. The weight of each of the iron chains was about forty-five pounds, but double that for two men. These restraints were usually fixed to their legs, but at work their respective chains were attached to their waist by a piece of rope to facilitate their labor. There were roughly four overseers or drivers for every hundred men and each carried a long whip that seems to be in constant motion. They showed little mercy to the poor sufferers in their charge. The slaves were whipped so cruelly at times that the victims were scarcely left alive. The prisoners were uniformly dressed in coarse red clothes and obliged to wear leather caps that had a tin or brass badge sown on them; each were engraved with a capital letter indicating the crimes for which they were condemned. When asked by strangers about the crimes that brought them to this state of affairs they usually said they did nothing wrong.

One extraordinary story involved the Count D'Artois, his majesty's brother. The prince, who had the reputation of being a kindly man, desired to see the slaves and give them some money. He asked several of them about the crimes that they had committed and all but one said that they were innocent. The prince then questioned him further to tell him what made him a convict. He answered that the crime that doomed him to the miserable existence is the worse-kind and it made him shudder to think of it. About six years ago his wealthy parents compelled him to marry a young woman whom he intensely disliked. His hatred for her was so bitter that he murdered her on their wedding night. This is why he was condemned to wear the galling chains. The Prince was moved that the slave seemed truthful even though talking about the incident, an emotionally painful episode for him. The letter engraved on the metal badge on the cap above his forehead corroborated the nature of his crime. Unexpectedly the prince, so affected by the poor slave's confession, appealed to the royal authorities and in time procured liberty for the man.

7. Adventures as a French Privateer

The port of Brest has the most convenient dry docks for warships that I have ever seen and they may be the best in the known world. They have a curious yet ingenious machine for hoisting and lowering masts of all sizes from those of first-rate men-of-war as well as much smaller vessels. It is done with great expedition. It could lift out a mainmast of a 74-gun ship and replace it with a new one in sixty-four minutes. I timed it with my watch to see just how efficient the mechanism was. The slaves are employed in this kind of work in the arsenals and do general hard labor in the shipyard.

While I was in Brest, the 80-gun *Couronne*, newly sheathed in copper after being hauled out of a dry dock, was tied alongside a quay and caught fire. It was burned to the water's edge in spite of the exertions of several thousand men to extinguish the blaze. It is fortunate that there was no powder onboard at the time and no lives were lost. A new ship with the same name and mold [plans] was soon ordered by the minister of marine to be rebuilt as soon as possible. I was informed by creditable persons that in seven weeks, counting the time the keel was laid, she was ready to sail with the fleet after all her guns and provisions had been brought onboard. I mention this fact because the British boasted in the House of Commons that they were the most expeditious in building, fitting out and commanding their navy.

On 7 April our privateer had been refitted and we put to sea setting a course for Ireland. We arrived there on the 10th of the month and took two prizes on the 12th. Cruising in sight of the highlands of Dungarvan through the 30th, we failed to capture any more vessels largely because the winds were mostly to the westward. The breezes finally shifted toward the east, a favorable omen. The fair air currents should entice some English shipping from Bristol or Liverpool. Sure enough, the next day we took three small sloops, two of which we ransomed and, after taking off her crew, sunk the third ship.

At 7 A.M. we discovered several square-rigged vessels and by 2 P.M. we had eleven new captives. At 5 P.M. we had issued ransom demands on all of them and had taken hostages out of each craft to secure our ransom mandates. At 6 P.M. we saw two tall ships with all sails set moving briskly before the wind on a course directly toward us. All hands were called to quarters and we prepared for them to be alongside us by about 8 o'clock that night. The foremost and largest of the two ships hailed us. As soon as she identified us as enemy, she fired a single cannon shot into our projected path. Captain Anthon thought that we should attempt to run from them, but I told him that if they were English warships we were too near to escape. If they were merchantmen however, we stood a good chance of capturing them both. Orders were given to fire a broadside into the larger and closer vessel. Once the smoke had dissipated she took down her topsails and begged for quarters. She then hove to and struck her colors. Now confident, we gave the smaller ship the other a broadside and she followed the example of her consort. After we lowered a small boat, I was sent to take possession of these prizes, send the captains with their papers and have them board the privateer. When I arrived on the larger vessel I found that she had cannon-ports for eighteen guns, but carried only eight of these arms and ten wooden false [Quaker] guns. She was manned by twenty-five officers, men and boys. The vessel was about three hundred tons burthen and from Bristol bound for Cork. I sent the captain in a boat to board our privateer.

The sun was setting and as it was getting dark, I saw a strange sail bearing down on us. By the way that she was maneuvering, I suspected that she might be the enemy. The *Count de Guichen* with Captain Anthon in command was not in hailing distance, so I decided to act independently. I had the small contingent of men that had accompanied me secure the prisoners below, man the ship's guns and prepare to engage the stranger. The unidentified visitor was a brig that ran to our stern and then hailed us. The master, in a bold and firm manner, asked about our identity and destination. The lights of the *Count de Guichen* were just coming in view so I ordered him to board the privateer and its captain would have the information that he requested. When the captain of the brig received my terse response, he swore repeatedly and almost broke his speaking trumpet to pieces on his quarterdeck rail. Arriving onboard the privateer asked to see the captain. One of our lieutenants who spoke English introduced him to Captain Anthon who, through his interpreter, immediately asked who he was. He replied that he was master of the brig that the captain of the other vessel directed him to board the lugger. Anthon said that he had previous business to attend to at the moment. He had to deal with the other masters who recently came onboard. The poor captain of the brig did not understand what all this meant, then indicated that he hoped that the captain was an Englishman and that this was a British privateer. He was certain that the first vessel that he encountered was a British letter of marque. Captain Anthon responded in broken English that this was perhaps recently so, but now she was my prize—as is your brig. Such are the fortunes and misfortunes of war and he should put himself at ease.

In time we threw overboard the guns of the captured ship, took their powder, etc., as was the custom and ransomed them for three thousand two hundred guineas, the brig and her cargo for five hundred. These sums were less than half the value of the vessels, but we thought it more reasonable than to run the risk of sending them back to France. After this we set sail for Morlaix with our total ransom bills of ten thousand, four hundred and fifty guineas and our eleven hostages as assurance that the money would be paid. On our return voyage between Scilly and Land's End we were approached by the English frigate *Aurora* of twenty-eight guns. She gave chase and in the fresh breeze that blew upon us she out ran us and we became her captive.

7. Adventures as a French Privateer

We were then brought into Mount's Bay, the site of a small town known as Penzance that lies about forty miles west southwest of Falmouth. The captain of the *Aurora*, a Scotsman whose name was Collins, treated us well and made sure that his crew did not take anything from us. Captain Anthon managed to save the spyglasses, quadrant and charts that belonged to the privateer.

We were captured on 4 May. During the day our hostages were released and that night we were searched for the ransom bills. Captain Anthon delivered two parcels to Captain Collins, one of which did not contain the genuine documents. During the chase we believed that we might be taken so bogus papers were made. The originals were retained and concealed in Anthon's trousers. Although we were put through another search, the English officers were unsuccessful in finding them. (The real bills of ransom were smuggled to France by a safe conveyance and will be addressed later in this memoir.)

During the last war, a supplementary clause was attached to each ransom bill. The article specified that the master of every vessel, after having been subjected to being ransomed by an enemy, was bound to pay the amount specified in the bill by himself, his heirs, his executors or assignees. This meant that in the event a privateer was apprehended and the hostages released unharmed, if the owners of the privateer produced the original bills of ransom after the fact in England, the pecuniary sums mentioned in the ransom and the holders of the bona fide bill(s) should be paid in full. This was the reason for the very strict search and our wanting to conceal the documents. More recently the British Parliament passed a law asserting that no ship's master or commander of an English ship should allow his vessel to be ransomed.[3]

On 7 May the captain of the *Aurora* ordered all of us, with the exception of our first lieutenant, pilot and boatswain, to get ready to go ashore. (These three excluded men were subsequently tried and unfortunately hanged. They had previously been in English naval service and were known by several crewmembers of the ship that had captured us.) As Captain Anton and I were ready to embark on the boats that came alongside, the captain of the frigate politely handed us our swords. He indicated to me that he hoped that I would never again unsheathe it in anger against whoever challenged Americans because he considered them respectable Englishmen. After we landed, the local king's officer invited Captain Anthon and me to his home where he politely accommodated us and demonstrated generous hospitality. The next day we were furnished with a post chaise, given passports by the same king's officer and were directed to proceed as rapidly as we could to Falmouth. Once there, we were told to meet with the mayor and he would formally parole us.

Accordingly, we set off in the post chaise without even a single guard to make sure that we followed the instructions we were given in Penzance. It occurred to us that we could have travelled all the way to London without a care, however we made our pledge to the king's officer and went directly to Falmouth. On our way we passed through Helston in Hampshire where we saw several French officers who had been paroled in the town. Some of them were men we were acquainted with in France. We arrived in Falmouth in the early evening and called upon the mayor. The gentleman treated us with graciousness and shortly thereafter we were presented to the English commissary of prisoners of war. The mayor then stated our case to this magistrate as the commissary carefully scrutinized us. He then gave Captain Anthon a longer look and said that he recognized him as the man who broke his parole at Helston some months ago. Anton admitted that this was true therefore the captain's parole was refused. The official then turned to me and inquired if I wished to be conditionally released as a parolee. I replied something to the effect that if my captain was to be imprisoned, it was my duty to accompany him—and therefore this was my preference. The commissary complimented me for demonstrating my loyalty to Anthon and said he would act in accordance with my choice. A guard was called and we were transported to a prison about two miles from Falmouth. This was among the filthiest most loathsome building that I had ever seen. We had no sooner heard the prison doors slam behind us when we were attacked by swarms of sizeable lice as well as bed bugs and fleas. They may have been of Dutch extraction because there were a number of Dutch prisoners of war who had been there for some time. The poor fellows were now extremely dirty and appeared quite miserable. That first night I did not close my eyes, even though I was extremely tired. I must confess that I began to regret not accepting the offer of parole when it was presented the day before. I waited with anxiety when the securely locked doors were reopened at sunrise the next morning. I was now able to get out of reach of my maddening insect tormentors by walking in the prison yard. During the course of the day some of our fellow prisoners generously offered Captain Anthon and me a small corner of the grassy plot that they had occupied and had cleaned as best they could. We then built a screen of some sheets to form a shelter of sorts. We then made a swinging hammock wide enough for the two of us to sleep in. This arrangement enabled us to live a bit more comfortably and keep out all but the most persistent pests—at least to some measure.

On the 15th the commissary sent orders to the jailor that the Captain Anthon and I were allowed to walk outside the prison every day from sunrise to sunset, but we had to return to our confinement in the prison every night. Also, our excursion was to be limited to one and a half miles from our place of confinement. The two of us readily agreed with pleasure and were fastidious about not tarrying any longer than the appointed time. There were many farmhouses within the limits of our restricted perambulations and the inhabitants of these dwellings treated us with kindness and munificence. I

7. Adventures as a French Privateer

spent many delightful hours with the Cornish girls who are generally quite attractive and good company. Alas I felt that they were not very worldly and at times naive.

We happened upon an exhibition of cockfighting in a cockpit constructed for this purpose. I frequently saw the mayor of Falmouth at this diversion as well as merchants, ladies of distinction as well as people of the lower classes. The cockfight was advertised in colorful printed posters that stated when and where they were to take place. Although these events were technically prohibited by law in England, cockfights drew great crowds of people. Those in attendance made substantial bets upon the cocks that were to fight as soon as they were identified and then brought into the pit. At one contest that I attended, I believe there must have been at least two thousand men women and children present. Two hundred guineas were staked on the head of one highly favored cock, but the usual bet was from one to twelve guineas each for a single battle. This kind of diversion that I considered barbarous could last almost all day. During this time a great many cocks were slain in battle. I would also not be surprised if perhaps there were a few broken heads among the men who made ill-fated bets.

After spending approximately six weeks of imprisonment, Anton and I were exchanged towards the end of June and arrived in Cherbourg, France. One hundred twenty-five about to be released prisoners of war were transported that day by means of a cartel. Shortly thereafter we were marched under guard to Brest to help man the grand French fleet of war that lay in the harbor. The distance between Cherbourg to Brest was about two hundred and sixty wearying miles. While we made the journey the greater part of my clothing was stolen. I did not receive any compensation and nor did I find out who did it. I suspect that one of the guards that accompanied us was the culprit. We were only ten days along in our march when I noticed that our number had diminished to about seventy out of the initial group that had started the journey. The rest had deserted along the road. Arriving at Brest I applied for a passport to go to Morlaix to the French commissary with whom, by chance, I had a prior acquaintance. He granted my request and at the same time suggested that if I arrived before the grand fleet sailed, I might have the honor of serving in the Royal Navy of the King of France, at least for one more campaign.

Soon after this reunion, I set out from Brest to Morlaix where I arrived in a few hours. It was not long before I found a French brigantine letter of marque about to sail for the West Indies and arranged for passage and space for some freight that I wished to transport. I made a partial settlement with the owners of my previous privateer, the *Couronne* that had been captured, and also obtained some wine and a quantity of dry goods that I bought for five thousand *Tournois*. I then had them stored for safe keeping onboard the new privateer.[4] I was in high spirits with the thought of returning, at least partway, to my native country. On 12 July 1781, I left my French friends as we set sail with favorable winds for our destination.

The brigantine that I had embarked upon had originally been built as a cutter and therefore was an excellent nimble sailor. She mounted 16 guns, carried forty-one officers, men and boys besides seven men passengers. On July 14th, about five leagues northwest of Ushant, an English frigate chased us for four or five hours. When darkness fell we lost sight of her. Later that night we experienced a powerful gale that forced us ashore a few leagues west of the Isle de Bas, not far from Morlaix. Regrettably the brigantine and its cargo were totally lost on the rocky coast. It was very difficult to make our way ashore and I lost every farthing and property that I possessed in the world. I feared that I was about to become a beggar out of necessity. After I arrived safely on dry land, I started to reflect on my past misfortunes that seemed never to end. I soon recovered from these depressing images, calmed myself and became determined to not attempt to cross the Atlantic Ocean until the war had ceased to waste the blood of the people of the western world. I realized it made little difference whether I fought under the striped American flag or French fleur-de-lis as long as it was against the English. I also reaffirmed that the French were the best allies and friends of the American people.

I once again set out for Morlaix once more and arrived on the 17th where I was graciously received by my many acquaintances. My leisure hours were spent visiting the many diversions of the town. By this time I had a passable facility with the French language so that I was able to converse with the ladies. They seemed eager to give me instruction and correct me when I made a mistake or mispronounced a word. This is common among beginners with only a smattering of knowledge of a foreign tongue. Sometimes my mispronunciation turned a simple word into an indecent term that caused a great deal of amusement.

During the end of August, I set out for Dunkirk, about six hundred miles north and east of Morlaix. Once there, I planned to find my old friend Captain Anthon who had recently been given command of an 18-gun cutter and cruise with him once again. The first day I arrived at Dinan, a town situated far inland lying on the eastern boundary of Brittany. The town is rather large and defended on all sides by formidable castle walls. This was also a place where many English prisoners of war were confined and it is said to contain ten thousand men, about four thousand were the British detainees. The next day I entered the province of Normandy that is the largest domain of all of France. I passed through many towns and villages, some walled and some not, and eventually arrived at the city of Caen, this province's economically stressed capital. Throughout my travels the small towns and villages all seemed to contain one-story houses mostly made of stone. Living in these domiciles are families of men, women, children plus cows, horses, goats and pigs all huddled together in a single room with a dirt floor. The people who dwell within the simple buildings sleep upon straw that is shared with assorted livestock.

The public roads in this country swarm with beggars. Whenever a carriage or people on horseback pass, the inhabitants dressed in rags, run after them pleading for charity. I have upon occasion thrown a handful of small coins among them to prevent them from following me any farther. While they scrambled I was able to make some progress and get out of their sight. Before long however, I met others of the same description. These vagrants were so incessant, the only way that I could continue on my way was to throw more loose change among them.

Many of the beggars live with their families beside of the road in caves dug out of the earth or in simple huts. These poor folks were for the most part dirty, did not appear to have any household utensils and laid upon nothing but straw. One member of the family stood on watch at the door of each simple residence. Whenever they heard or saw a carriage or person on horseback approaching, the person on watch alerted the rest of the hoard. In a moment the road would be filled with vagabonds. This frenzied activity went on night and day and it was difficult to impossible to pass by without giving them some money. Adding to the problem, the few coppers that they pick up were rarely shared. Those who were not lucky enough to come up with some pitiable amount of change followed after you. The young boys were capable of running nearly as fast as the fleetest of horses on these occasions. I remember one instance on the road while I was traveling on horseback with another gentleman when we were overtaken by three of these beggar boys who had crept unseen out of their den. These boys appeared to be eleven to fourteen years old. They were virtually naked except for a few nondescript rags. They lacked hats and their hair appeared as if a comb had never touched their heads.

We had no coinage with us. As they descended upon us pleading for charity, we quickly agreed that if we spurred our horses we should be able to make our escape. We set off at a full gallop, but the band of boys remained close to our horse's heels. We rode a few miles when the youngest or at least smallest boy began to fall astern of us. The other two held out and seemed to be just as close to us as when we started our flight. Before long I became tired of riding so fast and my mount was noticeably more difficult to control. I shouted at my companion that we should halt and we both did. I then gave the largest boy a crown and asked him to share it between the three of them. The boy acknowledged that they were brothers and dwelled in one of the caves with their father and mother. The young scrounger trio seemed satisfied and we continued on our journey without further incidents.

Upon reflecting upon the source of the appalling social situation that produced a multitude of beggars in France, I pondered what I had seen with care. Having resided among the French people on several levels of society, it became obvious that it must be the result of their government. The king, with his swarms of nobles, military officers, miscellaneous magistrates, tax collectors and other royal leeches, continually prey upon and devoured the earnings of the people. These circumstances were becoming intolerable among the peasants.

I am extremely pleased that Providence had placed me in America. Thank God that there are no royal bloodsuckers there. I sincerely pray that there will never be any of those outcasts of society about whom I have described. No, I predict that if ever a class of quasi-nobility attempts to establish itself in the United States and it would result in beggary with the same dreadfulness and torments. It must be deterred and should not succeed. My hope is that the greater part of our North American inhabitants will live well and accordingly prosper in a nation content with freedom and opportunity for all. I hope that God, in his infinite mercy, will protect the good citizens of the United States.

I believe that those whom we call poor in America know nothing about the poverty of the scroungers in France. Any traveler must have little compassion if they refuse to give these people a small pittance of the riches that providence has placed in their hands. To see hundreds of aged, halt and maimed fellow humans begging would melt the heart of stone. I see them crawling on their caves like four-footed beasts crying for charity. *Mon cher Monsieur, le prie au bon Dieu pou vous* (My dear sir, I will pray to God for you). Little naked children, fifty and sometimes seventy in number, running after people in carriages and on horseback for miles and making the most woeful noises. This scene can move the most obdurate heart to have pity for them and persuade them to contribute a few coins to these needy people.

Focusing upon the city of Caen; it had a large population and attractive buildings almost like those in Paris in their beauty and majesty. Granted there were no palaces, but the buildings were generally more elegant, the streets better looking and the city more pleasantly situated in some respects, possibly because of its location about nine miles south of the English Channel. The local taxes were extremely high, but similar to those in other parts of Normandy. I understand that this resulted in a rebellion that took place in the province many years ago. The citizens were obligated to pay the king a high duty on the wine that they consumed in sizeable quantity. In fact, about every article that one needed was subject to a substantial duty unless it was smuggled into the province. They had to buy their salt from the officers of the crown who had a monopoly on the necessity. The duty was three *sous* per quart and every family was mandated to buy a quantity annually based upon

7. Adventures as a French Privateer

the number in one's household whether they wanted the commodity or not. If anyone was detected having sea-salt in his house that was taken from the ocean by evaporation, that person was liable for a fine of twenty-five guineas payable to the king. If the person was convicted of this "crime" and unable to pay the required amount, he or she could be imprisoned for one year unless the bondsman determined that the fine was likely to be paid within a reasonable time. The king's officers however had to approve this act of leniency. There was nothing in this province that was not taxed either by the king, the nobles who owned large estates in the province or other titled parasites. An Englishman who had lived in Normandy for upwards of twenty years told me that this province alone provided the crown with one hundred million *livres* per year. That sum was equivalent to over four million pounds sterling. This was the sum collected in peacetime, but it could easily double in time of war.

From Caen (where I feel the handsomest women of France reside) I set out for a place called Honfleur where I arrived in six hours. Once there I had to wait about two hours for the current to slacken in the mighty river that ran between Honfleur and Havre de Grace. The small town of Honfleur was known for producing the whitest and best bread of any place in the entire kingdom. At 4 o'clock in the afternoon I crossed over the river to Havre de Grace in a flat-bottomed boat with a single sail. While making the short passage I observed that these boatmen appeared to me as not being very good seaman. This town was a very large seaport situated on the English Channel at the mouth of the Seine River. It had no real harbor. Vessels that wished to stop there could enter the very large basin, but this had to be done at high tide when the river flow was favorable. I note that the water's flow could be as rapid as any that I have ever encountered and the watercourse reminded me of New York's Hell Gate in America. It was low water when I made my crossing and consequently the there was hardly any current motion.

About an hour later I saw a large galliot that appeared too late for a favorable tide. The ship attempted to pass into the bay because she had a favorable fresh following wind to aid her in making entrance and an incoming tide.[5] When she got abreast of the estuary, the people onboard lowered the sail and tried to carry a line to a quay ashore by way of a small boat. They were unsuccessful because by this time the current was so rapid that it carried the galliot away. The people in the small boat retreated to their mother ship and then the galliot let go an anchor. In performing this maneuver, they failed to check their drift. In time, the swiftly flowing water forced the galliot up the river about three leagues [about nine miles] where she struck a rocky shoal. In a few minutes the vessel was dashed to pieces and all onboard perished. I was informed by some people in Havre de Grace that they had never seen or heard of a ship successfully entering the river's mouth when the tidal current was at its swiftest without being forced upon the many shoals along the river banks. The current was so swift and dangerous that almost all those who failed to heed the warnings lost their ship and often their lives.

The town of Havre de Grace was very well built, strongly fortified and its streets attractive. The public walkways a short distance from the town's center were quite beautiful in every respect. The open country that surrounds the township was lovely and most pleasing to the eye.

I must however discontinue my description of the seaport city since I was only there for about three hours after which I continued my journey. The next place that I came to was Calais, a city in the province of Picardy lying twenty-two miles southeast of Dover, England. Because of its proximity to England, this large town was well fortified. Its buildings were mostly built in gothic architecture, but a great many had been destroyed or torn down because of their age. The seaport had a fine harbor, but its entrance was very narrow and difficult to access owing to a sandbar that laid almost completely across its mouth. No vessel over one hundred tons burthen could come over it at high tide or even during spring flood tides. There were a number of packet boats that plied the waters between Calais and Dover in peacetime. The nobility and gentry wishing to travel to either London or Paris generally used these packets as this was the shortest cross-channel route between the two national capital cities.

I only stayed long enough at Calais to partake of some food and drink and to change horses. From there I set off to Dunkirk and made the trip in eight hours. Soon after arriving, I was employed in assisting with the fitting out of Captain Anthon's cutter *Eclipse*. One hundred and ten officers and men staffed the vessel when we were ready for sea. She carried eighteen six-pounders of French design. We were ready to sail round the middle of November, so all the crew was ordered on board and we prepared to enter the Roads of Dunkirk. On the night of 20 November Captain Anthon left the cutter, but before he departed he gave me directions to take good care of the vessel, keep a sharp lookout and pay particular attention to the small details onboard the ship. At about midnight a very violent gale blew in from the north-northwest that created a turbulent sea and forced us toward the lee shore. Trying to leave the harbor for the roads at that point turned out to be a bad idea. We had a pilot onboard who advised us not to stay where we were much longer. He suggested that the mainsail be reefed and the storm jib and foresail be made at ready for hoisting at a moment's notice. Shortly thereafter we set the cutter's northern-most anchor for added security, but by 2 A.M. we observed that both of our anchors were dragging and we were being driven toward the shore. We now balanced the mainsail with a reef, slipped our cables, hoisted the storm jib and foresail and attempted to get into the roads and hopefully into the North Sea. The tide was at half flood making it impossible for us to enter the piers at Dunkirk. With the wind blowing so strongly and our sails shortened, we opted to set a course for the neutral port of Ostend that was about three hours east northeast of us. The initial part of the journey was a challenge. It was very difficult to cross the bar at the harbors entrance because of the unfavorable tide. The next morning Captain Anthon learned of our difficulties and sent a boat to our aid. This vessel had the cables that we jettisoned and our two anchors that we had left on the Dunkirk Roads. Later that day we were ready for sea but were further delayed, this time because of contrary winds.

Ostend was a considerable seaport and subject to the Emperor of Germany. Situated in the Austrian Netherlands, it was one of the most strongly fortified towns in the area.[6] Because it was a neutral port, most nations in the region traded there. The result was both prosperity and a large influx of immigrants. The population increase produced a high demand for simple necessities such as food, drink and other provisions. This became an expensive stopover because of the inflated price of goods. Even worse, the break in our journey allowed our crew to become decimated. Almost half deserted our ship while we were there.

On the morning of 1 December an English ship mounting fourteen guns arrived at Ostend. As soon as the British vessel learned who we were, the captain sent a boat with a challenge to meet them outside the bar on the following day. She then sailed a considerable distance beyond the harbor's entrance, displayed the English colors on her mainsail for all to see and set her jib sheets to the windward to lay in wait for us—or as we supposed. We had accepted the challenge to engage the cutter in battle, but we stipulated that we would do so only after we complied with the local law.[7] The British cutter remained in her position a fact that we could easily observe from the walls of the Ostend fort. When darkness fell, we lost sight of the vessel. On the morning of the 2 December, as soon as the tide was favorable for exiting the harbor, we got under way and come to a standstill about six leagues off the Ostend pier-head. The Englishman, however, was nowhere in sight. The swaggering enemy seemed to have sulked away in the night; we assumed that she was afraid of us. Actually this may have been a wise decision on their part. The English cutter must have realized that we were an overmatch for her.

This is how they may have become aware of this. When both cutters were anchored in the harbor, her first lieutenant was invited onboard our ship and we drank a glass of wine together. During this social call he had the opportunity to see the number of guns we carried, their size and could approximate the number of men we had onboard. During our customary maritime officer conviviality, he casually declared that if we fought, he thought that they would have the better of us. I responded that if that did occur, he would learn about the extraordinary proficiency of Yankee warriors. He asked what I meant by that remark. I said that shortly after we exchange broadsides, we immediately board an opponent and beat them into submission. He then admitted that we would have a good chance of capturing them since they were out-manned by us. I then added that most of the crew was fearsome Yankees. After this conversation with the English officer, I got the feeling that they did not intend to engage us in battle.

At 11 A.M. we hailed a neutral boat bound from Dover to Ostend and asked if anyone on watch had seen our intended antagonist. They replied that they had not, so we set our course for Dunkirk Roads, arrived by 4 P.M. and moored our ship. The next day we replenished our crew with a fresh supply of seamen. We soon set sail on a six-week cruise in search of enemies of the United States and France. On 10 December we seized two vessels under English colors. We ransomed one for four hundred and seventy guineas, manned the other with a prize crew and sent her off to France. The next day we encountered a large English letter of marque that mounted eighteen carriage guns. She carried forty-five officers and men plus thirteen men and women passengers. After a bloody battle that lasted three-quarters of an hour, she finally struck to us. Shortly after we took possession of her, the smoke and an opaque sea-fog burned off. We were startled to see an English frigate was nearly within gunshot range of us. It was likely drawn to us by the noise of the distant cannon action. We were compelled to abandon our prize and immediately left the scene. After crowding on as much sail as possible, in about one hour we were able to out-sailing her. She was determined however and chased us for four hours. Finally, we left her so far to our stern that she was forced to abandoned the pursuit by hauling her sails into the wind and raising her lighter sails aloft. We then steered a course for Land's End where we arrived on 15 December. On the way to this destination we captured two small sloops that we ransomed and a large English brigantine that was carrying a valuable cargo of dry goods and other miscellaneous articles. A prize master was assigned to this vessel and ordered to sail for France. At noon the next day we saw another ship close by and before long discovered that it was a frigate. We made sail away from her, but she pursued us. This went on until about 4 P.M. and then she came within gunshot range. She fired her bow cannon and successfully carried away the top part of our topmast. She was now chasing us before the wind and, since we were damaged, she was rapidly gaining upon us. Being close to the English shoreline with the sun having set and darkness setting in, we lightened our sails and hauled close to the wind. The frigate did the same, but we found that we were capable of out-sailing her in this sail configuration. After 9 P.M., in total darkness, we happily lost sight of her. The next day we put into Cherbourg and set to work cleaning our vessel's bottom so that we could enhance our speed and maneuverability.

The port of Cherbourg, on the English Channel in the province of Normandy, had an excellent harbor for men-of-war except when the wind blew from the north. The town itself was rather large and its buildings appeared to have been very elegant some time ago, but now they were decaying badly. The basin was quite spacious and could contain twenty men-of-war, there being about twenty-four feet of water at high tide. Vessels that warp [move by hauling on a line] into the small-enclosed body of water in order to clean or grave their bottoms laid with safety at the nearly dry bowl-shaped area at low tide. We hauled our privateer into the spot where she was laid upon her keel on sand that was kind to our fragile bottom. We shored the vessel up to grave one of her sides with tallow during the first low tide and did the opposite at the next low water. At high tide, we were able to warp back to the deep part of the basin and then anchor near the Roads.

The government was nearly finished building a very costly dry dock in the port. It was purposely designed for the overhauling and repair of ships of war. The Roads of Cherbourg were bleak, open and quite exposed to northerly winds. I am certain the French administration continued to create an important harbor facility in this city. The government employed several thousand people. Here and there were many flat-bottom boats, wagons and carts that were used of by local inhabitants to assist in the overall construction project. They had already built a half-moon shaped breakwater that extended from the western shore out onto the Roads as a northern barrier. This mini-harbor was about seven fathoms deep and its bottom excellent for holding an anchor. In fact, several warships were able to ride from the prevailing wind under this new manmade land with relative safety. Once the entire complex and breakwaters was completed I have little doubt that a fleet of ships-of-the-line was able to moor here in absolute security in almost any weather. In any case, this facility was a source of irritation to the nearby English in times of war.

There was a daunting fortification on a rocky island outcropping about two leagues from the entrance to the basin. This bastion completely commanded the Roads. Although it was still a work in progress, once the construction projects in the harbor was finished it would provide formidable protection from invaders, particularly the English who had a history of attacking the town many times in the past. The English did not have a safe seaport for their warships along the channel east of Portsmouth. They often anchored in the Downs, but it was an austere and dangerous place to lay as they were exposed to almost every wind that blew.[8] Cherbourg's harbor was well situated being located on the channel roughly mid-way between Portsmouth and the Downs. It afforded a significant advantage over the British when these two great maritime powers went to war.

I had the pleasure to meet a celebrated American, Continental Navy Captain John Manly. The Marblehead, Massachusetts Captain had made several very important captures of English ships during the early years of the Revolutionary War. Manly arrived in Cherbourg with a group of Americans who had escaped from Mill Prison near Plymouth, England. The men had been confined there for around three years, had no money and their only clothing was that which they were wearing. They looked very shabby and drawn, but extremely pleased to be free once more. I provided each of them a small amount of money, but advanced Manly one hundred fifty dollars, a sum that he requested from me. In return he gave me a note that said a Mr. [Jonathan] Williams of Nantes would repay me once I delivered the receipt to him and would be duly honored a few months later. I was pleased to be able to help a distinguished brave countryman and fellow mariner with this small loan. (I took so much personal satisfaction in this gesture that it may appear to the reader as evidence of vanity on my part for mentioning it, but that was far from my intention.)

On 23 December we set sail to continue our cruise and the next day we were pursued by an English frigate for six hours. The chase put a physical strain on our vessel and she sprang a leak thus forcing us to sail back into Cherbourg. We spent the next two days repairing our bottom. Once everything was in order, we put to sea again and set a course for Land's End. This was a difficult place to be because English warships chased us every day until the first of January. Eventually we found some prey, an English letter of marque mounting twelve carriage guns. She engaged us in battle and there were many exchanges of fire between the vessels before we gave orders to board her. Once our men got on the ship, their people quit their stations and quickly descended to the hold below. When the captain saw so many Yankees on his deck, he struck the British flag and yielded his ship to us. She was from Plymouth bound for Saint Kitts in the West Indies. At the beginning of the action she had thirty-five officers, men and boys. During the battle four were killed and seven wounded. Only two of our men suffered slight wounds and none were killed. This vessel was a valuable prize that was laden with English goods, so we had a prize master secure the English crew and sail the captured vessel for Brest.

On 3 January we encountered a heavy gale that lasted until the 12th. We sealed our gun-ports and battened down all the hatches. We sailed under a reefed foresail for much of the time and managed to get a storm foresail and jib raised. This kept us off the nearby English shore. It was plainly in sight when the weather cleared for a few brief moments. We counted upwards of thirty wrecks along the nearby coast during this time. We learned that even a greater number of ships had been driven ashore from that fierce storm and most of their crews were lost. On 13 January, the weather had moderated and gave us the opportunity to capture an English brig carrying sea coal. We manned the collier and sent her to France. On the 14th we put into Morlaix to make some minor repairs and recruit more seamen. We were short of crewmen since we had sent a number of them as prize crews. Our plan

7. Adventures as a French Privateer

was to sail on 20 January, but the wind remained contrary until the middle of February. At last we were able to cross the channel once again but the coast seemed lined with English cruisers. It was difficult to capture a vessel and get it off to France without its being retaken. We were constantly chased by frigates that were superior in force to our privateer, but we did manage to seize one large ship off Dover and sailed her to Dunkirk. This vessel was from Ireland bound to Norway and carried mostly Irish linens. Once we anchored in Dunkirk's harbor, our privateer was disarmed and the officers and crew discharged. The owner of the same privateer than offered the command to me and I accepted. My next chore was to employ another crew and refit the ship for another cruise.

8

French Privateer Captain Fanning

Having some time on my hands I decided to visit London. With all the hostility I had toward the British described in this memoir, this might seem to be an unlikely journey. What made this adventure possible was that I became a naturalized French subject due to the large amount of time I spent in Morlaix.[1] I was given a large sum of money plus letters of credit for fifteen hundred guineas from several merchants in Dunkirk to be fulfilled by Messrs, Charles and Edward Hague of London. My creditors suggested that I travel incognito and, if asked, say that I have some private business to transact in that capital city. If I paid close attention particularly in coffeehouses, I might hear something of importance of commercial advantage to my creditors. I advised them that if I tarried longer than expected in London, they could give the command of the privateer to someone else. However, if they would patiently await my return, I definitely looked forward to taking command of the *Eclipse*. The mutually agreed upon goal was for my return to Dunkirk by the middle of May.

I set out on this surreptitious business to London in mid–March. My first stop was at Ostend thirty-three miles overland from Dunkirk and from there I booked passage to Dover onboard a neutral packet boat. We sailed before fair winds and arrived in about ten hours. When we reached in port and came alongside the quay, the customhouse officers came onboard to perform their inspections by rummaging through the passenger's baggage in search of contraband. This alarmed me because it would not do to have my belongings inspected too closely. I slipped a guinea into the hand of the officer who was zealously searching and overhauling the baggage. As soon as he felt gold among his fingers, he desisted from any further examinations. Seeing the rest of his comrades busily searching other passenger's effects, he signaled to a nearby porter to take my belongings to the nearby inn and indicated to the baggage clerk that this gentleman was in a great hurry. He gave me a wink, signaled to follow him and I readily did, not wanting to take the chance that another inspector might decide to search my baggage. When I arrived at the inn, I tipped the porter and purchased a glass of wine for the officer that I had bribed.

I hired a post chaise and went overland to stop at the famous city of Canterbury. I spent the next day sightseeing, especially its ancient gothic cathedral that occupies more ground than St. Paul's in London. The stained-glass windows inside were beautifully painted in variegated colors and exceeded any that I had ever seen. Inside the building were magnificent marble statues that represented some of the early kings of Kent and several bishops of that city. I was told that King Ethelbert founded the city of Canterbury and the surrounding county in 589. A guide also told me that the cathedral and its adjacent buildings were nearly twelve hundred years old.

While I was visiting, a large throng of people entered the city that had just returned from a hanging of English sailors at Deptford upon the Thames River. Some of these people were staying at the inn where I was lodging and related what they had witnessed to the landlord and other guests. They described how eleven convicted sailors were brought from a place of confinement under an escort of mounted soldiers and foot guards to their execution place. Once they arrived at the specified point on the riverbank they were herded upon a wooden raft, and placed in irons affixed to their bodies, legs and arms so that it was very difficult for them to move in any direction. After that, a sturdy rope noose was put around each of their necks. Once all these preparations were made, the floating platform or raft was slowly towed before a multitude of bystanders to an offshore-gallows that appeared to have been erected only for one purpose. The raft carried the criminals plus a hangman to a mooring under the gallows at precisely high tide. There was about twenty-five feet of water in the river at that time.[2] The executioner than secured each man to a halter [noose] to hooks on the gallows that were just above each man's head. The executioner then left the raft in a boat so that the criminals were left to slowly die by strangulation as the tide fell; a horrible death by inches at a time. This mode of punishment was new to me and deserves notice because of its singular barbarity. This was another example of the British inhumanity that is not seen in the United States and elsewhere. The poor sailors, hanged as described, took almost four hours to die. Their sobs and final groans were heard a great distance from this tragic scene.

The landlord told me that this the kind punishment was imposed upon every prisoner taken by the English who had sailed under the American or French flags—if they had ever been in the British Navy or Army and proved to have been British subjects whether they had deserted or not. This particular method of execution frequently took place upon the Thames and exceeds the terrible treatment of American prisoners onboard the prison hulk *Jersey* in New York's harbor or those that I had witnessed while incarcerated in Forton prison. When all these cruel dealings performed by the British toward their fellow creatures are held up for review, I defy anyone to produce anything in history, ancient or modern, by way of barbarity and cruelty, that has a parallel in any nation—or even in nature for that matter.

After I paid the landlord for my lodging at the inn, I was about to step into the chaise in order to continue my journey when the owner asked to speak to me in private. When we entered a secluded room and were alone, the man asked me if I was provided with guineas. I did not understand and requested that he explain why he asked me such a personal question. The innkeeper said that he perceived that I was likely a stranger and if so, suggested that I should be concerned about being robbed on the road between Canterbury and London. He went on to explain that there were a great many highway robbers on that thoroughfare. In fact, several of his guests had been accosted in the last few days on that road, even while they were traveling in carriages in the daytime. He then placed a large satchel on the table next to us, opened it, explained that it was filled with counterfeit guineas, and then suggested that I purchase some. These coins would serve as a defensive decoy against being robbed of genuine guineas; that is they were something that appeared valuable to present to those attacking you. I was initially startled at the prospect of being robbed, then I was intrigued by the thought of being able to hoodwink the highwaymen. I was at a loss about what to do. Next, I thought about what could go wrong. If I purchased these bogus guineas, carried them on me as robbery foil and then was stopped by the English authorities I would also be in trouble. I was a visitor in this country and the officers of justice might commit me to prison upon suspicion of all sorts of crimes such as being a spy or more likely one who was sent by France in order to circulate false guineas. On the other hand, I knew that being robbed was the more likely event and staying in England on a mission without funds would be disastrous. This was a difficult decision, but I finally acquiesced, purchased twenty of these counterfeit gold pieces for a few crowns and continued on my journey to London.

On the way we passed through the populous town of Roxbury. At one point we came upon a large tract of land that was overgrown with thick bushes as high as a man's chest. I was told that this vegetation was called black heath and, as it turned out, an ideal place for highwaymen to wait for quarry. Once we rounded a bend in the road two smartly dressed masked men mounted on handsome horses stopped the carriage. One of them grabbed the reins and bridle of the foremost horse while the other firmly ordered me to deliver my purse. He said that if I stirred, he would shoot the driver. As I fumbled for the purse containing the counterfeits, a coach and six appeared just ahead accompanied by several men on horseback. The robbers quickly noticed them, abandoned their booty, spurred their horses and galloped down the main road. The would-be thieves then leaped over some ditches and fences and were soon out of sight. We passed the coach and six and I concluded that it belonged to an English nobleman because some of the men who were outriders were dressed in elegant livery.

I believed him to be an aristocrat because the mounted escorts were armed with hangers [short swords hung from their belts] and each carried a pair of pistols. This retinue must have appeared too formidable for these two highwaymen and accounted for their swift departure. I was now about nine miles from London and near enough to the city where I could just make out steeples above a black cloud of smoke in which the city seemed enveloped. This was the result of the common practice of burning large quantities of coal and very little wind to dissipate the grimy veil. As I got closer I observed the domed St. Paul's Church soaring over the rest of the spires. On 18 March at 4 P.M. I arrived at my London lodgings, the Sign of the White Bear on Piccadilly Street. The next day I contacted the gentlemen to whom my letters of credit were addressed, Charles and Edward Hague, merchants who lived on Fen-Church Street. Mr. Hague kindly offered me any assistance that I might need while in the city.

I discovered by chance that an uncle of mine, then a colonel in the British Army in America, had frequented the inn where I was lodging.[3] I did not want to take the chance of meeting up with him, so I changed my lodgings to a private house not far from St. Paul's. While I remained in the city I frequented the coffee houses and taverns where I overheard a great many conversations among military officers about their attitude toward Americans in general. At one of these houses I heard a British officer who, by his uniform and his shoulder epaulets appeared to be an army colonel, describe his time fighting in the rebels in America. He had spent almost four years overseas and was now home on furlough. He engaged in conversation with another officer and amused himself by imitating the peculiar Yankee way of speaking and what he considered their wide-ranging ungentlemanly manners. He told his fellow officer that he recollected meeting a person who arrived in Boston about the time that the rebellious colonials were collecting their forces nearby. The man went on to relate that the main road leading from New York to Boston was filled with men marching in a single file heading to join the rebel forces under the command General Washington. These bedraggled men were called the militia rather than the army. Some of these poor souls were clothed in rags with a knapsack or something like it on their backs. Each carried an old and sometimes rusty musket upon their shoulders. Some of these weapons appeared to be missing locks. These men carried their firearms with the butt end in the air where the muzzle should have been with the gun resting either on their right or left shoulders. This untidy band of amateur soldiers frequently marched several rods from each other.

He struck up a little banter with a few of these men and inquired where they were going. The answer was to Boston to fight the enemy and then would curse and deliver low class invectives. Then they accused me of being an animal-like Englishman or Tory. The same question was asked to others along the long road and it was answered in a similar way.

The colonel, a veteran of the ongoing war, then asked the officer how effective the American Army would be that was made up on these types of men. Could these half-naked, half starved, poorly paid, almost barefoot rebels dare to face the well-drilled, properly clothed and equipped British regulars and expect to win? It seemed unlikely if not impossible. Yet he responded to his own question by saying that they had done so on a number of occasions. There were instances where the rebels had beaten British troops even when our numbers were equal or superior to theirs. We learned that a regiment of these Yankee troops often beat a British regiment provided that each unit consists of an equal number of officers and soldiers. This was especially true when the contest became pitched and it became necessary to decide the outcome at the point of a bayonet. This was the case at a place known as Bunker Hill. The colonel then opened his tunic to show his bosom and pointed to an ugly healed wound he received at that battle. He went on to say that he had seen enough of the bravery of the Americans. If his government ordered him to rejoin his regiment and return to America when his furlough was over, he was determined to resign his commission. He concluded by saying that in his view the English will never be able to conquer the Americans with its fleet and army. The officer who heard this tale was upset, but the colonel chided him and said that he did not care; this was his view and he would maintain his belief even in the presence of the military ministry itself.

The colonel and his friend soon left the room and I entered the summary of this conversation into the pages of my notebook. I became a frequent guest in this and other coffee houses where I overheard descriptions of the attributes of my countrymen. There were more positive Yankee stories than I had ever heard before. Many were so amusing that I had to control myself to avoid bursting out with laughter. There were other instances of similar tête-à-têtes, that made me deduce that, at this time, there were a great number of British officers in both the army and navy who held similar opinions. It certainly indicated there was a likelihood of an approaching peace between Great Britain and the United States.

My business with Messrs. Charles and Edward Hague was completed and I remained in London for about three weeks, but without gaining any additional information. I set out to return to Dunkirk by retracing my previous journey and safely arrived on 8 April. The next day the gentlemen who had sent me on my expedition to London met me at a house in town. There they gave me new instructions together with several letters from the French court

8. French Privateer Captain Fanning

to British Lords Shelburne, Stormont and Keppel among others. The significance of the directives and letters were largely two-fold: first for the prospect of peace and secondly for the English court asking for the liberation of two Irishmen, Captains Ryan and McCarter. They had commanded privateers in the service of France, seized a number of British vessels and were confined at Newgate Prison. Both men were under sentence of death because they had been British subjects, but sailed under French colors. Their execution was postponed twice and now the French government pressed the British to spare the lives of these two mariners that held commissions as lieutenants in the French Navy and had provided important service to France.

I left Dunkirk once again on 9 April and proceeded to London, passing through Ostend, taking a neural packet boat and arrived at Dover on the10th at 5 A.M. The customs official attempted to search my bags but I avoided their rummage by telling them that the French government sent me as a messenger of peace. As proof, I showed them the addresses of the letters that I carried. Upon recognizing the names on the correspondence and my insisting that I must not be detained because my business was of the utmost secrecy and importance, they quickly released my baggage and me. They believed my story, but since I was not fully aware of the contents of the documents I was not sure if my description was true. I hired a post chaise, set off to London and arrived there in four hours. I delivered the letters to the addressees as directed. The message that they contained proved to be just soon enough to save the lives of Ryan and Carter. They were scheduled to be hanged the next day, but were granted a reprieve and thereafter were given liberty. I remained in the city for a few more days, but incognito. Eventually I was given documents of protection signed by Lord Stormont among others that allowed me to appear in public as myself. A Lord Mansfield questioned me about some ransom demands that had been sent for collection by Messrs. Charles and Edward Hague. His Lordship asked if I was a French subject and whether I had seen the signatures that appeared on the bills. I was put under oath and replied to the affirmative. He then assured me that the amount on the bills would be paid to the Hague brothers.

I now had sufficient leisure time to see the wide variety of curiosities that abound in the city. The first was the Tower of London. I paid half a guinea to the gatekeeper dressed in a crimson coat that was largely covered with gold lace who was one of the king's pages. After I entered the Tower, a guide took me on a tour and showed me everything that I wished to see. The first stop was a very specious hall filled with statues of both men and horses. All were as large as life. I was told that they represented all the kings of England from Alfred the Great, in succession, down to the present king. Some of these men were monarchs of Great Britain after the kingdom had annexed Scotland to England. All the kings were on horseback and the sculptured figures were kept spotless. I also saw a statue of Queen Elizabeth that was kept behind a curtain in one end of the hall. Her horse was particularly elegant, being decorated with a bridle, saddle and other riding accouterments. A British grenadier, as large as life, held the animal by the reins of the bridle in one hand. In the other he clutched his cap. He appeared to be bending toward her majesty that had just descended from her mount splendidly dressed. My guide told me that it was a representation of the moment the queen received the news in Portsmouth of the total defeat and ruin of the Spanish Armada. Fascinated by the details of the scene and artistry involved in fabricating it, I was then told that these figures were made of wax and are considered to be masterpieces by most connoisseurs. I was next conducted to a very large hall that was said to be three hundred feet long and a hundred in breadth. This contained one hundred and twenty thousand small arms, bayonets, pistols and the like. My guide informed me that the entire contents of this room had been removed and replaced three times during the bloody war in America. How many more times it will be emptied before the war ends, only God knows. I learned that roughly one hundred men were employed to keep the arms well-polished and clean. The next place I visited contained the trophies of English victories taken from the French, Dutch, and Spaniards as well as a few other nations. Some were magnificent objects as well as a large number of battle standards formerly belonging to these powers and forfeited with blood.

I was then shown the regalia of his majesty. There were many curious and valuable articles, but the most impressive were the imperial crown worn by all the kings, the bejeweled orb that was held in their left hand at the coronation, and the royal scepter topped with a dove, the emblem of peace. The hall also contained St. Edward's Curtana, an old rusty sword with one edge known as the sword of mercy whose blade supposedly represented both temporal and spiritual justice.[4] Nearby was a silver gilded font used for royal family christenings. There were objects presented to Charles II, Queen Mary's crown, globe and scepter, the ampulla what holds the holy oil that is used to anoint the kings and queens of England plus the golden spoon from which the bishop poured oil. The Crown of State that the monarch wears when on his throne in Parliament is adorned with an emerald. I was told that it is seven inches around, in addition it contains what many felt was the finest pearl in the world and a ruby of inestimable value. The female guide illuminated these stunning items by candlelight and handed me those objects that I was permitted to touch, but only by putting my right hand through iron bars. No visitor was permitted to enter the vault where they were kept. The last articles that my guide exhibited to me were several miniature Towers of London and city scenes that were made by a lady who had been imprisoned in the tower for a number of years. They were very skillfully fashioned and displayed admirable workmanship under particularly taxing circumstances. I was also shown a great variety of natural history objects; curious seashells, stuffed wild beasts and birds from foreign countries around the world, the most memorable of them was a five-foot high gray eagle.

After seeing all that was curious at the Tower, I went to the British Museum where there were many wax figures of different sizes and in various positions on display. When I first saw them, they appeared to be alive. On one side was a full-size woman seated in a graceful chair in the act of suckling an infant. On the opposite side of the room was a youthful man on a bended knee in a supplicating position at the feet of an attractive young lady. His humble posture and the scene suggested that he was addressing the love of his heart in a proposal. There was also a replica of an infant after it had been taken out of their mother's womb and animated in such a way that it appeared to have just emerged. Other similar wax models depicted the embryonic stages of fetal maturity as it develops in utero. I found this fascinating, but wondered how the artist knew so much anatomical detail of the embryotic tissues.

My next stop was at Westminster Abbey where there were even more statutes, plaques and historical oddities beyond my capacity to describe. This was followed by a trip to Spring Gardens where I saw a real giant who measured eight feet two inches tall. He lived in a special apartment large enough for him to occupy in reasonable comfort. The man was well proportioned in his body, arms, legs and features, especially considering his height. He was well dressed with a superfine broadcloth red coat, white bluff vest and matching breeches, white stockings, and shoes with silver buckles. The giant wore a black cocked hat adored with a black cockade and gave the smart appearance of a gentleman of military bearing. I asked him a few questions and he responded with appropriate polite answers. He told me that he was twenty-three years old, born in Ireland to poor working parents who were normal in size. The man had completed an education paid for by an Irish lord. He was then obligated however to reimburse the nobleman after he took him on a tour of Europe.

For lighter entertainment I made it a custom to pass my evenings at Covent Garden, Drury Lane, Astley Riding School or the opera in the Hay Market. I attended the opera one night when His Majesty George III entered. The spectators greeted his arrival in the theater with unexpected hissing and fits of laughter. This was startling, but even more astonishing was the opposite greeting afforded the Prince of Wales who arrived shortly thereafter. He was welcomed with favorable shouts, applause and echoes of *bravo*, the same accolade or expression of praise given to performers in France.

Mr. Hague generously provided me with tickets for plays every night that I wished to go to Covent Garden. The seats were always excellent, either in the pit or in his personal box without cost to me. The enclosure had a silver plate with his name engraved on it, hence I knew these were his private seats.

At one point he mentioned to me that he paid the theater managers for his reserved seats annually, a common practice by numerous heads of prominent families in the city.

On the night of 10 May, I left Westminster and crossed the bridge over the Thames that bore the same name, a noble and distinguished architectural specimen. The other two bridges that cross the River Thames are called the London and Blackfriars. They are not nearly as stunning as the Westminster. Once when I ventured on the other side of the river, I was quite pleased to find two rows of lamps in a straight line that extended along each side of the road for two miles. I took occasional walks in St. James Park where I frequently saw members of the royal family waking on foot for exercise. When the king joined the entourage, he was plainly dressed. Some of the princesses who were seen in the gardens were indistinguishable from other women of quality. In fact, I noticed that the ladies in waiting to the queen, who were rather ordinary and certainly not very attractive, were more elegantly attired than the princesses.

Once I ventured to the king's palace at Whitehall to see his majesty. I waited for a long time in a large hall that the king had to pass through on his way to attend a religious service in his chapel only a short distance from the palace. A good size crowd of people had gathered there in the hope of seeing their king. In time he walked very close to me accompanied by lords in waiting. Someone, perhaps one of his guards, authoritatively shouted that we should make way for his majesty to pass and the throng moved aside so that the king could walk between them. I noticed that several of these people knelt when his majesty was near them and attempted to pass him a folded paper, presumably requests to the monarch. One of the king's accompanying servants gathered these papers from the petitioners, but neither the king nor the lords in waiting stopped. On the contrary, they seemed to accelerate their pace through the gallery. At that moment I thought of my country, a people now without a king. I hope that they may never be cursed with one and all the leeches of royalty that surround the throne; people with greedy appetites consume the earnings of the hard-working people. My country was so fortunate compared to that of Old England. So many of its current subjects were in a state of abject oppression, yet they submit with embarrassing obsequiousness to royalty that may be contrary to their well-being. The king, so adored by most of the English people, was merely an awkward man with round shoulders and a large skull. Some who were critical of the sovereign said that his head was not well stocked with common sense. I noted that there was nothing in his appearance or behavior that was significant to command respect. On the other hand, the queen was far more physically appealing and drew more favorable attention. Their majesties' subjects generally admired her. The Prince of Wales was a handsome figure and highly regarded by the fairer sex.

8. French Privateer Captain Fanning

I also had occasion to visit Parliament and heard speeches by the celebrated orator Charles James Fox. I noticed that he was toasted more often than the king at formal dinners, some of which that I attended included some of London's most prominent residents. At this time Fox was a strenuous advocate of liberty and the United States, both of which were often heard in his speeches on the floor of Parliament. I heard him say that the best way to reconcile the Americans to the people of Great Britain was for the British ministry to declare the North American colonies independent and open free trade. By these steps they would have the honor and glory of bringing about a lasting and sincere friendship between the two nations. These were, as near as I can recollect, a reasonable recounting of his words.

I remained in London for about four weeks and then departed for France. My route took me back to Roxbury and on to Dover. While staying at an inn along the way I heard several people say that they heard peace was in the offing and I had no reason to dispute this view. Shortly I walked out on the quay and boarded a neutral packet boat bound for Ostend. The trip took about ten or twelve hours because of very choppy seas. After I landed with my baggage, I hired a post chaise and arrived at Dunkirk at about 9 at night.

On 12 May 1782 I was given command of the privateer cutter *Eclipse*, the same vessel in which I had sailed with Captain Anthon as the second captain. The ship carried eighteen French six-pounders mounted on carriages and her officers and crew numbered one hundred and ten. The crew was very international consisting of French, English, Irish, Dutch, Italian, German, Flemish, Maltese, Genoese, Turk, Tunisian, and Algerian members. There were also about fifty-five American seamen. All spoke either French or English and some could converse in both languages.

It is important to note the way privateers were fitting out in this part of the country. The common practice was that owners of the vessels advanced large sums of money to the officers and crew before sailing on its intended cruise. Usually the captain received forty-five guineas, each lieutenant twenty-five, the gunner, boatswain, sailing master and carpenter fifteen each, and so on to other petty officers according to their rank. Each able-bodied sailor received ten guineas, while ordinary seamen or landsmen five. The French owners advanced these different sums of money as a kind of bounty. The early payments I described were for a six-week cruise. These sums were increased for the officers and crew if the privateer ended up making a longer cruise. All these advances, however, were deducted from the total prize money after the cruise was finished. If no prizes were taken or not enough money was acquired from enemy vessels that were sold to cover the advanced payments, the officers and crews were not liable to refund their money to the owners.

We got underway on 6 June, the wind being favorable to journey northward for the coast of Scotland. Finally, on the 10th we captured in English brigantine laden with coal. We put a prize master and crew onboard her, and ordered them to sail for Dunkirk. Not long thereafter we came across a large sloop near the Scarborough shore. We attempted to capture the ship, but did not succeed. The next day we seized two large coastal sloops and, after taking out the crews and putting them on board our privateer, we sunk them. On the 15th we captured a large English ship off Buchan Ness near Peterhead. She was carrying valuable cargo, principally Irish linens and other effects. Once again, we put a prize master and fifteen men onboard and order her to sail to Dunkirk. At sunset on the 16th, we made for the Orkneys, the desolate islands that lie off the northern frontier of Scotland.

On the 17th we sent the boat for shore and ordered the magistrates of a small town on one of these islands to provide us with fresh supplies, especially vegetables. We made this demand as a ruse by saying that my name was Captain John Dyon of his majesty's cutter *Surprise*. The subterfuge was successful and our small boat returned with a large quantity of fresh provisions. At 4 P.M. several boats rowed from shore and came alongside with native Orkney Scots manning the oars. Their regional accent was so strong and distinct that we could scarcely understand them. Never the less we managed to communicate sufficiently to hire a pilot to help us get into a little port called Hope's Bay.[5] We dropped our anchor when we arrived at 6 P.M. I had received intelligence before leaving Dunkirk that several vessels were expected there from Quebec laded with furs and other goods. They likely would not have the protection of a convoy since it was rare to have a French privateer venture into these inhospitable and dangerous seas.

The majority of my crew was conversant in English. Therefore, I kept the pilot on board and ordered all those who could not speak English confined to the hold. This done, I declared restrictions on seven sailing vessels that were anchored in this port and waited for the arrival of the fleet from Quebec. During this time, none of the residents of the port suspected that I was the enemy. On the 27th in the early afternoon some my officers who had recently been ashore said that there were two English ships on the far side of the island. They were headed our way and were likely to enter the harbor where we were anchored. Upon receiving this intelligence, I went aloft with my spyglass and was able to discerned a large ship that appeared to be a twenty-eight-gun frigate accompanied by a cutter mounting fourteen guns. The cutter's sails were rigged differently from those customarily configured onboard French cutters and both were flying English colors. They were obviously enemy vessels. This was a perplexing situation and for the moment I was at a loss to know the best strategy to employ. I did realize that I had to come up with some sort of a plan fast. By chance the pilot informed me that these relatively large warships could not enter the port of Hope's Bay without a pilot.

8. French Privateer Captain Fanning

I then made my move by utilizing a strategy commonly employed under the rules of war recognized by most nations. Legally, as a declared belligerent, I had the option of obtaining a ransom from the town or burning it. I knew that it could be considered to be in retaliation for measures used by commanders of British ships of war. It was frequently inflicted upon American coastal settlements, particularly by James Wallace, captain of the sloop of war *Rose* who, with the assistance of this officers and crew, burned many small towns. In July 1776, during the Revolutionary War, *Rose* played a significant role in the British invasion of New York state, firing on fortifications and making forays upon villages far up the Hudson River.[6] They committed wonton barbarous acts in the course of some of their invasions. After conferring with my officers and gaining their approval, we determined we would either ransom or burn the village opposite where we had anchored. I ordered a number of armed marines to go ashore and have one of my officers present the village's authorities with a demand; they must present us with ten thousand pounds-sterling in one hour or the village would be decimated. In the meantime, our marines were to arrest three of the town's principal magistrates. They were then to be detained as hostages onboard the *Eclipse* until the ransom was received.

The lieutenant received orders that spelled out exactly how to conduct this affair after landing his men and convening the principal inhabitants. Once ashore he identified himself and our vessel as that of the enemy and communicated our business. The leaders of the town asked our officer for one quarter of an hour to consult about this costly matter and this request was granted. During that short interlude the lieutenant and his men started to plunder the residents of silver plate and other valuables. In addition, some attempted to have their way with a few young maidens and commit other abusive acts—all against my orders. The village's inhabitants now became agitated and some quite angry. They grabbed clubs and large stones and attacked the lieutenant and his landing party, driving them to their boats. Once they were safely off the shore, our men were now under the protection of the privateer's guns. The lieutenant realized, however, that he had not executed my orders to take hostages and obtaining ransom money. He quickly rallied his men, rowed ashore once again and rushed the villagers who now were in a disorganized retreat. Several of the privateer's cannon fired grape and canister shot at the villagers and into the village's buildings. The officer started to set the town on fire and burned the small boats aground nearby. The landing party then returned onboard with no one being seriously injured. The men also brought a great deal of silver plate and other purloined loot.

There was one other surprise however; a very beautiful girl about sixteen years of age who was attractively dressed was brought onboard. The lieutenant begged me to allow him to leave her in his charge onboard until we reached France and, in turn, promised to marry her once they arrived in France. However, I knew that he was already married and was particularly distressed that we had deprived this comely young lady of her liberty, an act of kidnapping. I ordered the lieutenant confined to his quarters for disobeying my orders and for abducting this damsel, an unwilling passenger on our privateer.

When I asked the young lady if any of my officers or men had attempted to harm her in any way, she said no then fell to her knees. The maiden pleaded that she did not want to leave her parents and friends, begging me in moving but in difficult to understand English. Because she could not bear to be separated from those to whom she held so dear, her only wish was to be allowed to go ashore. The adolescent then grasped me tightly around my knees and began to mutter words that I could not fully understand but it seemed like a prayer. I lifted her up, seated her in a chair and asked her to settle down. I then promised that I would see her safely brought to shore. She apparently misunderstood me, became hysterical tearing at her hair and talking wildly like a person who had gone mad. She might have misinterpreted my comments and assumed that I intended to carry her away. This was possible because the cutter was now just starting to get underway. I then took the time to write a letter to the woman's parents that I had no hand in causing her to be brought onboard my vessel and she was not harmed while onboard. As proof that I had no intention of waging war on women and children, I would personally return the girl to shore unscathed. I asked that they receive her into the bosom of their family still as virtuous as when she was forced away from them.

Accordingly, I ordered the boat manned and embarked with the young Scottish lady and me onboard. When we approached the beach, a shower of thrown rocks greeted our landing. In spite of the battering, we alighted as the assembled crowd retreated back a few paces. Many stood with their arms folded across their chests in defiance and perhaps in astonishment at our boldness. Having brought the young women ashore, I gently hugged her and [platonically] kissed her. She returned the favor in earnest and said "taunky, taunky, guid mon."[7] She then tripped away from me on dainty light heels.

After this I returned to the privateer and about 10 o'clock that evening we set the pilot ashore and paid him five guineas for his services. By midnight we were clear of the Orkneys and had successfully avoided running into the two English ships cruising in the area. The next day we captured two English sloops, manned them and sent them back to France. The following night we seized three additional sloops and sank all of them. I had all the prisoners onboard placed on the largest of the three vessels and had them sign a letter purporting that they had been captured by the cutter *Eclipse* sailing under

French colors identifying me as the privateer's commander.[8] They retained a signed copy as well. I then gave the prisoners the sloop to sail wherever they pleased, wished them well and then departed, sailing to the southwest.

On 29 June we arrived off the island of St. Kilda, to the west of Scotland. There we sank two sloops loaded with pipe clay and took shelter in a small harbor to find an anchorage and obtain fresh vegetables and other provisions. The next day we arrived off the northeastern part of Ireland where we encountered two English frigates. They pursued us for twelve hours. During the first part of the grueling chase they were positioned to the leeward of us, but the head of our mast sprung loose and we were obliged to shorten our sail. Because of this misfortune the frigates were rapidly gaining. We debated the best course of action and concluded to put the wind on our stern even though the frigates were to our lee. We got our sails ready, crowded as many as we could aloft and the *Eclipse* turned directly before the wind. One of the frigates was now very near and the other tacked and stood across our forefoot. This situation was dire so I decided to take a risky move. I ordered the after-yards secured, the throat and peak tied to the mainsail with chains and instructed every officer and crewman to lie as flat upon the deck as they could in preparation for action.[9] As we approached within gunshot range of the two frigates who were standing next to each other in order to prevent us from sailing between them. Our privateer's helmsman became agitated and then quite frightened. Noting this, I took the helm from him and steered directly between the two frigates. When they saw this maneuver, both of them began firing at us. Someone on the larger of the two hailed us and shouted, "Haul down your sails and strike your colors, you Irish rascal."[10] I made no reply and they repeated the same words a number of times in loud shouts coming from both ships. We were now abreast of both vessels and within a pistol-shot of each. The officers on the deck then fired their small arms into us, but we were moving at a greater velocity than the frigates and were about to pass them. They then directed their whole broadside into us and we were fired upon by their marines stationed in the tops. Most of the cannon shots went through our waist, but only damaged our boat stowed in their chocks on deck. One twelve-pound ball went through our main boom and fell into my cabin. We finally got so far to the leeward of them that they ceased firing their broadsides, but kept firing their bow guns at us. Several of our men were wounded as a result of the action, but no one was killed. Our rigging was not damaged, but our boom and mast were splintered but fortunately largely intact. The wind began to fall off and we set more sail. As the darkness descended, we thankfully managed to get clear of the two frigates.

On 1 July we were in sight of Slime Head or Twelve–Pence. The headland was also known by the second name because it appears as twelve small hills near the middle of the western coast of Ireland. There we discovered a non-descript ship to our windward sailing in our direction. We prepared for action. She displayed English colors and we did the same. We then requested that she heave to. Now I could see that she had twelve guns on each side and that she appeared to be a letter of marque. Our men were ordered to their stations and to prepare for boarding. We approached within gunshot, exchanged hails and, indeed, she identified herself as English. I ordered our British pennant hauled down and French and American raised in its place. As soon as this was done, the English opponent unleashed her starboard broadside into us and a rancorous battle commenced. We countered with four successive broadsides as our well-armed men crouching on deck cried out "*A la Bordage, mon capitaine*" (Let us board her, Captain). We then ran the *Eclipse* alongside the enemy and the boarders bounded upon the enemy's deck. This caused most of the opponents to quit their quarters and scurry below. In short order the English flag was struck and we took possession of the *Lovely Lass* that was in transit from Nevis, an island in the West Indies bound for her homeport of Liverpool. She was a valuable prize loaded with sugar, rum, cotton, and miscellaneous other West Indian products. A large vessel of five hundred sixty tons, she carried twenty-four long nine-pounders and several short eighteen-pound carronades mounted on carriages, besides swivels and small arms. When she engaged us in combat her ship's company was seventy-five officers, men and boys. The battle resulted in her losing a mate, boatswain, six sailors and two boys killed and eleven wounded. We lost two men killed and seven wounded out of the crew of sixty-eight that was onboard when the clash started.

Our third lieutenant was assigned as prize master along with sixteen sailors and ordered to keep company with us until we concluded our voyage and landed in France. The next day we took yet another prize, a brig loaded with provisions bound from Ireland to Portsmouth. We manned her and ordered her to sail to Morlaix. In pitch-blackness of the following night, we lost sight of our convoy. On 3 July we plotted our course for L'Orient to be refitted with a new mast and boom and obtain needed provisions. An English frigate and cutter chased us for two days, but we arrived safely in France on the 7th.

On 24 July our somewhat battered privateer was completely refitted and furnished with everything we needed. We set sail again from L'Orient in order to complete our cruise. Steering for the coast of Ireland, we arrived off the highlands of Dungarvan. At 5 P.M. we took a large galliot loaded with sugar and coffee and a sloop from Glasgow leaving with bails of broad cloth and linens. We put a prize master onboard each, manned them, and ordered them to sail to Morlaix. On the 29th, we captured a small English sloop from Bristol. The master of that vessel informed me that sixteen merchant ships were anchored in Bristol Harbor. They were mostly privateers waiting for a fair wind so that they could proceed from Bristol to Cork. He understood

8. French Privateer Captain Fanning

that the vessels were to sail as a convoy, but under the protection of a man of war's tender that carried fourteen guns. After the sloop's captain provided me this valuable information, we took out a few bails of her goods and other valuable property on board, returned the vessel to the captain and dismissed him. At noon I sent my boat on the shore with the first lieutenant and a party of armed men in order to procure some fresh provisions and vegetables. I told him not to molest the inhabitants if they did not oppose his executing my orders. I furnished him with money and told him not to take anything without paying for it. By 2 P.M. the boat returned with one plump ox, a few of the fattest sheep that I had ever seen, plus geese, turkeys and other assorted fowls. In addition, they brought a young gentleman and his rather beautiful sister with them. It seemed that the lieutenant had invited them on board telling them that he belonged to his majesty's cutter *Surprise*. He promised them that they would be treated courteously while on board and were at liberty to return to shore any time they pleased. It turned out that the youngsters were the son and daughter of the Earl of Keith. They had been out hunting and, on their return, met my lieutenant and his party of sailors. They accepted the lieutenant's invitation because they had never been onboard any of the king's vessels. The couple was very dignified, handsome and well dressed. The young lady was wearing a riding habit and the young man wore cloths that were suitable for a gentleman hunter or perhaps for informal business. When they first came alongside and I was informed about who these strangers were. Therefore, those officers who could not speak English were ordered below deck so as not to rouse suspicions about our true identity.

I made them feel very welcome. We provided them with food and good wine set up on a table because they appeared somewhat fatigued from their hunting expedition. We chatted amicably for a while together and cracked a few jokes. This was accompanied by a great deal of glee and mirth on everyone's part. As soon as the young Irish people had taken refreshments, they said that they wished to go upon the deck to see the great guns, as they termed them. The lady was very inquisitive and asked me many questions regarding what she saw. At one point she asked if we might fire one of the guns. We fulfilled her wish, but she appeared to be somewhat frightened by its loud report. She then requested that we discontinue the cannon fire. Suddenly there was a shout from a man stationed at the masthead about a sail approaching that drew the attention of everyone. He said that she was a large ship and showed English colors. I now ordered all hands to quarters on deck including the non–English speaking men who had been confined in the privateer's hold. The young gentleman and lady understood French and when they heard so many of my crew speaking that tongue, they began to realize that their hosts were in fact foes. I then assured these two very surprised "guests" that our privateer was a French vessel and indeed the enemy. Upon hearing this they were dumbstruck with astonishment and likely fearful. The young lady first broke her silence and said she hoped that we did not intend to carry the two of them to France. Before I could reply, the young gentleman said he would pay a thousand guineas if we did not take them to France. He then bargained a bit by saying that we could hold him hostage, but he respectfully requested that his older sister be set on shore. The lad noted that their parents were very old people and that it would nearly break their hearts to lose both their children at once. The young lady then replied with exuberance that if I set her on shore and gave her four hours to raise some money, she would provide three hundred guineas as the ransom of herself and brother and that I could detain him on board as hostage until she delivered the remainder that she had promised. After that she burst into tears and cried for her beloved parents.

Having no inclination of detaining either of them onboard longer than they wished, I ordered the boat manned and told these young people that they could go ashore whenever they pleased. When they heard this news, their joy knew no bounds. Their expressions of thankfulness were warm and grateful beyond description. The young gentleman now asked to know my name and declared that if I ever became a prisoner in either Ireland or England, he would aid me with his influence and fortune. I however declined giving him my name or the name of the privateer that I commanded. He then stepped into my cabin and left me his address. I was about to assist the young lady over the side when I begged her for a parting kiss. She complied without hesitation and I thought at the time that this Irish kiss was sweeter than the Scottish one I had exchanged earlier. They two young people then embarked for shore and I had the pleasure of seeing them safely landed. When the boat returned, it was immediately hoisted into its chocks.

The weather became calm, but just after we set the young Irish couple on shore the ship that we had been spotted earlier was now within a league of us. She appeared to be a warship with thirteen cannon ports on each side. I consulted my officers about whether we should attack her. A majority was in favor of engaging the vessel as well as the crew. We accordingly put out sweeps [long oars] and tried to row either alongside her or under her stern before nightfall. When we got within the range of her guns, she opened fire on us. We positioned ourselves off her stern so that she was only able to shoot her stern chaser. That was more of an annoyance than a serious threat. Just before sunset we had gotten within musket-shot close under her stern. We could now see that she had a great many soldiers onboard. The helmsman now gave the privateer a rank sheer [abrupt turn] and we fired a broadside into her stern. Our cannon balls poured across the length of her deck causing a great deal of confusion onboard the enemy vessel.

After repeating the broadside several times, we rowed alongside her with our boarding party fully prepared for an assault. They then leapt over the rails and onto the warship's deck at just the right moment. After seeing a number of almost naked men jumping onboard, many of the English crew quit their quarters. About thirty of our men were Maltese, Genoese, Turks and Algerians who are generally stout, brawny and athletic in appearance and they took delight in boarding and intimidating the enemy. Upon occasion they would strip themselves to nothing but a pair of draws and some sort of belt around their bellies. When attacking, they used long knives or dirks secured to their waists by a cloth band. Frightened and overwhelmed after five minutes of intense melee, they bawled out "Quarters!" and their flag descended upon its staff.

The ship we captured proved to be the *None Such*, an English letter of marque out of Bristol bound for Cork and laden with British manufactured goods. She mounted twenty-six six-pounders made of brass rather than iron and before the battle carried eighty-seven officers and men. Our assault killed fourteen men and boys upon her decks and forecastle plus several of her men were thrown overboard in the hand-to-hand action that lasted thirty-one minutes. Besides her complement of sailors, she had one hundred and twenty-seven British soldiers that were destined for America and were to be joined by others at Cork. Our privateer lost three killed and seven wounded. We assigned our first lieutenant as the prize master and manned her with a crew of twenty-five handpicked men. We took her captain and his two mates and part of her crew as hostages. We also took care to see that all the British officers and soldiers onboard the prize ship as well as any other Englishmen employed on the vessel were confined below deck. I ordered the prize master to refrain from letting any of them on deck until he reached port. I also suggested that they try to make for the nearest French port that I determined was Brest.

A few days after the battle I was sorry to learn some distressing news from some of the Irish citizens that came onboard the *Eclipse*. My lieutenant who took ashore the two young people that we released had stolen the young man's gold watch. That officer, however, had now sailed to France in one of the prize vessels and I would most likely never encounter him again. If I did see him, I certainly would demand that he either return the watch to the owner or make restitution for it.

After spending a short visit in Ireland, we sailed for the Isle of Man in the Bristol Channel. Once there, we cruised for several days in the hope of capturing some rich prizes as part of the Bristol fleet. Before long a violent storm producing a fierce gale forced us to change our station. We made for Land's End with a great deal of difficulty under shortened sail. The storm tested our seamanship as we struggled against being cast upon the coast. Once we got into the English Channel, we heaved to and laid without moving for thirty-six hours under a balanced trysail. On 9 August, the weather finally cleared and the sea became moderate. Towards nightfall we took two prizes, a brig and a sloop. Once again, we put prize masters onboard each, took out most of the prisoners and sent them to Morlaix. At 10 o'clock that evening we landed a party of armed men on the Cornwall coast and obtained some fresh provisions that were badly needed for our wounded men and prisoners. The next day we captured two English brigs that were within sight of twenty-eight English ships-of-the-line; several frigates and cutters at anchor in Torbay, Devon. The two prize vessels were laden with provisions that were bound for the fleet anchored nearby. We manned them and sent them to the nearest French port that they could safely reach. Our next foray took us to a bay near Falmouth where we discovered a brig and sloop under the protective guns of a small fort. We got within cannon-shot range and heaved to. The guns from the fort began to rapidly fire at us, but to little effect. We silenced the fort after discharging a few broadsides at its walls. After the smoke cleared I ordered our boat with a few armed men to approach the two ships. When they came alongside, they found them abandoned. It appeared the crews of these vessels recognized us as the enemy, deserted their two craft and fled toward shore. My second lieutenant with a party of men was dispatched to take possession of the fort. Once they landed they were astonished to see a dozen women retreating from the still smoldering ramparts. Still more were in sight in the distance, but evidently no men had been in the fort. The women who had withdrawn were armed with muskets. Every so often they would stop and fire their weapons at my men. When all became quiet, we took inventory of the fort's armament. The bastion had four four-pounders and six three-pounders all mounted on carriages. My lieutenant and his party spiked the guns making them useless for the enemy. Upon leaving the fort, they brought a fair quantity of powder that had been left behind by the fleeing artillery-ladies.

We put a prize master and crew on the brig that had a valuable cargo and ordered her to sail to Morlaix. I presented the sloop to the English prisoners that had been incarcerated onboard. The number of detainees had risen to one hundred and ninety-five officers, men and boys. The sloop that I gave them was carrying nothing but ballast. The Englishmen were thankful for both their liberation and gift of a ship that would allow them to return to their respective homes. Before we parted they, like the young Irish couple, showed their gratitude by promising to do everything in their power to be of assistance if we were to become prisoners of war in England. I gave them a certificate attesting to their capture and release and kept a copy as was the custom on such occasions. The released men gave us three cheers as we made sail leaving the British shore behind us.

On the morning of 11 August, we came across HMS *Jupiter*, a fifty-gun ship escorted by two frigates.[11] The warships bored down on us from a dis-

8. French Privateer Captain Fanning

tance of nearly five leagues and the wind was blowing a fresh gale from the west-southwest. We sailed away before the wind and raised every sail we could upon the privateer. The three vessels gave chase and spread all of their canvas aloft in order to catch as much of the brisk wind as they could. We soon saw a good-sized cutter directly ahead of us flying English colors. The ship off our stern of us raised signal flags. The cutter took note and heaved to ahead of us partly obstructing our passage. I immediately called all hands to quarters onboard our privateer. As we rapidly approached the English cutter, we observed that she mounted fourteen guns. While barely moving in her hove to position, she hauled up the tack of her mainsail in preparation for engaging us in an exchange of canon fire. The ships that were chasing us were now so close that, in order to avoid them, I had to sail within pistol range of the cutter. We exchanged broadsides as we passed each other. The *Eclipse* did not incur any significant damage from the altercation. When we came about, we gave her another broadside that carried away her topmast, jib-tack and part of her peak. In the English cutter's crippled condition, we left her and continued our course sailing before the wind without adding a rag of sail because the other ships were on our heels. One of the ships pursuing us came alongside the enemy cutter and appeared to offer her assistance. The cutter soon disappeared from view and we assumed that she had sunk. Later we saw the impaired cutter in tow behind the ship and making for the nearest point of land. By 3 P.M. we had out-sailed them and lost sight of all of our pursuers except the fifty-gun ship that was now about three leagues from us.

We shortly realized we were heading directly for an English fleet of men-of-war. The armada roughly extended in a long line for about nine miles from abreast of the east end of the Isle of Wight towards the south. In order to sail to safety, I tried a desperate move. I ordered our French flag hauled down and an English ensign and pennant raised aloft. Soon thereafter we attempted to count the vessels in this fleet. There where twenty-eight ships-of-the-line several of which were three-deckers. There were also a number of frigates, sloops of war, and cutters. Signal flags were now on display on the ship that had been tracking us and it was still to our stern. The grand armada hoisted an assortment of signals in response. I now had confidence that our ploy could succeed; we just might be able us to avoid the danger that waited us.

Our cutter had been built in England with distinct British lines and rigging and was painted exactly like the king's royal cutters. Most of my officers and crew spoke English and I ordered all of the crew who did not to go below. I had our officers dress like their English counterparts to facilitate the deception. We then approached the fleet with boldness, entered the center of their line and passed between two three-deckers. When we were only about a hundred yards from them they hailed us asking for our identity. Our cautious response was that we were his majesty's cutter *Surprise*. We dropped our peak so that we dipped our colors as were passed these formidable wooden castles, but did not take in a fragment of sail. We had nearly gotten outside hailing distance when we were ordered to heave to. We promptly answered with an "ay, ay," but kept both our course and speed. We had now given them the slip and intended to show them a Yankee leg bail [escape by flight].

This appeared to work when suddenly the ships-of-the-line in the center fired their cannon at us. The shot carried a considerable distance beyond our bow, passing well over our heads. Realizing that we did not halt as we agreed, three frigates, a sloop of war and a cutter separated from the fleet and gave chase. The fifty-gun ship that had been dogging us passed through the grand fleet and joined what became a maritime posse. The cutter out-sailed all the other vessels and gained on us. Observing this, I ordered the helmsman from time to time to give our privateer a rank sheer [put the rail almost under water] so that the hull would slightly slow us down. I also sent a drag [sea anchor] overboard to retard our way through the water. The English cutter came within musket shot, began firing at us, but none of our crew was hurt. In return we gave her a broadside that sliced away some of the cutter's rigging. She was forced to halt in order to make some repairs and did not attempt to follow us. This happened just at dusk and about this time the other ships hauled down the wind and gave up the chase, with the exception of the *Jupiter* that appeared to be gaining on us. As darkness enveloped us we were unable to see her with the naked eye, but she was visible with our night-glass.

I was now exhausted from the multiple trying diversionary tactics we managed in the course of that day and went below for some food and rest. I did not think that we would be taken by any of those ships that had chased us, but the *Jupiter* was close-by and still posed a threat. I had no sooner gone below than our helmsman broached the cutter and the upper most portion of our topmast was carried away.[12] The steering sail, ringtail and water-sail halyards gave way, all parting at the same instant causing the officers and crew great confusion.[13] I ordered the ringtail and water-sail cut clear and took charge of the helm myself. Because of the rough sea, my gunner fell off the main boom in an attempt to execute my orders. We did all that we could to save him, but were unsuccessful. The poor fellow who was a good man, drowned within sight of us. We effectively got the cutter before the wind again and the light sails secured onboard. All hands were expeditiously employed to get the spare topmast set in place. Before we could accomplish this, the formidable *Jupiter* came upon us, ran under our stern and luffed up [dumped the wind from her sails] under our lee. The English warship commanded us to strike our colors, drop the peak of our mainsail, haul down our windward jib sheet, lower our boat into the water and come onboard his majesty's ship. I replied that our boat was so full of holes that she was unseaworthy and we were unable to comply. It was now four o'clock in the morning, nearly three

8. French Privateer Captain Fanning

hours before daybreak on a moonless night. They said that they would put their own boat over the side and ordered me to hoist a lantern at the peak. As I abided by their wishes, the *Jupiter* took in her light sails; her courses were hauled up and ready for action with her bows pointing to the southward while ours were faced in the opposite direction.

My officers now prepared to surrender and become prisoners of war. They dressed themselves in their best clothes and each wore two shirts that would serve them well if they were incarcerated for a long period of time. I, however, suggested a wild plan; one that offered a slim chance of escape from the enemy. We were to lay low in the vessel and then make a run for it even in the face of a hail of fire. I told them that I would take the helm if we get out of reach of the enemy's shot. Most of the officers and men agreed to this truly hazardous scheme. Then we all proceeded to act as one. At the time the enemy was visibly employed hoisting out their boat because we heard the familiar boatswain's call for this action carrying over the waves. I ordered some men to make their way up to the peak and let out the jib sheets. Once this was accomplished, I directed every man and boy to lie flat on the deck. The *Eclipse* had just begun to gather headway when the enemy's small boat left the *Jupiter* to board us. I repeated my warning that everyone obey my orders and we must quickly get away from our nemesis. I did not have much faith that we would succeed with our plan at the time. The Englishmen quickly perceived our intentions and their boat returned to the large warship. She instantly fired upon us from all parts of the vessel and, for a few minutes, she had the appearance of a luminous body of fire. We were so close to her that she was also able to use muskets against us. Realizing that we were determined to make our escape, they wore-ship [changed course with the wind to her stern]. This maneuver was time consuming in a square-rigged vessel and when she had almost completed her 180 degree turn, the *Jupiter*'s crew set all her sails in order to pursue of us. While doing so she continued to fire her bow chasers at us. We became vulnerable once again and were forced to expose ourselves to another broadside as well as fire from their musketry. I knew this to be the important moment of the escape plan and cautioned everyone once more to lie as close to the deck as possible. The *Jupiter* blazed away at us from every part of her as we passed by. At this moment I received a flesh wound in the leg and another in the forehead from a splinter. These two injuries stunned me and knocked me down. I was later told that I remained motionless on the deck for some time. Several of my officers and men were wounded as well and some cried out that we should strike. When I recovered, I seized the helm and shouted back at my men that in ten or fifteen minutes our vessel should be out of the warship's gunshot range. We were now evading the enemy at a very rapid pace and found it best to tack often, then ply to windward. I tacked *Eclipse* again and, when passing her, hoped to remain just out of reach of her cannon shots. It was easier to maneuver our privateer then the enemy could manipulate the ungainly and more complex square-rigged ship. We gradually, but steadily opened up a good stretch of water between us. The next time we passed the ship, she fired her broadside at us. As predicted, her cannon shot failed to reach us and made splashes to our stern. It the morning's daylight the enemy was at least four leagues to our lee. Apparently disheartened, the *Jupiter* soon gave up the chase and bore away. It is my opinion that the enemy expended more powder in shock firing at us then she would have used in a two-hour engagement with an enemy ship of equal force. They called us all sorts of disparaging names. "So much for the Irish rascal—as they called me—but the bird had flown. And now, messieurs bragadocio [sic] Englishmen, you may return home to tell your royal master, 'that you catched [sic] an Irishman and lost him.'"[14]

In this very mobile battle, we did not fire a single gun. We had enough to occupy our crew maneuvering our privateer while trying to avoid the reach of the enemy's shot. During this incident thirteen of our men were wounded, but none were killed. Our waist and boat that was in the chocks were pierced many times with eighteen and nine-pound shots. Our sails were also tattered and full of holes. Once we got clear of the *Jupiter* we counted in excess of seven hundred and fifty of these punctures in our mainsail alone. Fortunately, during the time that she was firing into us, her cannon balls, chain shot [two small cannon balls attached together by a chain] and angel-shots [two headed half balls attached together by a rod] failed to cut away a single piece of rope or rigging of any kind as they were intended to do. Now we took the time to treat our wounded men and take a bit of nourishment. There were no other vessels in sight except for the *Jupiter* barely discernable far to the leeward.

At 10 o'clock the next morning we found ourselves close to the small English seaport of Rye. Here we captured a brig laden with coal, put a prize master onboard and ordered her to Dunkirk. We also took a small sloop that was in ballast and gave her to our ninety-four English prisoners. Our captives were given prisoner of war certificates and we took copies from them. They offered their friendship, wished us well, gave us three cheers then British sailors departed as free men.

At about noon of the following day, the wind being at the southwest by south and the weather thick and cloudy, we discovered a sail to the windward. The vessel was on a course heading directly toward us. We heaved to, waited for her to come close to us and prepared for action. As she came nearer, we could discern twelve guns on each side and she appeared to be transporting troops. The vessel passed within gunshot range, but did not attempt to hail us. We were flying English colors, but I decided to haul down the union jack and hoist the French fleur-de-lis aloft. As soon as they discovered our true national identity, they took in their sails and hauled by the wind for us. Our boarding men were at their ready stations and began their usual shout asking me to give the order for boarding.

Meanwhile the Englishman, having gotten within cannon shot of us, gave us a broadside. We returned the fire, but only with ineffective musket shot. The English ship fired briskly for fifteen minutes and then the discharges began to slacken. During the exchange I received a musket-ball wound. The projectile passed through my left leg, but I did not feel the ball strike nor did anyone notice my injury until the action was over. The bullet wound bled so profusely that my shoe filled with blood. I took out my handkerchief and bound it around the wound to create both a bandage and tourniquet. This first aid measure allowed me to remain at my station on deck during the remainder of the action. We could now hear the groans of the wounded and dying onboard the English ship, but one of my lieutenants noted that we had not lost a single man in the skirmish. In order to quickly end the clash, I ordered the privateer laid alongside the English vessel where we heard a great deal of flaunting, demanding we strike and they would not allow us quarters. The majority of our boarding party waited below the rails and a few other members huddled in the yards and bowsprit. All were in full spirits and eager for the hand-to-hand action to begin. At length we maneuvered to a position under her stern and poured a broadside into her. We then raked her main deck fore and aft dreadfully slaughtering many poor blokes. We luffed up under her lee and our men leapt onto the enemy's deck. They engaged in a bloody conflict for about six minutes and once again we gained a victory. Many of the Englishmen quit their quarters and scurried below decks shortly after the *Eclipse*'s sailors got onboard. They soon begged for quarters and we noticed that the number of men surrendering on their deck appeared to be about double that of our boarders. It became evident that the courage of the Englishmen failed them when they saw fearsome men leaping on their deck or dropping down upon their heads from above. I feel that when they see unexpected or unusual sights like these, they become cowards and sniveling poltroons. They turn out to be shadows rather than men. I speak of this from my experience; spectacles that I have witnessed many times.

Having struck, the ship proved to be the *Lord Howe* from Cork, bound for the Downs, under the command of a lieutenant in the Royal Navy. The vessel was roughly six hundred tons-burthen and mounted twenty-four six-pound cannon besides a few short carronades, cohorns and swivels. The ship's company was eighty-seven officers and men (mostly older men-of-war sailors) at the start of the battle. In addition, the *Lord Howe* was transporting one hundred and ten officers and soldiers that belonged to a regiment that had been stationed in Ireland. The army personnel that were lost in the action were one major, one lieutenant and twenty-one soldiers. The king's warship lost one master's mate, one boatswain, seventeen seamen and three boys killed and thirty-eight officers, seamen and soldiers wounded. We suffered the loss of one quartermaster, one gunner's mate, one boatswain, seventeen seamen and three boys killed on board the privateer plus twenty-two officers and seamen wounded. I believe the entire number of the *Eclipse*'s officers and crew at the time of battle did not exceed seventy-two. The prize, so costly in English lives, turned out not to be very valuable. The warship was largely sailing in ballast and carried only beef, pork and butter as provisions.

We had just managed to transport all the prisoners to our privateer and, for our safety, put them in irons when a fog that had largely engulfed us started to clear. A thirty-two-gun frigate suddenly appeared out of this parting murkiness. While we had the opportunity, we abandoned our prize and began to escape. We removed all personnel from the prize, threw most of their guns overboard and spiked those that remained. A lieutenant wrote some of the particulars of the battle in chalk in the quarterdeck as our own calling-card and retained the colors of our antagonist as a trophy of our victory. The frigate was now closing upon us and fired several shots. This caused us to spread all the sails that we could on the privateer and give us the chance to test the strength of our newly repaired topmast. We saw the frigate come alongside the prize that we had abandoned in the distance, but she did not stop. The English warship continued to pursue us before the wind. After three hours, the gap was widening and her chase seemed fruitless. We had outdistanced her, so she took in her light sails and braced her yards by the wind.

I now decided to set our course for Dunkirk and return to France. There were many reasons to justify this choice. I had a great many wounded men onboard and most were obliged to share crowded space with the English prisoners in the hold. None of the men on either side could receive adequate care in this situation. Since I had many able-bodied prisoners onboard, we ran a risk to our own lives if these men rose up and overpowered us. With only about thirty men, including officers as part of the privateer's crew at that point, we were in no position to engage in battle with an enemy of roughly equal force. I was wounded myself and was largely confined to my cabin. My leg was very uncomfortable sometimes producing excruciating pain. A bone had been fractured in that leg and I could not bear to put any weight on it. We also were running low on provisions. I entered all these different reasons into my journal in case the owners questioned my judgment as to why I chose to discontinue the cruise.

I arrived in Dunkirk two days after our battle with the twenty-four-gun ship that I was forced to abandon. As soon as we entered the port and tied up at the quay, people flocked from all parts of town to inspect our shattered privateer. The commandant of the city's fort offered his services, helped me get into his personal coach that then carried me to his house. While there, I was waited upon by nearly all the king's officers who were then in Dunkirk. The commandant's family was especially attentive to me. Three days later I was carried to the Hotel D'Estaing where I usually lodged when in Dunkirk and where my wound confined me to my room for about three weeks. During my convalescence I was visited by both the most important gentlemen of the town as well as the ladies, the latter of whom seemed to be quite interested in my recovery. The owners of the privateer visited me more frequently than the others and appeared anxious for my restoration to good health. My recuperation was prolonged because of some complications that often accompany a severe wound.[15] The owners told me that they had built a new brig with me in mind and it was sheathed in copper with a new hull design. Those who saw her thought that she would likely be the fastest sailing ship ever built in Dunkirk. The vessel was to mount eighteen nine-pounders. Her masts were being shipped from Norway because at that time there were no masts in Dunkirk. Spars of any type were in short supply except for those in the king's shipyard and those were reserved for use in large royal warships. None would have been suitable for the masts of the brig under construction. One of the owners kindly invited me to reside at his house after I had recovered enough to walk. I accepted his offer and lodged there as my temporary home.

His daughter, a part owner the privateer-brig, paid close attention to me bordering on ardor. It was not uncommon in France to find young ladies of fortune who fitted out privateers as investments. I was too much of a warrior to have thoughts about love at the time. Besides she was around thirty-five years old about eight years my senior, very pompous, formal in her manners and ordinary in her looks and figure. She was the kind of female that might be called in my home country "an old maid." In order to avoid any sexual weakness that might develop related to her persistence while waiting for the brig's masts, I purchased a part of a forty-ton English built cutter. I set some people to work to prepare the ship for a cruise. As soon as the rather wealthy lady in question knew about this, she insisted upon purchasing a few shares in this privateer for herself. The other owners of the cutter accepted the partnership arrangement and the vessel was ready for a cruise by 20 October.

9

Lieutenant in the French Navy

I waited for the admiralty's judge to grant us a letter of marque for the cutter that we named the *Ranger*. The judge appeared surprised that I would ask for a commission for so small a vessel. He inquired about the fate of the large cutter I commanded. I replied that she was laid up. She had become so old and cranky that I choose not to venture out on another cruise on her. This was especially true because winter was about to set in and she was now leaking badly. The *Eclipse* had become so difficult to manage in the last gale we encountered I did not consider the cutter safe with the number and size of cannon that she carried. The judge listened attentively and then said that he wished to introduce me to Monseigneur the Marquis de Castries, the king's minister of marine because he was aware of my courageousness in support of France demonstrated in many instances. The minister was so impressed by my daring, especially during our last cruise, that he wished to appoint me as a lieutenant in the French Navy. As part of this commission, I would be entitled to half pay at my present rank for life as long as I resided in France or remained within territories governed by France. He then asked me to be seated and ordered a servant to go to the customs house to get my appointment. He soon returned with a parchment scroll that was proof of my king's commission. I told the judge that I was honored by his offer, but I had made other plans at this time. I requested that he keep it for safe keeping in his office for the time being. After more convivial conversation, he granted my letter of marque request for the *Ranger*. I then recruited an officer as my first lieutenant, a former printer from New York named Thomas Greenleaf who had been a fellow inmate in England's Forton Prison. I also hired a boatswain, a gunner and twenty American seamen. Each man was advanced ten guineas as "earnest money" for a fifteen-day cruise. That was as long as I expected this particular foray to last. The cutter *Ranger* mounted only three four-pounders upon carriages, six swivels and an assortment of small arms necessary for boarding an enemy vessel. This was our chief means of capturing English

9. Lieutenant in the French Navy

ships. Because our guns were relatively ineffective, we did not intend to be very reliant upon our cannon.

I set sail from Dunkirk with fair winds for the English coast on 23 October. My destination was to be the Downs. At daybreak the next morning we found ourselves amidst an English fleet of sixty odd sailing ships. They were not far from Dover and seemed bound for an unknown western port. We moved leisurely propelled by a light easterly breeze. Our situation was obviously perilous so we covered our guns with sailcloth, unshipped our swivels, stowed them away and hoisted English colors. Next, we steered along the same course the members of the fleet were following. I ordered all crewmen to go below except for the helmsman and two others. This disguised our privateer as much as possible by making *Ranger* look like an ordinary coastal vessel. As soon as it was broad daylight, I reconnoitered the fleet. I determined that there was only one thirty-two-gun frigate among them and that warship was the commodore's vessel and flew a broad pennant. However, there appeared to be several letters of marque in the fleet that mounted four to sixteen carriage guns and two large sixteen-gun cutters. At noon the wind shifted to the west, remained very light and followed the direction of the coastal current. The commodore signaled the members of the fleet to heave to and drop their anchors. This was largely done, but several of the fleet's small boats kept passing and re-passing one ship and another. I expected that one or more of them would pay us an uninvited visit. If they did, they would likely discover our true identity. This concern waned when we saw them start to retrieve their boats and hoist them onboard. At 5 P.M. a signal was made that appeared to indicate the fleet should get underway. We did the same and steered along with them. My lieutenant and I joked that somehow the two of us had inadvertently become British prisoners again. We spoke to two ships and a brig towards nightfall, passing within pistol-shot range. We engaged in a fairly long conversation with the people onboard one of the ships because the wind was so light and the sea so calm. On the first night we considered sneaking away and getting clear of them that very night, a plan involving little risk if we opted for it, but we decided to stay with the fleet until we succeeded in capturing one of them. We could not see the logic of being forced to leave so many valuable vessels without trying to seize one or more of them. By further conversation with some of them that we learned the entire fleet was bound for Portsmouth. We kept company with the motley convoy and I believe that none of the English suspected us of being the enemy. It was now becoming dark and squally. The commodore made a signal by firing three guns and hoisting several flags that meant the ships were to disperse and seek shelter in the nearest port. That was Rye, too far distant to the northeast. At 9 o'clock we ran under the lee of a large ship with our men ready for boarding and hailed them. We enquired if they were acquainted with the port to which they were heading. If not, we said that we would be pleased to put a pilot onboard. They replied "Ay, ay." It was now very dark and nearly all her crew was in the yards reefing her topsails. I then ran the cutter under her lee quarter and ordered the lieutenant in command of the boarding party to go aboard the English ship. They did this instantly and with ferocity. The captain of the enemy ship and his men on deck offered only faint resistance. After a short skirmish the Englishman yielded and were taken prisoner, as did those who descended from their stations in the yards. Not a single cannon or musket was discharged by either party during the conflict with the exception of three or four shots from pistols. Several of the enemy were slightly wounded. Our first lieutenant and three other members of our crew were also wounded, but not seriously. The English ship proved to be the *Maria*, a letter of marque mounting eight double fortified [extra heavy casting] six-pound cannon, but the weapons were placed on a gun deck below the upper deck. The ship had an unusual configuration that enabled them to fight in close quarters with nearly all her rigging controls operated in a space between decks. Therefore, she could be maneuvered reasonably well without exposing her men to very much gun fire. The ship's company consisted of thirty-five men, the captain, officers and crew plus three gentleman passengers. The vessel was bound from the Downs to Portsmouth carrying a variety of supplies for the English Navy. As soon as all the prisoners were placed in irons and secured in our cutter's hold, I ordered the first lieutenant to take charge of the prize ship. He selected ten men to assist him. I gave him a copy of my privateer's commission, directed him to sail across the channel with as much canvas as the vessel could carry, and then put into the nearest French port. Several of the lights of the fleet could now be plainly seen in the darkness, but no alarm guns were fired by any of the vessels. We next ran alongside a large brigantine, boarded her and took the ship without resistance. She was the *Speedwell* mounting four carriage guns and manned by fifteen men and boys including the captain and mate. This ship was laden with sheathing for coppering the bottom of the navy's ships. I put a prize master and six men onboard the *Speedwell*, took its crew as prisoners and had them join the others in the hold. I once again ordered the prize master to make for the French shore as fast as the ship, the weather and the increasingly choppy sea would allow. Our next undertaking was to attempt to capture a large sloop. We now ran a great risk when we ran alongside her because the breeze was fresh from the west southwest and the sea was running rather high making the cutter pitch and roll. Water was coming in very fast into the hold where the prisoners were incarcerated and they frantically yelled that we were sinking. All this commotion failed to deter me from attempting to take this last prize to France. I put the boatswain and gunner onboard this prize, but neither of them understood much about navigation. I added one seaman to help work the sails. I gave the boatswain a copy of my

9. Lieutenant in the French Navy

letter of marque commission and repeated the same destination orders that I gave to the other two prize masters. This vessel turned out to be the *Dolphin* from the Thames River also bound for Portsmouth and carrying bales of dry goods, pig-iron and coal.

After taking these three prizes, manning them and securing the prisoners, I took some much-needed rest for the greater part of night. I began to think that it was time to head to France, but I was in an awkward situation. My crew was now down to only two Irish lads without experience in steering or navigating. Clearly it would not be safe to release the prisoners from the hold to assist me in operating my privateer. In spite of this, we set sail and left the fleet. At daybreak we could distinctly hear alarm guns fired in the distance. At 6 A.M. I had overtaken two of my prizes, the brigantine and the sloop. At about the same time I saw a large cutter bearing down on us likely from the fleet. We were then roughly abreast of Dieppe, a small port on the French coast. I hailed my prizes and ordered those in command to endeavor to make that port, but thought that it would not be wise to remain with them. If the cutter approaching us was English, I might have made a successful escape with the *Ranger*, but the prizes would likely be retaken. I decided to haul onto the wind to the northeastward. The large cutter at the same time stood nearly directly in front of us. When we were out of sight of the prizes, I bore away directly before the wind. The unidentified cutter did the same. I could not set any more sail since I was obligated to stay at the helm. The two lads left onboard lacked knowledge of how to properly set the needed topsails.

The unidentified cutter was rapidly closing in. At 2 in the afternoon she came alongside and our only choice was to surrender. She mounted fourteen carriage guns, was in the king's service, and was commanded by a Lieutenant Lane of the Royal Navy. (After the *Ranger* was taken, if she was managed correctly and had sufficient sail set upon her, she would sail faster than the large cutter that had taken us.) It turned out that the commander of the king's cutter and I were well acquainted. I had seen and conversed with him in Ostend sometime before when we had taken lodging in the same place. He treated me with friendship and kindness while I was his prisoner. Both cutters now set a course for Dover. The captain of the large prize that I had taken out of the English fleet made several attempts to kill himself as he was embarrassed at having been boarded and captured by such a small apparently inconsequential privateer. Only the night before he was taken, he had bragged that he was able to subdue any French privateer of sixteen guns. Once captured however, his own countrymen reproached him for his ineptitude and perhaps pusillanimity. The English cutter's captain was now concerned about the man's mental health, confined him to bed and a sentinel was stationed to watch over him to prevent him from taking his own life.

At 10 o'clock on the second day of this new captivity, we arrived at Dover and anchored close to town. When it was learned that they had found the person who went by the name of "John Dyon," alleged the captain of his majesty's cutter *Surprise* and was now a prisoner onboard a king's ship lying off the town, it caused an uproar.[1] The next morning I embarked to shore onboard a cutter's boat that carried me, my baggage, plus the two Irish lads that had been taken with me under the command of the second lieutenant. As we approached the quay I saw it was crowded with approximately two hundred people, almost all women. They had heard of my capture and it seemed by their conduct that they were determined to execute an Old Testament, *Book of Leviticus* law upon me; that is, stoning to death. They started to throw stones at us as we drew near the quay. They became so thick in number that it was impossible to avoid getting hit. To my great surprise I heard the ladies cry out incongruously "Welcome, welcome, Captain Dyon." Shower of stones of all sizes pelted me accurately and repeatedly, followed by strident shouts. My head started to swell and become very painful. By chance I was wearing a stiffly varnished sailor's hat on my head, otherwise I believe that I was in danger of losing my life. I quickly pulled it down over my face to protect my eyes. The oaths, curses and threats were extremely vile. They were unlike that I had heard uttered by women or other human beings. At length a guard of one hundred officers and men was sent to disperse the mob and then escorted us to the fort. Once there, a very young man who was said to be the illegitimate son of a nobleman and the commissary for prisoners of war examined us. In attendance was his assistant, a surly looking one-eyed fellow. The man had once been the first lieutenant onboard the sloop of war *Rose*, stationed at Newport and had taken part in one of the earliest battles of the American Revolution.[2]

This former lieutenant boasted about his knowledge of the American coastline from New Hampshire to Georgia and that he knew the way in and out of every seaport within these two geographic coastal regional extremes. He also knew the bearings and distances between all the capes and headlands along the seacoast. He was stationed there with the title of the port's regulating captain [superintendent] by appointment of the king. His duty was to examine all the prisoners brought here or to nearby ports by cruisers of all description, whether navy or letter of marque. His impressive knowledge of the American coast was the reason for his appointment under the crown—or so I was told. I concluded that his boasts may not have been empty because of the questions that he subsequently asked.

The two lads were examined first by the commissary and the regulating captain. The superintendent determined that they were Irish boys and consequently were sent onboard the guard ship lying off Dover. Afterwards, since they were British subjects and were taken sailing under an enemy's flag, they were hanged.

9. Lieutenant in the French Navy

I was then conducted into the presence of the king's two officers. When I entered the room, the regulating captain swore that I was an Englishman. The commissary, after asking me a few questions, declared that in fact I was an Irishman. The interrogatories that they intended to ask were written down and laid on a table before the king's officers. The first question asked was where was I born? When I had answered, they had a great deal of conversation among themselves. The regulating captain told several Yankee stories relating to the town and the people about where I claimed to be born. He said that he knew Long Island Sound well, so then he asked very specific questions to me such as: Exactly where is the lighthouse at the mouth of New London Harbor located? On which hand would you leave the lighthouse heading out and which side would you have it coming into port? How far is that lighthouse to the west end of Fisher's Island and on what course? How far is the mouth of New London's harbor from the mouth of the Connecticut River? Who was His Majesty's Tax Collector in New London before the rebel war broke out in America?

I answered all these questions and more to convince these officers that I really was an American by birth. I succeeded in my quest and the commissary told me that I might be eligible for conditional release if I choose, but advised me not to accept parole. The reason was if I consented to be imprisoned, I would likely receive liberty sooner by way of a prisoner of war exchange. However, I could choose whichever option pleased me. I then decided to accept confinement. The commissary assured me I would be given a small apartment in the prison by myself and should have the liberty of the yard during the time I remained there. He then pledged on his word of honor that I would be among the group to go to France on the first cartel vessel dispatched from an English seaport and thought it would probably go to Calais. This exchange was likely to occur within eight to ten days. I also knew that if I had accepted parole in Dover, it was likely that my board and lodging would have mounted to a considerable sum of money. I recalled that after my first landing in that port not long ago, I paid a half guinea for my simple breakfast of coffee, toast and some dried beef that had been shredded thin.

When my examination concluded, I was dismissed from the guardhouse. A corporal and four soldiers conducted me to Deal, a small town about eleven miles from Dover situated near the mouth of the Thames River. Although I was placed in confinement as a prisoner, every indulgence that was promised to me by the commissary was forthcoming. After only 10 days, I was exchanged and arrived in Dunkirk on the 17th day after departing on my cruise on the *Ranger*. Upon arrival I discovered that all my prizes that I had taken from the British fleet were safely anchored in the harbor. This meant I was about to receive a thousand guineas for my efforts.

I now learned the brig that was being built before my cruise on the

Ranger was nearly ready to be launched except for its masts. I purchased a quarter of the vessel and, not liking to be idle, I also purchased a small lugger that was used as a privateer and had recently returned from a cruise. Her burthen was twenty-five tons, carried six three-pound cannon and shipped twenty-one officers and men. I paid them the customary bounty and sailed again only five days after returning to Dunkirk. After putting to sea for two days I was sighted by an English twenty-eight-gun frigate called the *Belle Poule*. Previously she had been a French Navy ship. After a ten-hour chase, we were finally brought to and forced to surrender. One of her boats came alongside and took me to the frigate. Every officer upon her quarterdeck then examined me. The captain whose name was Phips was quite inebriated and insulted me in a rude manner. He called me a damned Irish renegade scoundrel and, threatened me by putting his fist in my face a number of times. I had the courage to tell him that by abusing a fellow officer and prisoner he was not acting like the gentleman he was expected to be. This upset him and he instantly ordered one of his officers to call the master at arms who appeared soon after. I had my commission as a privateer with me and by chance I also had taken my commission as a lieutenant in the French Navy. One of the English lieutenants who spoke the French language read it to the captain and the other officers and provided a translation of the documents. In doing so they made a great deal of sport about the papers and appeared highly entertained. The frigate's captain laughed heartily when the translator finished reading it, grabbed it from his hand and then pushed it into my face quite a few times. He then asked me why I was not ashamed to carry a commission granted by the French scoundrels, he repeated the latter disparaging phrase by phrase with unwarranted frequency.

The Captain Phips then ordered the master of arms to put me in irons between decks, bind me hand and foot and that I was to be feed nothing but bread and water. He then sneered and said to his first lieutenant stating that he intended to punishment me as a scoundrel. The master of arms stripped me of every rag of clothes that I wore and gave me, in return, a very dirty frock and baggy pair of trousers. I was then dragged below to the gundeck, put in irons, and chained between two guns so that I was securely restrained according to the captain's orders. The sailors on the gundeck then mistreated me by kicking me several times about my body enjoying the malicious diversion.

There were three American merchant captains held captive onboard at this time. One by the name of Davis who had damned King George was dragged to the gangway and whipped by one of the boatswain's mates on his naked back. He was given three-dozen lashes with a cat-of-nine-tails by order of the brute in command of this warship. My daily allowance while onboard her was a half-pound of dry stale bread and one pint of water. The ankle irons that I was compelled to wear were too small and made them swell badly and created raw wounds. I often begged the master at arms and other officers to take off the irons on my ankles and replace them with larger ones, but my pleas were in vain. He replied that he wished that the restraints were smaller and that my treatment was only half as bad as I deserved for going to battle against my lawful sovereign and for accepting a French naval commission. And for some reason they kept labeling me an Irish rebel in their incessant curses. I was puzzled why these arrogant Englishmen, who sailed under the British flag, insisted that I was an Irishman. I am sure that my Yankee accent and manner of speech could not justify this belief, not that it made any difference.

They also refused to allow me to have anything to lie upon, not even a single rag of cloth to put under my head. I largely sat in this situation with my hands and feet in irons upon a damp deck between two guns for six weeks. Making matters worse, I was almost eaten alive by vermin that dropped down by the scores from the hammocks suspended above me and into my face. My hands were so restrained I could not brush them off and the ship's officers would not allow any of my fellow prisoners to come near me. The insult and pain that I suffered during my captivity in irons was beyond my words to adequately relate.

One night when we were cruising between the Isle of Wight and the coast of France the *Belle Poule* blundered. It found itself in the center of a French fleet of twelve ships-of-the-line, a number of frigates, sloops of war and cutters. The British warship attempted to escape, but was subsequently captured close to midnight. French officers came onboard to take possession of their prize soon after and they released me from my cursed irons. I do not recall being happier in my life at this liberation. I quickly realized that I now had the power to avenge the insults that I had endured at the hands of the dastardly English. Early the next morning French Admiral Count de Guichen had learned of my sufferings and sent a barge to transport me to his ninety-eight-gun *Invincible*. When I arrived on deck, the French officers suggested that I exchange my attire for suitable apparel. I thanked them, but told them that it was my choice to appear in the admiral's presence outfitted in the garb that I was forced to wear and that still harbored scores of lice.

I was introduced to Admiral Count de Guichen in the great cabin by one of his lieutenants. As I entered he arose from his seat, took my hand and heartily shook it. While I was still wearing the filthy frock and trousers, the admiral then asked me to take a chair by his side. Almost immediately after I was seated, I briefly explained why I elected to come before him dressed as I did. I then asked permission to retire to a stateroom to change before I related my story to him about the cruel treatment I received from the English naval officers and crew. Sympathetic and understanding, he quickly consented. A boat was dispatched to bring the English captain onboard the admiral's flagship. Captain Phips had been confined on one of the other ships of the fleet. As soon as I dressed myself I returned to the cabin and found the admiral surrounded by several principal officers of the fleet and Captain Phips alone in a corner looking very despondent. Admiral Count de Guichen requested that I relate to the assembled officers my account of the treatment I received as a prisoner of this officer and of the English crewmen. I did so in my now reasonably fluent French and as concisely as the atrocious subject allowed. I purposely emphasized what the captain said that I could do with my French commission. This produced some harsh expressions from the usually dignified admiral as well as other French officers with regard to Phips's conduct as I related my story. The admiral demanded my commission from the English captain that he had on his person, produced the document and handed it to the Count. The admiral wrote down my name along with the threats that the captain had made. He paused and explained what he intended to do. He then handed my commission to me and told me that whatever the English captain had done to me while I was a prisoner on his ship under his command, I had his permission to inflict similar punishment upon Phips as retribution. The English captain had by this time transformed from an extremely arrogant fellow into an abject fawning disgusting man. I decided not make use of the permission granted to me by the admiral. Therefore, the English captain went unpunished for the barbarous cruelty that he meted out upon me. The admiral however ordered Captain Phips to restore all the effects that had been taken from me by his officers and crew or compensate me financially for what they were worth. Having little choice, the captain agreed with the order, a source of humiliation for him.

I was assigned a duty station onboard the French Navy flagship that was fitting for my rank of lieutenant. During our cruise in the English Channel we encountered eleven English ships-of-the-line with whom we offered to do battle. They declined and we chased them almost to Spithead the roadstead off Gilkicker Point in Hampshire England.

At another time we saw thirteen ships-of-the-line and challenged them. We received no reply and by nightfall they had slinked to nearby Plymouth where they anchored. We patrolled off that active port for three days in a line of battle, but were unable to induce any of them to get underway and engage us. During the cruise the French fleet captured several English frigates, sloops of war and a merchantman.

The sixty-year old French admiral was an experienced commander who was dauntless. Most important, he was greatly beloved by his officers and men. Admiral Count de Guichen had a somewhat curious but charming habit of calling those under his command his children. Every day at dinnertime the admiral made it his custom to visit all his men and boys. The messes are divided into groups of eight or ten each as was customary on a warship. He would ask if they had enough to eat, if the provisions tasted good and were properly prepared. Upon these occasions he would frequently sample the soup, meats and wine. If they did not meet his standards, he would complain to the cooks and order that men to be served with better foodstuffs.

Our cruise being completed, we put into Brest with a number of prizes. Upon landing we learned that peace would be declared within the next two months. This was an incentive for me to return to Dunkirk as soon as possible. I wanted to make one last short privateering cruise before the hostilities ended and I informed Admiral Count de Guichen of my desire. It was my wish to take leave from the navy for a few months. He granted my request after giving me a certificate attesting to the time I served onboard the *Invincible*.[3] He then suggested that I call at the customhouse's Admiralty Office in Brest and receive my pay. Finally, he gave me a magnanimous and gracious letter of recommendation to the French minister of marine and the promise of his continuing personal friendship.

I then set out for Dunkirk as rapidly as that manner of overland transportation allowed. When I arrived, I found that my privateer owners had recently obtained the long-awaited spars for the brig's mast and the ship was in the process of being fitted and almost ready for a cruise. The news that peace was close at hand made us accelerate our work so that the brig might be ready for sea by 30 December. The officers and men received their customary bounty or advance from the owners and were on board the privateer. We were in the act of casting off from the quay and hoisting our sails when a proclamation posted in the town of Dunkirk announced that the preliminaries of a peace treaty was signed by commissioners in Paris. Because of this incident I lost five thousand guineas, my shares in the brig, the bounty money that I advanced, plus my part of the loss incurred from the sale of the brig, captured guns and other arms that they brought at auction.

An unforeseen event happened to me at a dinner about the same time. I was at the White Hart Tavern playing a game of backgammon one evening when two officers of justice [policemen] entered the room and placed me under arrest in the king's name. I was jailed without knowing of what crime I was being accused. I happened to know both of these officers and I asked them what my offense was. They made no reply. The next day officers of the admiralty extensively questioned me. Soon thereafter I was released from prison and, on behalf of the king, paid one thousand five hundred livres as compensation for being unjustly imprisoned. I also received an apology from the commandant who had me arrested under the king's authority.

The story behind this accusation is complicated and multifaceted. First one must remember that privateering is a cat-and-mouse game of deception and counter-deception. When one sees a potential prey, by law the vessel must be the ship of an enemy nation or one of its allies. Because vessels often change hands and their design and rigging appearance, typical of that of another nation, can be easily modified. Every ship carries a set of false flags that can be raised aloft to mislead an interceptor. If a privateer believes that a quarry appears vulnerable and could easily be subdued, it is customary to hail the ship and ask for its identity. If the captain answers that it is that of a neutral nation, occasionally an officer and men are sent over to confirm this by physically inspecting the ship's official documents. During my second cruise on the privateer *Eclipse*, we ordered what purported to be a neutral Danish ship in the English Channel to heave to so that we could inspect the papers of the captain. A ship's officer said that it had left from St Croix and was bound to Copenhagen. I ordered my first lieutenant to perform this routine task of inspecting the officer's documents, the manifests and cargo of the neural ship. He was ordered not to molest or take anything from the passengers onboard nor remove anything out of the ship if it proved to be neutral. These were routine directives given for every such encounter on the high seas. By chance, a French passenger by the name of Segur, the brother to Marquis de Segur was onboard. The Marquis held a high French governmental office, was a close friend of the king and was one of his majesty's favorites. It turned out that the lieutenant stole a prized gold watch from Mr. Segur and also took several other valuable pieces of jewelry of which I was completely unaware.

After a considerable time, Mr. Segur, while travelling from Copenhagen to Paris, stopped for a few hours in Dunkirk to visit some old acquaintances. While strolling along the quay, he noticed the *Eclipse* anchored in the harbor's basin. At that point the cutter had been stripped of most of her rigging, her guns removed and no longer had a warlike appearance. In spite of these significant alterations Mr. Segur recognized her and asked for the name of the ship's captain and the principle officers who had been on the cruise when he was robbed. Remembering the details of that event very well, when Mr. Segur arrived in Paris he made a formal complaint joined by a representative of the Danish court to the king's Minister of Justice. Thereafter orders were issued for the arrest of the captain of the *Eclipse* and all officers and crew, if they could be found while still residing in the kingdom of France.

I assumed that the first lieutenant and those who looted the French passenger had fled the country because they knew they were guilty of a criminal offense. In time two of the boat's crew who had been accomplices in this affair were captured and punished by receiving thirty whip lashes each and then branded with the letter R on their shoulder.[4] The lieutenant, an American, was the same man who plundered the young Irish nobleman of his gold watch off the Irish coast. He left Dunkirk in the night without informing anyone and was pursued by the *Maréchausseé* as far as L'Orient and managed to embark for the United States.[5] All his share of the prize money, however, was

9. Lieutenant in the French Navy

seized and placed at the disposal of the king's officers at Dunkirk. The alleged thief was tried in absentia, convicted and sentenced to death. Because he was not available, he was hanged in effigy upon gallows erected on a Dunkirk quay just for this purpose. A sizeable parade was held with troops officers and civilians for the bizarre event. It attracted a great crowd estimated to be five thousand. I did not mention the lieutenant's name because I learned that he later died and left a wife and children in Newport, Rhode Island. This tragic ending caused me a great amount of mental anguish. I felt particularly regretful concerning this affair because I had personally rescued the man from an advanced state of poverty and appointed him as my privateer's first lieutenant. The reward for my generosity was a burdensome metaphorical noose that tarnished my reputation.

The lack of appreciation that this lieutenant exhibited toward me was perhaps the worst I encountered during our revolution. I have frequently experienced the sin of ingratitude from not only from strangers, but near relations as well. I can say unequivocally that my conscience is perfectly free of guilt in every part of my conduct toward neutral subjects and vessels during the entire time that I commanded the privateer *Eclipse*.

10

Aftermath of War

Upon the news of peace, all privateers in this port were embargoed. The money that I had received at the customhouse amounted to twelve thousand guineas. Of this amount, I had expended nearly one half as expenses of owning and outfitting my portion of several French privateers sailing out of Dunkirk. In addition, I had advanced my countryman five hundred and fifty guineas to those who had fled from Britain's bondage and landed in different French ports. Now these men found themselves among strangers, nearly naked and again without money. I therefore assisted them by advancing the former prisoners of war as much cash as their needs required. I must note to my disappointment that some of the larger sums that I advanced were never repaid such as the one hundred and fifty dollars I loaned to Captain John Manley, plus another one hundred dollars given to another person.

I now had time to explore the populous town of Dunkirk at my leisure and go to the many public diversions available here. First, however, I shall share my observations about the town's inhabitants and manners. Most of the local people were Flemish. You were not allowed to fill any of the official posts under the crown unless you were French-born. The city is situated in the province of Flanders in a section known as French Netherlands on the English Channel at the mouth of the Coln River. It lies fifty miles east southeast of Dover. In 1713 this town had an excellent fortified port with a dry dock and other conveniences for ships of war. These facilities were destroyed by order of the British to conform to agreements put forth in the Treaty of Utrecht. Since then, only small vessels such as cutters, sloops, brigs, galliots and coasting vessels could go in and out because of the shallowness of the water at the harbor's entrance. The town is still walled, but the enclosure is crumbling and had tumbled down in many places. In my opinion, at the present time the protective battlements are insufficient to hold back any invader with a small regular army under an experienced commander for more than three days.

A three hundred-foot high tower had been constructed at the center of the town. A man was stationed on top of the turret with a very powerful spyglass. It was good enough to plainly see people walking near Dover castle. This tower also had a small dwelling to shelter those on watch duty from storms. In fair weather an observer stationed in the tower had the potential of seeing all ships going in and out of the Thames River. This offered a great advantage to the owners of privateers who reside in Dunkirk in times of war. This turret-like structure had a tall flagpole that was used to display signals to inform the inhabitants of vessels that were in the offing, their number and whether they were friend or foe. Most people in the town were acquainted with the meaning of the different signals when they were hoisted on the staff.

About a mile east of the town was a place known as the royal gardens that contained pleasant walking paths, white marble statues and several gazebos where musicians put on excellent concerts. The orchestra was comprised of about seventy persons that played delightful music especially in the evening. I believe that it also features the best public theater in any part of France that I have visited. The manners of the Flemings were generally unrefined and appeared appallingly rude to strangers. They were for the most part greedy among themselves, yet remarkably kind and hospitable to visitors. Among those that I put into the last class of Dunkirk citizens were those in my circle of acquaintances and many were the best friends that I had made in any part of the world. (I wish to say that I do not exempt my own and nearest relatives.) In time of peace the chief means of support of these peoples was coastal trade, fishing and, because of high taxation, smuggling. In time of war it was privateering and they were quite fond of this endeavor. During the recent war, one hundred seventeen privateers of various sizes sailed out of Flemish ports. Their manner of dress mirrored that of the Dutch and Germans. All articles of considerable bulk were conveyed on flat-bottomed boats drawn up and down the canals with horses on tow paths on each side of the waterway. Some of these vessels could carry eighty tons of freight that usually moved at three to five miles an hour on level ground. This speed was slower when ascending a canal bank and faster when descending. Most common were smaller boats frequently seen on the canals pulled by two animals. Some of the much larger boats had eight or ten horses attached by ropes to these vessels. These barges were so big that they had the services available one would expect at a hotel or tavern onboard. I frequently traveled in this way and dined there with a number of gentlemen and their ladies. After dinner we frequently danced in the dining room while traveling at a stately five miles an hour. Boats kept to the right so as not to interfere with one another. This province and the Austrian Netherlands, at this time a considerable part of Germany, abounded with canals along with canal boats or flat-bottomed barges and were the greatly preferred mode of transportation.

The Manner of Hanging Criminals in France

Gallows were erected outside the walls of the city or town. Typically, one would find a platform or stage with wheels under it. The place of execution usually drew a large crowd. The grand-bailiff or high sheriff ascended the platform with the convicted criminal that had a noose around his neck. The government official loudly proclaimed to the nearby multitude that he needed a hangman or as the French called him, "Jack Ketch."[1] He then asked if anyone would be willing to perform this task, in the name of the king. Then a sort of macabre auction began requesting if anyone was willing do it for one crown, two crowns, etc., each time adding one crown until the amount reached perhaps one hundred or more. I once heard of the sheriff escalating to a ghoulish bid of around five hundred crowns to procure a "Jack Ketch." This was certainly the extreme since it was more common to "hire" a hangman for ten crowns. As soon the hangman accepted the offered price, he mounted the stage as the bailiff descended from it accompanied by a shout of *bravo* from the populace. The hangman then fastened the halter to the horizontal beam of the gallows and adjusted the other end tightly around the criminal's neck. He would then signal with his hand or a handkerchief. At that moment a number of people dragged the wheeled stage from under the criminal and hangman. The hangman then leaped upon the shoulders of the criminal and they both swung in the air for some time. The hangman often pounding the condemned man in the stomach or under his ribs with his knees as hard as he could until he was sure that the man was dead. The hangman then released his hold, dropped down to his feet and strolled over to the bailiff to receive the agreed upon fee. The criminal was left to hang for a few hours, then he was cut down so that his body could be delivered to friends or family. I have been told that in England the body of the executed criminal was commonly delivered to surgeons for dissection, however this custom was looked upon with great abhorrence in France.

The Manner of Hanging or Executing Criminals in Germany

Nearly every town or city that I passed through in my travels through Germany had a large ten-foot high post planted in the ground on its outskirts. On its eastern side were several stone steps. The sheriff, the criminal and a hangman had previously been engaged, presumably without the auction, arrived at the post. The criminal, with the assistance of the German version of "Jack Ketch," walked up the steps and turned around with his back against the post that had been slightly hollowed out at various heights to stabilize the man's head. The criminal was then tied to the post so that he could not move his body, even his feet. The hangman now appeared with the instrument of death, a rope with the two ends spliced together just long enough to reach around both the post and the criminal. In his other hand he carried a piece of wood about the size of an axe handle that acted as a toggle. Thus prepared, the executioner waited for a signal from the officer of justice. Behind the post a temporary stage had been erected where the "Jack Ketch" stood ready to execute the criminal. When the bailiff waved a white handkerchief, the hangman put the special rope around the criminal's neck and the post. Through a bite in the rope he inserted the wooden toggle and tightened the rope by a series of rapid hard twists almost in the fashion of a whirl-a-gig. In this manner the criminal died quickly. The body was cut down and delivered to the friends of the deceased a few minutes after the execution. Occasionally the bodies of criminals were delivered to surgeons for anatomy studies as in England. The only body I personally saw slain and disposed of in this way was that of a non–Christian man executed in Ostend. I was informed that this mode of execution was commonly practiced throughout most of Germany.

In Dunkirk, as well as in other towns in France, auction sales were very common and they were done in the king's name. Normally before they begin, a sergeant, drummer and two soldiers bearing arms went throughout the streets and made a tour of every square in the town or city where the articles were to be sold. At every corner the drummer beat his drum loudly and the sergeant clutched and sometimes distributed a printed list of all the articles that were included in the sale. The accompanying soldiers stood to one side, their muskets loaded at ready and their bayonets fixed. With a dignified display, the sergeant raised his cane high in the air, removed his hat and loudly proclaimed "*Par le Roy*" (for the king). Woe to the man who did not doff his hat on the sergeant's words "*Par le Roy.*" He took a chance of having one of the bayonets plunged into his body for neglecting the sign of respect to the king's name.[2] At that instant the sergeant read the list of articles to be sold. At the end of this formality, the drummer resumed his beating. When the sergeant flourished his cane high in the air once again the drumming ceased. The soldiers then marched off to another street corner and repeated the same maneuvers until they had finished their rounds.

On 26 July I left Dunkirk for Paris and went as far as the city of Lille on a flatboat drawn by horses. I was well accommodated and had sufficient food and especially for drink. The vessel was especially well supplied with the best claret and other wines. The lodging was comparable to that of a good public inn. I arrived in Lille that evening and was put up at a celebrated hotel that was largely full of foreigners. This city is large, quite populous and located southeast of Dunkirk. A great many British people vacationed in the area during times of peace and the English language was prevalent among its citizens. Many Englishmen who had done business there for a number of years had become very wealthy. This was because the city was renowned for its manufacture of rich laces of all kinds, the best that could be had in the kingdom. The citizens were thoughtful and very welcoming to strangers. Their homes were neat and commodious without any great show of grandeur.

The next day I proceeded on my journey to Paris travelling very rapidly in a stagecoach drawn by six horses at a rate of twelve and sometimes fifteen miles an hour. The roads leading to the French capital city were generally excellent, very wide upon its sides and paved in the middle with round stones. The passengers had the choice of travelling on pavement or an unpaved road and had only to direct the coachmen to drive along as he desired. The coachman usually complied with their passenger's wishes and were very obliging. The travelers paid the coachman ten to a dozen sous each at the end of every stage that was usually ten to twelve miles from each other. At certain points the horses and drivers were changed. As the coachman arrived at the entrance of the next stage station in the following town or village he made up a particular snapping sound of his whip. This was a signal that he has generous passengers onboard. If he considered the passengers tightfisted, the driver did not crack his whip at all.

There were two vastly different ways for a person to travel on horseback in this country; one was on the so-called King's Post and the other *Les Postes de Matelots* (the sailor's post). The King's Post furnished the traveler with an excellent horse, a pair of large riding boots that could be drawn on one's legs with ease, a crop, a pair of spurs, and a servant guide mounted on another horse of similar quality. Thus equipped, one might travel at the rate of eighteen miles an hour or much slower if he wished. *Postes de Matelots* furnished a wretched horse and no guide or servant. For the King's Post charged six sous per mile for the hired horse; the *Postes de Matelots* costs four sous.

The internal regulation of French police was unique. The grand superintendent of this institution lived in Paris with a great number of officers who worked under him, but were scattered all over the kingdom. Besides these, there were several thousand *Maréchauseé* who were under the control and received orders from the lieutenant of Police or his subordinate officers. Most of the *Maréchauseé* were the younger sons of noblemen. They dressed in distinct uniforms, blue blouses with red facings, red cuffs, red waistcoats and pantaloons. On the left sleeve of their coats, just above the cuff, they wore gold lace that extended broadly all around that arm. The *Maréchauseé* were mounted upon fine horses, armed with a pair of large pistols, a broad sword, and sometimes a short light horsemen's musket slung over their backs to be used as a sort of carbine. Dressed and armed in this distinguishing way, their mission was to scour and secure public roads to apprehend highwaymen, catch deserters and arrest criminals who had fled justice or escaped from jail.

10. Aftermath of War

These *Maréchausseé*, sometimes called officers of justice, were paid for their services by the king himself and I was told that this could be a considerable sum, enough to support them to live as gentlemen in French society. They traveled on public roads in groups of two, four, six and as many as ten together and seemed never to be out of sight because they rode day and night. They sometimes shed their uniforms and put on disguises so that those in whom they were in pursuit may not recognize them. Since this police force extended throughout the country, many kinds of crimes rarely occurred such as highway robbery, house break-ins or even shoplifting. During the time I lived in France I never once heard of a highway robbery or burglary being perpetrated.

On the evening of 28 July, I arrived in the city of Paris. The next day I visited and paid my respects to Dr. Benjamin Franklin.[3] The distinguished American diplomat resided in Passy, a small village situated on a knoll between Paris and Versailles. This relatively high location offers a good view in either direction, of Paris three miles away and Versailles six miles distant. Because of its elevation, almost the whole city of Paris is visible from this charming village. Stretched out before me were nearly three hundred towns, great villas of noblemen that look like so many palaces and county seats scattered as far as the eye can see. The building where the diplomat and his secretaries lived was spacious and adjoined a beautiful garden. Dr. Franklin received me without any ceremony, but with the tenderness of a parent greeting his child. He had the habit of calling all Americans that paid him a visit his children, somewhat reminiscent of Admiral Count de Guichen. When I met him, he was in the company of [Marie-Joseph Paul Yves Roch Gilbert du Motier] the Marquis de Lafayette and several other gentlemen. About a half hour following my arrival they left and he asked me to follow him into his study. After we were comfortably seated we had a long conversation about many different subjects. He gave me good advice concerning the conduct I should observe while in Paris in the familiar style one would expect from one's father. When it was time for me to go he invited me to call upon him whenever I wished. Because of his polite unpretentious behavior, I shall always admire him.

Dr. Franklin was highly esteemed not only by the French, but all the foreign ministers that resided in the Court of France and his royal reception. His respectability exceeded that of the Count de Vergennes, the king's favorite minister and the American people's friend. After my first interview with this American statesman, I called upon him several other times and was always treated with the same kindness and amity as on my first visit. On all occasions his dress was unusually plain which made him admired by all classes of people.

I managed to visit much of this great and densely inhabited city over several days where there were so many wonderful sights to be seen. The *Place*

Victoire (place of victory) was among the first that arrested my attention. It is near the center of the city and occupies about half an acre laid out in a square. In its center was a statue of Louis XIV on a marble pedestal with a truncheon in his right hand and the other simply clasping his waist. He was attired in royal robes, but without a crown on his head. An angel was represented carrying a light in his left hand with a foot on the pedestal. In his right hand he was in the act of crowning the monarch with a laurel wreath. At each corner of the pedestal were images of four kings that the French say Louis XIV took prisoner in his wars. They were wearing their crowns, coats of armor and badges of royalty, but they were lying at the feet of the French conqueror and their feet were in chains. This *chef d'oeuvre* (masterpiece) is made of bronze. The monarch was depicted on horseback as large as life. At the Place Vendome the horse and the king seated upon him also stand on a marble pedestal, but they were elevated twelve feet above the pavement. Near the old palace gates was a statue of a horse with Louis XV mounted upon him. At the four corners of this pedestal were four female figures that were an allusion to the four cardinal virtues. Some cynics said they actually represented his four mistresses who were sisters and great beauties. This much is known however, Louis XV with all his faults was a monarch who was universally beloved by his subjects during his entire reign. In fact, many knew him as "Louis the beloved." All of these impressive statues were made of bronze.

Not far from this palace was *des Champs-Élysées* or the Elysian fields. It was a park of about twenty acres of ground planted with beautiful trees and divided by pleasant walkways, the best that I had ever seen. There were many ornamented arbors that provide ample shade and among them were kiosks offering food and drink. When the weather was clear and serene, several thousands of the nobility, gentry and others gathered there in the latter part of the day. They would linger there until it is time for a play, opera or other entertainment to begin that was usually six o'clock in the evening. A considerable part of the crowd would continue to amuse themselves in these delightful pathways until 10 o'clock and, if the evening was pleasant enough, up until around midnight. I believe, as do others, that the city of Paris may occupy more area than London. Its houses and public buildings were both higher and their architecture more pleasing to the eye. The streets, however, were not comparable to those of the English capitol. Those of Paris were narrow, crooked and dirty. One's feet could easily be run over by coaches because the only shelter was in houses or shops on either side of the road. In London foot-passengers could walk on each side of the streets in safety. The pavements in the English city were raised moderately high in the middle in order facilitate drainage and therefore a narrow patch of dryness. On the right and left sides of the roadways there was a second pavement of flat stones, about eighteen inches above the lower pavement, to accommodate the pedestrians.

In spite of that fact, the streets of Paris were a disappointment. Most of the male citizens wear black silk stockings, the fashion here, but they easily show splashed-on mud. The French capital was divided into two parts by the River Seine, an expansive watercourse that meandered some three hundred miles and eventually found its way into the English Channel near Havre de Grace, the nearest port to the kingdom's capital. There were a number of old decaying palaces in the city that were former residences of ancient kings. I believe that the riches of Paris exceeded those that I witnessed in London.

The Duke of Charters had built a palace near the center of the city that cost him an immense sum. It was magnificent and I feel far exceeded that built by Louis XIV in elegance, beauty and grandeur where the present king resided. This is not surprising since the duke was said to be the richest prince in Europe. The comedies and operas were much grander in Paris than in London. The people who frequented these events here were more smartly dressed than those who visited similar places in London.

The infamous Bastille, situated not far from the Tuileries palace and gardens, was a large group of buildings and a very strong fortress that was said to be impregnable. It was the prison complex where enemies of the state were confined. I tried to gain admittance to the foreboding facility, but without success.

I was impressed by large number of spacious hospitals in the city. I have visited several and observed their general cleanliness, orderliness and empathetic care of the sick. Everything inside was kept well-organized. This surprised me because the French seemed not to keep their household and their furniture very clean. I visited the hospital where people with venereal disease are admitted and cared for. From what I saw, I believe that many of the poor miserable wretches were brought there so that the French surgeons could experiment upon them. I was told that the entire population in these hospital buildings approximates six thousand patients of both sexes. Except for those that were bed-ridden, almost all seemed deformed into bizarre shapes perhaps from the effects of mercury used in their treatment. I saw one with a face and head misshapen and twisted so far toward his back that it was difficult to tell where his back and face should have been. Another was without a nose, a third without eyes, and a fourth with most of his joints badly dislocated. These examples of human horrors caused me a great deal of disgust. In fact, I was forced to turn away and seriously reflect upon what I had seen. After remaining in this hospital until I felt that I could no longer stand the stench of these unfortunate people, I went to another institution, L'Hôpital des Enfants-Trouvés (child abandonment home and hospital). This facility contained seven thousand children who were fed, clothed and educated until they were fifteen and then set adrift into the world to seek a livelihood. This was all at the expense of a certain French noblewoman whose name I noted, but I cannot recall. They were poor children almost all of them orphans. Every morning large numbers of them were picked up and taken off the streets nearly as naked as when they were born.

The next thing that attracted my attention was a well-dressed fellow holding up the train of a lady's gown as she walked on the street. I assume that this was to prevent the garment from being soiled. Soon after I saw the lady enter a house and give the man what looked like a few coins. He deeply bowed to the woman and quickly left. I asked an acquaintance what this was all about and he laughed and said that there were a number of men of this class who live by the ladies' bounty. That is to say they received about twelve sous for escorting them around the city and to their house, an unusual manner of their employment. These men were attired as gentlemen, wore swords and were a distinctive type of servant. Their task was to provide physical protection for the lady, prevent her from being insulted by anyone and preserve her silks from filth when she strolled about the streets. These fellows were quite proud and were called *petit maître*.[4]

Many private dwellings in this city built of hewn stone were one to twelve stories high. The floors were of marble of different colors and because of this, it was rare to hear of one catching on fire. Conflagrations however were common occurrences accounting for the destruction of wooden buildings in the country and abroad. In Versailles, a small town to the west of Paris, was the palace of Louis XVI and his royal family. The grounds of the royal residence were in a perfect square except to the south where it was fenced in. There was a large double gate in the middle of the piquet that was open during the day and shut at night. Two grenadier guards were posted there and no person except for the royal family could pass through the gate without the password and a countersign issued by the king. This palace consisted of many tasteful buildings whose architecture was well executed and magnificent to behold. The enclosure between the two wings form a square attractively paved and was where the king's lifeguard parade.

When I arrived, I found lodging at a hotel near the palace gates. There I met an old colleague who had served in the French Navy, a captain of one of the ships-of-the-line in the division of men-of-war whose admiral was Count of Guichen. I mentioned to this officer that I had hoped to meet the royal family and he agreed to accompany me wherever I wanted to go. He was a young nobleman who was well known at the royal court. The two of us left my hotel to visit apartments in the palace and hopefully meet the royal family. Arriving at the gates my friend gave the correct password, but the guard refused to admit us into the courtyard. My friend than gave him the countersign, but a heated conversation ensued between the naval officer and the king's lifeguard. My acquaintance told the guard that I was an American who had served in the French Naval Service. I was there with the intent of seeing the royal family only out of courtesy. After this exchange he became cooperative and escorted us to the king's chapel adjoining the palace where I saw the king, queen and dauphin then an infant.[5]

The family had come in to hear the Sunday mass that was in progress. The king was very handsome, about twenty-eight years old, dark complexion, of average height but with a corpulent body. He had a pleasant majestic countenance. The queen was extremely beautiful with a Roman nose, light complexion and also a pleasing visage. I am sorry to say that her character with regard to goodness, modesty, virtue and other female attributes did not measure up to my expectations in a queen. There were many anecdotes heard throughout Paris about her intrigues and voluptuousness and particularly her infidelity to the king. Some even have said that the Count D'Artois, the king's younger brother, was the father of the present French dauphin. A short distance from Versailles was an island in the River Seine to which, because of the queen's unfaithfulness, has been given the name the Island of Love. She and some of the characters of loose morals among the ladies of the court went there for bathing. The Count D'Artois as her escort and other noble gentlemen served as partners for the ladies. The queen was known to act the part of Venus as the leading goddess of this company, but I shall refrain from making any more comments about this alleged sordid affair.

From the king's chapel we went to the great audience hall and on to other apartments in the palace. From there we visited the royal gardens and its nearby pond in which were marble sculptures of lions, tigers and other wild beasts including various kinds of serpents. These imaginary animals were continually spouting water from their mouths that rose several feet high in some cases. The fountains made a continuous roaring noise that vaguely resembled a waterfall. Near these waterspouts was a delightful footpath where I once again saw the royal family with a group of gentlemen of the court. Among them were the Count d'Artois and the Count de Vergennes. D'Artois was much handsomer than the king and appeared years younger. The palace at Versailles, situated upon a small hill, was built by the order of Louis XIV and was said to exceed any other royal palace in the world. I was told by one of the king's lifeguards that the spot of ground where the palace now stands was formally low sandy soil. The expense of raising the ground to the present level cost the French government several million livres. The buildings in the village of Versailles were neither as high nor as elegant as those in Paris, and not as crowded with families. Parisian buildings can be fourteen stories high with one family occupying each story.

On 9 August, I returned to Paris and paid another visit to Dr. Franklin where he gave me a passport for L'Orient. The next day I met with Mr. Thomas Barclay, Consul General of the United States. I gave him power of attorney to collect monies owed to me from merchants who resided in Morlaix and Dunkirk. After completing my business with him, I purchased a seat on a public stagecoach and set out for L'Orient. I arrived in this familiar port city in four days and engaged passage on a king's packet, a ship that carried four carriage guns. I understood that during the recent war she mounted twenty-two. While I was waiting for the packet to get ready for sea, I became ill with a fever called an "ague" [malaria] that stayed with me until we had put to sea.

11

Reflections on French Society

Now that I have a fair amount of time being a passenger at sea, I would like to share my observations concerning the manners and customs of the French people in general. The young unmarried ladies in this country were more physically attractive than their counterparts in England, though they were giddier and more volatile. They also carried these traits to a greater extreme. This seemed especially true when it came to dancing, a diversion of which they seemed remarkably fond.

As was the custom in England and United States, the ladies in France did not have tea parties, but in the afternoon or the early evening they spent time together at each other's homes. After chatting a while, the ladies usually served cakes, fruit and other delicacies while sipping a few glasses of excellent French cordials. Fermented drinks, instead of tea, constituted their preferred beverage and may have been far more wholesome. The French ladies and gentlemen commonly made their breakfast with wine, bread and butter and sometimes a salad containing garlic and onions. Their heartiest meal of the day was supper. They hung up all kinds of poultry after it was killed, and before the entrails were removed, let it remain there until it was quite green before cooking. They claimed this made the fowl more tender and easier to digest. Another cooking method being quite common among the French was stuffing a leg of mutton or veal full of garlic before being roasted. I must confess, I did not agree with either custom. I saw many a Frenchman make dinner or supper out of bread, wine, salad and soup. Yet I had also seen men set twenty meat dishes and fricassees on their table. In spite of these peculiarities, the French were hospitable, generous and especially kind to strangers. As proof of this, I traveled many miles in France without paying a single *sou* for food or drink. On these occasions I had only to show them my passport that identified me as an American and they would absolutely refuse to accept payment from me, whether for victuals, beverages or lodgings.

They had a custom that took place once a year in all populous towns and cities. It almost always happened in April and represented a celebration of the trial, crucifixion and resurrection of Jesus. Any description that

I give cannot do it justice, but I shall at least attempt to summarize what occurred.

At the initiation of this solemn religious event, a temporary building was erected in the public square. A judge temporarily inhabiting this structure was seated upon a richly ornamented chair. He represented the person who would pass a sentence of death upon Jesus Christ. A dramatic trial commenced and lasted for a number of hours during which many people appear playing different parts. Some were complicit in his death and others were his followers who wished to obtain the body to take for his burial. After the crucifixion and resurrection, a grand procession was formed of all classes of citizens led by Roman Catholic priests. One of the priests carried a large silver vessel in the form of an urn in which was the *Heavenly Host*. At the center of the march were several magnificent statues partially covered in a tent-like structure carried upon the shoulders of a group of men. I assumed that the figures represented saints, but I was not sure of their specific identity because of the partly drawn curtains on each side. I was always curious about the details of the event, but habitually withdrew into some house to avoid the crowd and the soldiers who formed a guard. I learned that the entire military in the town were obligated to participate except for those who were infirm. Young ladies in the pageant, from age six and or older, were dressed in white. The procession moved slowly without music through large throngs of citizens with soldiers on either side with muskets on their shoulders and bayonets fixed. A calamity could befall the person who drops even a scrap of paper or morsel of food on the street. If so, he had to kneel and remain in this posture until the rest of the procession passed or had a bayonet thrust into him. It made no difference if it was muddy or dusty. I was told that the soldiers had orders to punish and even to kill anyone who neglected to kneel. The French people were remarkably fond of their king. They seemed to revere the mere sound of his name. They generally say that he is the best monarch that they ever had, with the possible exception of Henry IV.

After the procession had passed through the principle avenues of the town, a process that could take up much of the day, they returned to the place from where it all started. Then the people were allowed to disperse to their respective homes. They spent the remainder of the day and part of the night in celebration and rejoicing. In some places this festivity went on for two or three days and nights in succession.

In my opinion the winters in the northern part of France were not terribly cold, nor did the snow fall as often or so deep in Charleston, South Carolina in the same season. I never saw the snow more than two inches deep in Dunkirk, the most northerly part of France during the three winters I spent there. The frosts seemed less severe than those I remember in Charleston.

I have often heard the English denigrate the French saying that they

11. Reflections on French Society

were terrible cowards, particularly their sailors. I adamantly disagree. On the contrary, I feel that they were as brave and courageous as the English sailors, or those of any other nation for that matter. I have been an eyewitness to their fearlessness in many instances. While cruising in French privateers I made it a rule to station men to the carriage guns among their fellow countrymen. Typically, I put five French sailors on one gun and the same number of Americans on the adjacent cannon in the same action. I always noticed that the French gunners fired as frequently and behaved with as much bravery as the Americans. In several bloody battles in which I participated, I never saw a Frenchman flinch or desert his quarters. On the other hand, I had seen many an Englishman abandon their stations.

On 30 September I embarked onboard a king's ship, a French vessel bound for the United States. I paid the captain twenty-eight guineas for my journey and storage for my belongings. We set sail for New York in the afternoon with a fair wind. There were a number of ladies and gentlemen who accompanied me on my voyage. Among them was Mr. J. Hector St. John Crévecoeur, later the author of *Letters from an American Farmer*.[1] Also onboard was the French Consul General for the states of New York, Connecticut and New Jersey. Mr. St. John Crévecoeur was a man about sixty years of age who spoke good English.[2] There was also a French vice-consul for the state of Virginia and his wife; a Mr. Thatcher, an American who had been secretary to an American consul; and a fellow Continental Navy veteran named Robinson with whom I had served on the frigate *Alliance*. Both of us had been midshipman onboard that warship. The third day after we left L'Orient my malaria-like fever called ague left me and I did not suffer another attack ever again. We experienced a very pleasant passage until we reached the soundings off Long Island that meant we were in sixty fathoms of water. From that point until our arrival we started to encounter repeated gales. The weather turned very cold and the sea became unruly. Most of the French sailors were unable to perform their duties because they came down with an unknown incapacitating illness. They could not tolerate the cold and became easily fatigued while on watch. The lack of a healthy crew caused our vessel to be driven off the North American coast several times. Mr. Robinson and I volunteered to keep watch, take our turn at the helm and perform duty onboard as seamen until our arrival. Because of this, Mr. St. John Crévecoeur and the Captain promised to refund the purchase price of our trip once we reached any port in the United States. (This promise was never fulfilled.) Although Mr. Robinson and I faithfully performed the services required of us day and night, Mr. St. John Crévecoeur would make it difficult for us get the rest we needed in our staterooms when we were relieved from our watches. He was so terrified by the repeating storms that he became uncomfortable and sometimes agitated unless he knew that we were both on the deck. To make the point, when the wind blew stronger than a normal breeze, he would continually bang upon our stateroom doors to urge us to turn out go upon the deck. He then would try to make up for this by calling us "good fellows" and "dear children." During this trying time there were only three French sailors out of a crew of fourteen who were able to do their duty. When the topsails were to be taken in, the two of us were obliged to go aloft and the bulk of the other duties fell upon us. In especially bad weather, out of necessity, one of us would take the helm. There was talk of changing course and bearing away for the West Indies. This is where the captain of the vessel would have directed the ship, but we prevailed by insisting that we complete our trip as planned. The stormy weather finally subsided allowing us to arrive at our destination. Our hands were so sore because of the rough duty the two of us were compelled to perform, we could scarcely hold onto a rope.

About the middle of November, we caught sight of the Western Board, the first division of the British fleet that was stationed in New York with soldiers onboard.[3] We were then at the southernmost part of the shoal of Nantucket Island. We spoke with several of the vessels and were able to obtain one of them as our pilot to New York. This was a stroke of good fortune for him, because he would have ended up at Halifax where the fleet was bound. Four days later we arrived off Sandy Hook, the entrance to New York Harbor. No pen, I am sure, could describe my joy at beholding my native land.

The next day we proceeded on to New York City. We passed a British fleet of warships and transports lying off Staten Island. Flying a French ensign and pennant, our vessel anchored in the East River. We had just taken in our sails when a boat from the British admiral's flagship came along side our vessel directed by a lieutenant who insisted on coming onboard. The lieutenant, an arrogant and haughty fellow, noisily inquired who was in command of the vessel. Our captain appeared on deck when he heard the commotion. The lieutenant then glowered at the captain and asked how he dared to display the French pennant when the admiral's flag was flying nearby. Our captain said that he had nothing to do with the British admiral. He knew nothing about him nor did he care to learn anything about him. His business was with the American commander in chief or government officials in New York. The lieutenant then condescendingly ordered him to haul down our pennant. The French captain quickly and bluntly said no. Exasperated, the lieutenant said that he would find a way to make him do so—and very soon. After this the officer descended into his boat and returned to the British fleet. In the interim the French captain went on shore and received permission to display his pennant from the American commander in chief. I believe it was General George Washington at that time. He then felt quite secure in defying the British threats and continued to ignore their untoward conduct. He then paraded ten marines upon the quarterdeck and ordered them to shoot the first man who attempted to haul down the pennant. Some sailors and passengers were also armed and were resolved to assist preventing the British from having their way. Before long the British lieutenant returned and came alongside accompanied by another boat. Both vessels were full of well-armed men. The Lieutenant hesitated to come onboard this time, but brashly told the captain that it was the admiral's orders that the French pennant must be hauled down. Our captain replied if that was his orders, then he should haul it down himself. The lieutenant shouted orders at a detachment of his men to haul it down, but when they reached the ship's gangway, the French marines stood in their way with raised muskets. The would-be boarders withdrew to their boats and, after a few more threats from their officer, they returned to the British fleet from whence they came. Unintimidated, the French ship continued to proudly fly her pennant.

FINIS

A Brief Overview of Nathaniel Fanning's Career

Revolutionary War Period

Seaman in mercantile trade, 1774, 1775, 1776
Captain's Clerk, Connecticut Privateer *American Revenue*
Prize-master, Massachusetts Privateer *Angelica* Prisoner of War, one year, Forton Prison, Gosport, England
Midshipman, ship *Bon Homme Richard*, Continental Navy
Midshipman, prize-ship *Serapis*, Continental Navy
Midshipman, frigate *Alliance*, Continental Navy
Midshipman, Sloop-of-War *Ariel*, borrowed French vessel
First Lieutenant, Privateer *LeCompte de Guichen*
Prisoner of War, Pendennis Castle, Falmouth, England
First Lieutenant, Privateer *L'Eclipse*
Captain, Privateer *L'Eclipse* Wounded in action
Prisoner of War, Dover, England
Captain, Privateer *LeRongeur* Shipwrecked, Isle of Bas, English Channel

Postwar Period

Captain, schooner *Good Hope*, West India Trade
Captain, schooner *Eliza*, West India Trade
Lieutenant, U.S. Navy, 1804–5
Lieutenant, U.S. Navy, commanding Gunboat No. 1, Nov. 5, 1804
Commanding Charleston, SC Naval Station 1805.
Captain Fanning died of fever September 30, 1805, at Charleston, SC, and was buried there the same day.

Editor's Postscript

Shortly after the United States entered World War I, the USS *Nathaniel Fanning*, a modified four-funneled Paulding-class destroyer commanded by Lieutenant Arthur Schuyler Carpender, reported for convoy and anti-submarine duty off the western coast of Ireland. Launched in 1912, *Fanning* was equipped with five 3-inch guns and six 18-inch torpedo tubes and was capable of a top speed of 29.5 knots.

On 17 November 1917, she was part of an escort protecting a convoy departing Queenstown bound for the United States. Besides *Fanning*, the escorts consisted of five USS destroyers, plus several much smaller British warships. At 1615 hours the convoy was forming near Daunt's Lightship off Cork when in the waning daylight, *Fanning*'s coxswain spotted the periscope of a submarine about 400 yards off her port bow. The officer of the deck ordered full speed ahead and mobilized the crew to report to their action stations. With flames and smoke belching from her four funnels, *Fanning* passed over the place where the U-boat had been sited and dropped depth charges. The subsequent explosion from their detonation was so violent that the *Fanning*'s generator was temporarily disabled. They waited and waited. Suddenly the stern of the submarine shot into the air. The U-boat's bow broke the water more slowly and the wobbly craft finally settled. *Fanning* fired three cannon shots at what was now seen as U-58 under the command of Kapitänleutnant Gustav Amberger. Thirteen minutes after surfacing, the submarine's crew spilled out on the deck, hands raised above their heads. Mortally wounded by the depth charge attack, the submarine had sunk to 278 feet. There was an emergency blow of the submarine's ballast tanks at that depth that brought her back to the surface, but the U-boat was a partial wreck. Shortly after the crew surrendered, an internal scuttling explosion detonated that caused U-58 to make her final fatal dive. Carpender was awarded the British Distinguished Service Order, personally pinned on his uniform by King George V at Buckingham Palace and promoted to Lieutenant Commander. The *Fanning*'s U-boat kill was the only one of the United States Navy for the rest of World War I.[1] This was a fitting event to commemorate continental naval officer Nathaniel Fanning's courage and fighting spirit.

Three United States navy ships have been named *USS Fanning* for Nathaniel Fanning:

> The first was *USS Fanning* (DD-37) the Paulding-class destroyer whose action is discussed above. It was launched in 1910, served in WWI and subsequently in the United States Coast Guard from 1924 to 1930. The vessel was sold in 1934.
>
> The second *USS Fanning* (DD-385) was a Mahan-class destroyer launched in 1936, served in the second World War and was decommissioned in 1945 at the close of the war.
>
> The third *USS Fanning* (FF-1076) was a Knox-class frigate launched in 1970 and decommissioned in 1993. The frigate was sold to Turkey in 1993, decommissioned in 2001, and later scrapped.

Chapter Notes

Introduction

1. William Bell Clark, et al., eds., *Naval Documents of the American Revolution*, 12 vols. to date (Washington, DC: Naval History and Heritage Command, 1964), 1: 714.
2. Louis Arthur Norton. "Dudley Saltonstall and the Penobscot Expedition, 1779," *Connecticut History*, vol. 42, #1, 2003, 19–39.
3. Louis Arthur Norton. "America's Unwitting Pirate: The Adventures and Misfortunes of a Continental Navy Captain," *Coriolis*, vol. 6, #1, 2016, 1–25.
4. Family archives of the Stonington Historical Society, Stonington, CT, compiled by Captain R.J. Ramsbotham, USN (Ret), R.W. Woolworth Library.
5. From official records in the Public Record Office in London, at Dunkirk, France, in the archives of the U.S. Navy Department, and Maritime Court records of Connecticut—while in the New England Historic and Genealogical Register, vol. 32, 266.

Chapter 1

1. The master-at-arms was the rough the equivalent of a chief petty officer charged with maintaining the ship's discipline and held the store of the ship's weapons.
2. Nathaniel Fanning, *Fanning's Narrative: The Memoirs of Nathaniel Fanning* an Officer of the American Navy 1778–1783 (New York: NY reprinted by William Abbatt, 1913, originally printed 1806 as *Narrative of the Adventures of an American Navy Officer who served during part of the American Revolution under the Command of Captain John Paul Jones, esq.*) 2.
3. *Ibid.*, Nathaniel Fanning, *Fanning's Narrative: The Memoirs of Nathaniel Fanning*, 3.
4. Biscuits, better known as hard tack were made of flour, salt and just enough water to form stiff dough. After cutting it into roughly 4-inch sections and punching it with holes, the dough was baked in a flat pan for several hours. The resulting biscuit, heavier by about a third than the grain from which it was made, was unappetizing, but could last for many weeks at sea.
5. *Ibid.*, Nathaniel Fanning, *Fanning's Narrative: The Memoirs of Nathaniel Fanning*, 5.
6. It is not clear how the Americans while being incarcerated managed to obtain enough vitamin C to prevent scurvy. There is essentially none in dried fruit and wine, but perhaps apple cider vinegar preservative and the fat on the preserved meat provided enough somewhat like an Eskimo's high fat diet.
7. *Ibid.*, Nathaniel Fanning, *Fanning's Narrative: The Memoirs of Nathaniel Fanning*, 7.
8. *Ibid.*, 7.
9. "Jack" was actually James Aitkin (or John the Painter), an American bumbler-painter and terrorist, who managed to cause a significant amount of damage to the famed British shipyard by starting a fire in the paint stores.
10. Forton Prison was located across Portsmouth Harbor and approximately a mile northwest of Gosport Harbor. Prison conditions were difficult. Captives had little to eat and both the quality and quantity of food was the subject of continuing prisoner complaints. Clothing was also a problem. Many of the prisoners had their posses-

sions taken during their shipboard captivity and some arrived at Forton half-naked. In November 1777 the Commission for Sick and Hurt Seamen petitioned the Admiralty to alleviate the need for clothing and of shoes and stockings for the prisoners.

While incarcerated, enterprising American prisoners dug tunnels including one from the prison privy, jumped the eight-foot high prison pickets and dug their way out under the fences. Some also bribed corrupt, ill-trained, or incompetent guards to turn their backs on escapes. An alternate plan was to feign a serious illness so that a prisoner might be transferred to the less protected Haslar Hospital. Recaptured fugitives however received serious punishment: forty days in the "Black Hole" at half-rations, and relegation to the bottom of the exchange list. Apparently this proved not to be serious a deterrent. The area immediately outside the prison at Gosport was conducive to hiding and guards at Forton had no standing orders to fire at fleeing inmates. Therefore, escape must have seemed more feasible and attractive than putting up with the tedious wait for exchange.

11. Fanning, *Fanning's Narrative: The Memoirs of Nathaniel Fanning*, 10.

12. Some who were foiled in their escape attempt were kept in prison until the peace treaty was signed.

13. The preferred small boats were called wherrys.

14. An extensive article concerning Rev. Wren and the aid he gave to Forton prisoners is: Sheldon S. Cohen, "Thomas Wren and Forton Prison," *Pennsylvania Magazine of History and Biography*, vol. 103, #3, 1979, 279–301.

15. Ostend was a neutral Belgium port about 33 miles from Dunkirk, France.

16. A cartel was a specially designated ship, used during wartime, to exchange prisoners between hostile powers or carry proposals from one to the other.

17. Fanning's stay at Forton lasted thirteen months.

18. The ordinary French citizens called all Americans Bostonians at the time.

Chapter 2

1. The *Ranger* served Jones well much as had the *Providence* before it, but the vessel had many shortcomings. He now demanded a faster and more formidable warship in France. Jones wrote many memorials to the Continental Congress and ultimately obtained command of the French 40-gun *Duc de Duras*. He changed the name to *Le Bon-Homme Richard* (*Bonhomme Richard*) in honor of Benjamin Franklin's *Poor Richard's Almanack* or in French *Les Maximes du Bonhomme Richard*. He admired the spirit of one of *Poor Richard's* sayings, "If you would have your business done, come yourself."

2. The *Bonhomme Richard* (or *Good Man Richard* as Anglicized by Fanning) became the Jones's flagship of the American squadron: the frigate *Alliance*, the converted merchantman *Pallas*, the cutter *Cerf*, and the brigantine *Vengeance*. In addition, two privateer vessels became part of the fleet for a share of prize money. (A cutter was a small with a single mast whose rigging was similar to that of sloops. It was sharply built, fast and highly maneuverable.)

3. The exact number of guns carried on these ships varies in the historical records. *Pallas* may have had 32-eight pounders, *Vengeance* 12 three pounders and *Cerf* as many as 18 nine pounders.

4. Captain George Waith Babcock was a native of Exeter, Rhode Island.

5. Jones's former first lieutenant was later given command of the 18 gun *Ranger*.

6. After another incident that will be covered in the memoir below, Landais questioned Jones's competency. In fury, the volatile Jones responded that Landais was guilty of slander. This enmity produced an affront to each man's honor to be settled according to the code of eighteenth-century gentlemanly behavior. The piqued Landais challenged Jones to a duel, but with swords. The choice of the sword as the dueling weapon would give Landais a distinct advantage having been raised in the French tradition of swordsmanship. Jones managed to subordinate his ego and vanity. He sensibly suspended the duel until they were on land. Jones later stated in his own memoir, that Landais was "a man of the most unhappy temper," not only disrespecting his commander, but acted as he pleased as an independent chief officer, refusing to obey the signals of the commodore. In John Paul Jones. Memoirs of Rear-Admiral Paul Jones (New York: Da Capo Press, 1972) vol. 1, 163.

7. An entry in the logbook of the *Serapis* that Jones captured later. It chronicles another instance when Jones lost his temper and castigated another officer. Nathaniel Fanning dropped one of the ship's chronometers and this incited Jones's wrath. The captain kicked Fanning out of the cabin, across the main deck, and down the hatchway. The logbook account is in the handwriting of Beaumont Groube, Fanning's fellow American midshipman.

8. This would be an example of one of many raids designed to frighten and intimidate local English coastal populations.

9. Ordinary crewmen did not have uniforms that distinguished them as belonging to any particular navy.

10. Other references suggest that the request was for £50,000, but regardless it was a large sum to accrue on short notice.

11. A commonly told variation of this story reports that Jones then identified himself as the very privateer the town's people feared. The stunned and startled, the official then pled for his life. Amused, Jones released the terrified man unharmed and sent him off with the barrel of powder.

12. A sloop in North America was a single mastered ship with a bowsprit and no topmast. A sloop in the Royal Navy was a similar vessel, but could have a different designation depending upon the rank of the commanding officer. If he is a captain it might be rated as a ship, but if led by a commander it may be called a sloop.

13. Fanning, *Fanning's Narrative: The Memoirs of Nathaniel Fanning*, 31.

14. The courses are the lower most sails on the mast. They are raised during a battle for visibility and so as not get in the way of men that may have to fight on deck.

15. This is a white flag with a red cross across it and the union as its canton. It was also known at the time as a white squadron ensign.

16. This red flag was the first national flag of the English colonies. It was widely used on all British ships during the colonial period and Cornwallis surrendered at Yorktown under this flag.

17. Fanning consistently misspelled Captain Pearson's name as Parsons in his text. However, the correct name is used through this edited version.

Chapter 3

1. This was a fundamental violation of leadership. A commander must never leave his men in a vulnerable position to engage in battle.

2. To support his intended raids, Jones initially embarked with one hundred thirty-seven marines aboard *Bonhomme Richard* instead of the usual sixty to provide security and musketry support normally assigned to a warship of that size. These were not Continental marines, but rather members of France's Irish Regiment of Walsh-Serrant, whose watchwords *Semper et Ubique Fidelis*—Always and Everywhere Faithful) became the basis for the motto of the United States Marines. Colonel Antoine Félix Wuibert (Weibert) in charge of *Bonhomme Richard*'s principal battery, the 12-pound guns on the upper deck, which were to fire split shot into *Serapis*' rigging in order to disable it. The Irish marines were sent to the poop deck and fighting tops (the highest parts of the masts) to fire down upon the enemy ship. Jones referred to another French Colonel de Chamillard who commanded twenty soldiers on the poop deck. In John Paul Jones, Memoirs of Rear-Admiral Paul Jones (New York: Da Capo Press, 1972) vol. 1, 184.

3. Fanning, *Fanning's Narrative: The Memoirs of Nathaniel Fanning*, 36.

4. *Ibid.*, 36.

5. Samuel Stacy. Fanning's description of how the maneuver was accomplished is complex and difficult to follow, but not a crucial part of the story. It was a remarkable feat of seamanship accomplished while the ship was receiving fire with many of her seamen killed or injured.

6. The shrouds are pieces of standing rigging which hold the mast up from side to side. A vang is a rope or tackle that extends from a boom to a deck fitting of a vessel in order to keep the boom from riding up.

7. Fanning, *Fanning's Narrative: The Memoirs of Nathaniel Fanning*, 38.

8. *Ibid.*, 38, this meant that one should not carelessly close the doors to heaven at a critical time.

9. Fanning, *Fanning's Narrative: The Memoirs of Nathaniel Fanning*, 41.

10. *Ibid.*, 41.

11. A trepan was used to relieve the fluid buildup in his skull and he recovered.

12. This is the origin of the well-known Jones rejoinder, "We have not yet begun to fight." His exact words are unknown and in dispute, but regardless the sentiment is the same.

13. "After the battle Landais confided to one of the French colonels that his intention was to help *Serapis* sink the *Richard*, to capture and board the British frigate and emerge victor of the battle. Later he had the impudence to claim that his broadsides forced [the *Serapis*] to strike." Samuel Eliot Morison, *John Paul Jones: A Sailor's Biography* (Boston, MA: Little Brown, 1959), 235.

14. Other historical documents suggest that in spite of *Good Man Richard's* highly visible lanterns, *Alliance* closed once again to engage the two ships and Landais ordered another grapeshot broadside to be indiscriminately fired.

15. Later the sailor was identified as William Hamilton.

16. Matthew Mease of Philadelphia, but he has also been identified as from Massachusetts with a French Huguenot name of Mathurin.

17. Fanning, *Fanning's Narrative: The Memoirs of Nathaniel Fanning*, 44.

18. *Ibid.*, 44.

19. Although Richard Pearson eventually surrendered, he accomplished his mission of protecting a convoy of merchant ships that, with only one exception, escaped capture by John Paul Jones' squadron.

Chapter 4

1. Stanhope was said to be the son of a lord. After the battle, he was cited for his "bravery" onboard the *Serapis* and was later given command of a British frigate. This was an example of the fact that promotion was not necessarily due to merit but often to the exercise of bureaucratic connections.

2. Some references rate her as a 20-gun vessel.

3. Thomas Berry was the leader of this group of seven that successfully made the daring escape.

4. The *Serapis* had been commissioned only four months before the battle. The ship's hull completely sheathed in copper, if preserved she would be a valuable addition to the American fleet.

5. Jonathan Wells, one of the gunners on the *Good Man Richard*, met Andrew Jackson in Boston and told him that he reminded him of John Paul Jones. Wells said that Jones and Jackson at each given the British the wickedest licking they ever had. It was said that Jackson was greatly pleased with the old seaman's compliment.

6. Fanning makes no mention of the American ensign being on the *Bonhomme Richard's* flagstaff when she sank.

7. Many sailors were wounded from wood slinters that were the result of canon ball shattered hulls, bulwarks or bulkheads. These usually triggered infections and, with no antibiotics, they often were fatal.

8. *Den Helder* (The Helder) is a municipality in the Netherlands.

9. When the Americans reached the safety of Holland, arrangements were made to exchange the British prisoners for American prisoners of war. Upon returning home, the British Admiralty at first court-martialed, acquitted his of the charges and afterward honored the defeated Captain Pearson for his gallantry.

10. Captain Denis N. Cotteneau (also spelled Cottineau).

11. Since the British government did not recognize the rightfulness of the rebellion, officers of an illegitimate navy were considered little more than pirates. By the protocol of the day, they were deemed not worthy of the usual courtesies afforded to officers commissioned by an established sovereign nation. Also, Pearson had lost his ship and being defeated by this brigand was a trying humiliation.

Chapter 5

1. On New Year's Day in 1776, Dunmore gave orders to burn the waterfront buildings of Norfolk, Virginia when patriot troops fired on his ships. The fire spread and burned much of the city and with it any likelihood that Dunmore's loyalists could return to Virginia. Dunmore retreated to New York. Some ships of his fleet of refugees were south, mostly to Florida. When Dunmore realized he could not regain control in Virginia, he returned to Britain in July 1776, but continued to draw his salary as the royal colony's governor until 1783 when Britain recognized American independence.

2. Goodwin Sands is a 10-mile long

sandbank about 6 miles off Deal on the Kent coast of England.

3. It was a common practice to humiliate the American prisoners of war. The British assumed that by making the detainees feel inferior, if and when they were exchanged, the men would be less inclined to reenlist.

4. Jones was very focused on his own place in history, regardless of the danger to others under his command.

5. Fanning, *Fanning's Narrative: The Memoirs of Nathaniel Fanning*, 72.

6. All dispatches from Jones while he was in command of the *Bonhomme Richard* were directed to the President of Congress. The Congress had to be aware that this was now an American warship.

7. Fanning, *Fanning's Narrative: The Memoirs of Nathaniel Fanning*, 75.

8. *Ibid.*, 77.

9. The verdict of the court was that Pierre Landais was judged guilty of a breach of "the orders of the Congress" and of the Navy Board in coming away with the *Alliance* without Benjamin Franklin's permission. Because he had acted on the advice of Arthur Lee, this was considered a mitigating circumstance. Second, Landais was also found guilty on a second count of a breach of bringing private goods to be transported for his private benefit on the *Alliance*. Third, he was found guilty of a breach of the first and thirty-seventh articles of the Navy Rules by "not exerting his utmost abilities" in not punishing offenders aboard ship, and in not setting a proper example to his officers by the discharge of duty. Fourth, he was held guilty of a breach of the order of the Navy Board in not delivering up the ship *Alliance*, her cabin and cabin furniture upon direct orders. But the court took into consideration the fact that Landais had no money or credit when he landed in Boston and had no place to lodge except the ship and that he had suffered from a mutinous disposition in his passengers, officers and crew. He was sentenced "to be broke and rendered incapable of serving in the American navy for the future."

Chapter 6

1. L'Orient is in the French province known as *La province de Britagne*.

2. Likely Major General John Sullivan of New Hampshire.

3. Fanning, *Fanning's Narrative: The Memoirs of Nathaniel Fanning*, 83.

4. *Ibid.*, 85.

5. Each state printed and issued its own currency. The problems with them were many-fold. They were easily counterfeited, may not be accepted in other states, and because of the cost of the Revolutionary War and rampant inflation, the currency's value depreciated at a variable and often a rapid rate.

6. John Paul was actually born on 6 July 1747 at Arbigland, Scotland, in the parish of Kirkbean, in the county of Kirkcudbright. His father, John Paul senior, was a gardener, a working-class common laborer. He was however the chief gardener of the estate of the wealthy landowner William Craik. Young John Paul's formal education ended in the parish school when he turned twelve where few children of the working class went much further. His home, on the north shore Solway Firth exposed Paul to a seafaring life at the nearby port of Carsethorn. One of the most common cargoes off-loaded from the holds at the port was American tobacco and Paul had the opportunity to converse with mariners from the colonies who were volubly discontented with the Crown. Jones likely sympathized with the growing anti-British sentiment uttered by the Americans because the Scots had similar feelings after the British brutally defeated them at Culloden in 1746.

During the summer of 1759, a merchant ship owner named James Younger signed on the twelve-year-old Paul as an apprentice seaman on the eighty-foot merchantman *Friendship* under the command of Robert Benson.

7. Modesty was not a prominent personality trait of Jones. Because he had served as years as a British merchant captain, he considered himself among the most qualified of the first group of American naval officers. Unhappily he found himself as a lieutenant under two men whom he would later disparage. Esek Hopkins, the commodore of the fleet, and Dudley Saltonstall, captain of the *Alfred* to which Jones was assigned. Native-born Yankees and experienced mariners, both had gained rank through political connections. He particularly developed a dislike for the well-bred Saltonstall who had

the reputation of being a highly condescending officer, a character flaw that Jones found offensive, but ironically a flaw of which he himself became accused of later in life.

8. Fanning, *Fanning's Narrative: The Memoirs of Nathaniel Fanning*, 97.

9. An alternate version relates a different story. The *Ranger* sailed into the harbor. When it came close to the *Drake* at anchor, a small boat was lowered from the *Drake* to reconnoiter the unidentified vessel. Jones masked his guns, hid the crew below to give the *Ranger* the appearance of a harmless merchantman. The officer in command of the small boat was deceived and, when invited on board the *Ranger*, he and his crew was taken prisoner. The Americans then ceased their *ruse de guerre* and prepared for battle. Now that the American's intent was evident, the *Drake* weighed anchor and came out to engage the *Ranger* strangely attended by several yachts and pleasure boats that hoped to watch the impeding mêlée.

10. According to official records, the death toll on the *Drake* was four killed, nineteen wounded and 133 taken prisoner. The *Ranger* listed one officer and two crewmen killed and five wounded.

11. Fanning, *Fanning's Narrative: The Memoirs of Nathaniel Fanning*, 101.

12. This personal reference likely referred to evidence that Jones's father may have been employed as the Count of Selkirk's gardener at one time, but the historical indicates that he worked for William Craik of Arbigland.

13. Fanning, *Fanning's Narrative: The Memoirs of Nathaniel Fanning*, 101.

14. Robinson will reappear briefly as an important figure very much later in this memoir.

15. Although it was said that Jones died in poverty, he had property in the amount of about $30,000 in the currency of the day plus ownership of some land.

16. Richard Dale was actually born in the town of Portsmouth in Norfolk County, Virginia. Only the French government that had financed Jones's privateer ventures recognized the rank of first lieutenant that John Paul Jones bestowed upon Dale. However, in recognition for his extraordinary services, the American Continental Congress now officially recognized his rank as well, and made him a first lieutenant in the Continental Navy. Dale spent many years in the service and was appointed as Commodore of the American Squadron in the Mediterranean in 1810.

Chapter 7

1. Fanning, *Fanning's Narrative: The Memoirs of Nathaniel Fanning*, 112.

2. A lugger is class of boat commonly used for fishing, particularly in France, England and Scotland. It is a small sailing vessel with lug sails set on two or more masts and occasionally lug topsails.

3. The Parliament of Great Britain banned payment of ransom in 1782, although this was repealed in 1864. It is not clear how a captain could prevent this if a privateer captured him and his ship.

4. The *Tournois* were French coins struck in Tours, but not as valuable as those struck in Paris as *livre*, but valued at about 19½ cents.

5. A galliot has a single mast. It is a common Dutch cargo boat or fishing vessel that can be either rowed or sailed.

6. The Austrian Netherlands (or *Belgium Austriacum*) was not an important Austrian possession and they had little interest in the region. The fortresses along the border known as the Barrier Fortresses were garrisoned with Dutch troops. The area had been given to Austria largely at British and Dutch insistence because these powers feared potential French domination of the region.

7. This was a time of war between many nations and there were rules to enforce neutrality in Ostend. Challenges between belligerents visiting the port were not uncommon, therefore no secondary vessel was allowed to depart the port until twenty-four hours after the first sailed out of the harbor that presented a challenge in international waters. The vessels, however, were ships of nations at war with each other and both warships were armed.

8. The Downs is a roadstead, a sheltered area from the sometimes-violent sea, in the English Channel off the east coast of Kent in southern England.

Chapter 8

1. Fanning, being an American, was still technically a British citizen because the

Yankees were considered rebellious Englishmen.

2. The mean ebb and flow of the Thames at that point is about twenty-two feet.

3. This reference was to Edmund Fanning, a prominent Tory and colonel in the Kings' American Regiment. After the Revolutionary War he moved to Nova Scotia and became a general.

4. This ceremonial sword used in the coronation ceremony end is blunt and squared on its point or end to symbolize mercy.

5. This was likely St. Margaret's Hope known today as Hope.

6. A poignant example is the burning of Falmouth, Maine [present day Portland] by a British naval lieutenant. Louis Arthur Norton, "Henry Mowat, Miscreant of the Maine Coast." *Maine History*, vol. 43, #1, 2007, 1–20.

7. Fanning, *Fanning's Narrative: The Memoirs of Nathaniel Fanning*, 166.

8. The convention of the day was that the captain of each French privateer was entitled to a crown for each English prisoner. That was to be paid even if they were released provide that there was proof of capture. This sum was to be paid by the French government. Another provision of this pact was that the English government was then obligated to release an equal number of French prisoners.

9. A gaff is a spar used to the heads of fore and aft sails. The peak is the upper corner of sails extended by a gaff. A throat is the hollow end of a gaff next to the mast or the opposite end of a peak.

10. Fanning, *Fanning's Narrative: The Memoirs of Nathaniel Fanning*, 168.

11. I learned the name of the ship from conversing with the vessel's second lieutenant long after this incident when we both happened to be in Ostend. We related several incidents that happened during the chase from his point of view and mine. I also learned that the captain intended to hang the captain of the privateer from the yardarm if they had succeeded in capturing us.

12. A Broach is when the boat heels excessively to one side or, in some cases, capsizes. The boat falls on a side with its bow usually driving into the direction of the wind. The mast tips sideways forcing its sails to sweep the water's surface or submerge.

13. The ringtail is a narrow stud sail set after a gaff sail, especially a spanker and extending beyond the gaff and boom. A water sail is a sail hung below the boom on gaff-rigged boats for extra downwind performance.

14. Fanning, *Fanning's Narrative: The Memoirs of Nathaniel Fanning*, 181. This was a sort of reference to a Yankee log book of a similar event that stated "catched a dolphin and lost it."

15. The nature of Fanning's wounds is not clear. In his text he the states that, "the bones having been a good deal shattered." This implies that it likely was a comminuted fracture, but it is not clear whether it is of the tibia or femur. He also said that it was accompanied by a great loss of blood that ultimately caused him to lose consciousness. It is possible the femoral artery or one or more of its related peripheral vessels were also compromised. He complained of the accompanying pain and the common effective relief was from laudanum, an alcoholic solution that contained morphine derived from opium. He also had a splinter wound. These were notorious for causing infections and this was before antibiotics were available.

Chapter 9

1. It should be remembered that when Fanning was in command of the *Eclipse*, he assumed that name and identified his cutter as *Surprise* that became a successful ruse.

2. In 1774, *Rose*, under the command of Sir James Wallace was sent to Rhode Island to terminate the rampant smuggling that had made Newport the fourth wealthiest city in America. The *Rose* was much larger than any American vessel of the time and Wallace, an effective commander, brought smuggling almost to a standstill severely affecting Newport's economy.

3. Although this vessel was rated as a ninety-gun ship, she actually mounted ninety-eight brass cannon. Those on her lower gun-deck were forty-two pounders French weight or fifty-eight pounders by English weight.

4. It is unclear what the brand of the letter R meant in the French legal system at the time.

5. The *Maréchausseé* are a provost marshal's guard, roughly analogous to the military police.

Chapter 10

1. Jack Ketch (also known as John Ketch, Jack Catch, or simply Ketch) died in November 1686. He was an English executioner who became notorious for his barbaric inefficiency. For nearly two centuries after his death his nickname was popularly applied to all of England's executioners. Ketch is believed to have received his appointment as public hangman in 1663. He is reported to have executed Lord William Russell (1683) in a brutal and inept manner, and in 1685 he took eight or more strokes of the axe to behead James Scott, duke of Monmouth.

2. This refers to *lèse majesté*, the crime of offending the monarch.

3. Franklin recently had been the brunt of satirist William Cobbett (whose pseudonym was Peter Porcupine) giving the amateur scientist the nickname "Old Lightning Rod" and linking him with the first man Gulliver (of Gulliver's Travels) encounters during his voyage to Laputa.

4. Literally little masters, but also known as coxcombs, vain conceited men, dandies or fops.

5. The dauphin is the eldest son of a king and presumably the crown prince.

Chapter 11

1. Michel Guillaume Jean de Crèvecœur. Letters from an American Farmer. (London, UK: Printed for Thomas Davies, Covent-Garden and Lockyer Davis, in Holborn, 1783).

2. Michel Guillaume Jean de Crèvecœur (December 31, 1735–November 12, 1813), was born in Caen, Normandy, France, to the Comte and Comtesse de Crèvecœur and became naturalized in New York as John Hector St. John a well-known French-American writer.

3. It is not clear what Fanning was referring to. Perhaps it was a transport ship or a small fleet of vessels that may have been called the Western Board.

Postscript

1. Steve R. Dunn. Bayly's War. The Battle for the Western Approaches in the First World War. (Barnsley, South Yorkshire: UK, Sea forth Publishing, 2018), 192–194.

Bibliography

Barnes, John S., edited and annotated. *Fannning's Narrative being the Memoirs of Nathaniel Fanning an Officer of the Revolutionary Navy 1778-1783*, New York, NY: De Vinne Press, 1912.
Clark, William Bell, et al., eds. *Naval Documents of the American Revolution*. Washington, D.C.: Naval History and Heritage Command, 19674.
Cohen, Sheldon. *Thomas Wren and Forton Prison*, Pennsylvania Magazine of History and Biography, vol. 103, #3, July 1979.
de Crèvecœur, Jean Michel Guillaume. *Letters from an American Farmer*. London, UK: Printed for Thomas Davies, Covent-Garden and Lockyer Davis, Holborn, 1783.
Dunn, Steve R. *Bayly's War. The Battle for the Western Approaches in the First World War*. Barnsley, South Yorkshire, UK: Seaforth Publishing, 2018.
Fanning, Nathaniel. *Fanning's Narrative: The Memoirs of Nathaniel Fanning 1778-1783*. Bedford, MA: Applewood Books, 1913.
Fanning, Nathaniel. *Fanning's Narrative: The Memoirs of Nathaniel Fanning an Officer of the American Navy 1778-1783*. New York: reprinted by William Abbatt, 1913, originally printed 1806 as *Narrative of the Adventures of an American Navy Officer who served during part of the American Revolution under the Command of Captain John Paul Jones, esq*.
Franklin, Benjamin. "Notes of Rufus King in the Federal Convention of 1787." Avalon Project, Yale Law School, New Haven, CT: 7 August 1787.
Frost, John. *The Book of the Navy Comprising a General History of the American Marine; and Particular Accounts of all the Celebrated Naval Battles from the Declaration of Independence to the Present Time*. New York, NY: D. Appleton and Company, 1842.
Hoehling, A.A. *The Great War at Sea: A History of Naval Action 1914-1918*. New York, NY: Thomas Y. Crowell Company, 1965.
Jones, John Paul. *Memoirs of Rear-Admiral Paul Jones*. New York, NY: Da Capo Press, 1972.
Jones, John Paul. *The Log of the Bon Homme Richard* (with an introduction by Louis F. Middleton). The Marine Historical Association, Mystic, CT,1936.
Morison, Samuel Eliot. *John Paul Jones, A Sailor's Biography*. Boston, MA: Little Brown, 1959.
Norton, Louis Arthur Norton, "Henry Mowat, Miscreant of the Maine Coast." *Maine History*, vol. 43, #1, 2007.
Norton, Louis Arthur. "America's Unwitting Pirate: The Adventures and Misfortunes of a Continental Navy Captain." *Coriolis*, vol. 6, #1, 2016.
Norton, Louis Arthur. "Dudley Saltonstall and the Penobscot Expedition, 1779." *Connecticut History*, March 2003, Vol. 42, #1, 2003.
Swift, Jonathan, *Travels into Several Remote Nations of the World. In Four Parts. By Lemuel Gulliver, First a Surgeon, and then a Captain of Several Ships*, Bejamin Motte, London: UK, 1726.
R. W. Woolworth Library, *Fanning Family papers*. Stonington Historical Society, Stonington, CT.

Index

Alliance 5, 19, 21, 23, 24, 31, 35–37, 39, 41, 43, 48–50, 55, 56, 58, 68, 75, 78, 151
American privateer 7; *see also* Fanning, Nathaniel
Amsterdam 45
Amsterdam 46–47, 75
Andromeda 6–9, 11
Angelica 7, 8, 9
Anthon, Nicholas 79–82, 85–88, 90, 94, 95
Antoinette, Marie 59
Ariel 5–6, 62–65, 68, 78
Arnold, Benedict 4
Aurora 86–87
Austrian Netherlands 95, 139

Belle Poule 132–133
Bonhomme Richard 1, 6, 18, 40–42, 52, 74–76, 78
Bordeaux 4
Boston, MA 104
Brest 4, 83, 85, 89
Bristol 82, 86, 114, 117
Brittany 90
Buchan Ness 110
Byrne, Henry 7, 8, 11

Caen 90, 92, 93
Calais 94, 131
Canterbury 101 102
Cape Finisterre 53, 54
Cerf 19
character analyses: 68–78; *see also* Dale, Richard, Jones, John Paul; Pearson, Richard
Charleston, SC 150, 155
Chaumont, Monsieur 56 57
Cherbourg 96–98
Connecticut River 131
Continental Navy 97; midshipmen 18–76
Conyngham, Gustavus 4

Cork 81, 86, 114, 117
Cottineau, Denis, 75
Countess of Scarborough 36, 41, 47, 48
Courier de l'Europe 6
Couronne 85–86
Crévecoeur, J. Hector St. John 151

Dale, Richard 1, 26, 32, 34, 42, 78
D'Artois, Count 84, 147
Deal 131
de Castries, Marquis 126
de Guichen, Count 79, 80–81, 86, 133–135, 146
de Lafayette, Marquis 143
Deptford 101
de Segur, Marquis 136
Dieppe 129
Dillon, Count 62, 63
Dinan 90
Dolphin 129
Dover 15, 94, 96, 99, 127, 130–131, 139
Downs 127
Drake 70, 71
Dungarvan 85, 114
Dunkirk 23, 90, 94–95, 99–100, 109, 127, 131, 135–139, 141, 148, 150
Dyon, John 110, 130

Eclipse 94, 100, 109, 112–113, 117, 119, 136–137
Edinburgh 22
England during the Revolutionary War 100–109

Fanning, Edmund 6
Fanning, Elizabeth Smith 6
Fanning, Gilbert 6
Fanning, Livinia 6
Fanning, Nathaniel 1, 5
Firth of Forth 22
Flamborough Head 26, 28, 44

169

Index

Forton Prison 12, 17; see also Hastley, David; Old crab; Wren, Thomas
Fox, Charles James 109
Franklin, Benjamin 19, 45, 143, 147
French naval officer 135–137; see also de Guichen, Count
French privateer 78–124; see also Anthon, Nicholas
French slaves 83–85

General Mifflin 19
George III 107, 132
Glasgow 114
Good Man Richard 18, 19, 21, 24–26, 28–31, 35–39, 42, 44, 49–57, 63–64, 68
Gosport 14, 16

Hague, Charles 100, 103–105, 107
Hague, Edmond 100, 103–105, 107
hanging, methods of 101–102, 140–141
Hastley, David 14
Havre de Grace 93–94
Hazel Hospital 11–12
Henry IV 150
highway robbery 102–103
Holland 44–54
Honfleur 93
Hope Bay 110
Hopkins, Esek 4
Hull 69

Invincible 133, 135
Isle de Bas 90
Isle of Wight 50

"Jack Ketch" 140
"Jack the painter" 11, 12
Jersey 6, 101
Jones, John Paul 1, 18, 26–30, 32, 34, 37–38, 40–55, 58, 60, 65–66, 70, 71, 74–78
Jupiter 118, 120

Keith, Earl of 115
Keppel, Lord 105
kidnapping 115–116

Landais, Pierre 19, 20, 45, 49, 56, 57, 59; see also *Alliance*
Land's End 83
Lane, Lieutenant 129
Leith 21, 23, 35
Lille 141
Liverpool 114
London 15, 100, 104, 105, 109, 144–145
Long Island Sound 131
Lord Howe 123

Louis XIV 147
Louis XV 144–145
Louis XVI 146
Lovely Lass 114

Manley, John 97, 138
Mansfield, Lord 105
Marblehead, MA 97
Maréchaussée 136, 142–143
Maria 128
Mill Prison 98
Monsieur 19
moonlight battle 25–35; see also *Alliance*; Dale, Richard; *Good Man Richard*; Jones, John Paul; Landais, Pierre; Pearson, Richard; *Serapis*
Morlaix 79–80, 82, 90, 98, 114, 118, 147

Nantucket Island, MA 152
Nates 16, 17, 98
New London, CT 131
New York, NY 101, 103, 152
Newport, RI 130, 137
Normandy 90, 96

Old crab 13, 14
L'Orient 4, 17, 18, 21, 54, 55–57, 60–61, 65, 68, 72, 74, 75, 114, 136, 147–148
Orkney Islands 21, 110, 112
Ostend 15, 95, 96, 100, 109, 141

Pallas 19, 21, 24, 35, 36, 39, 41, 45, 47
Paris 59, 60, 75, 76, 141, 144–145, 147
Passy 143
Pearson, Richard 1, 24, 26, 28, 31–32, 34, 37–38, 40–42, 45, 75, 77
Penmark 61
Philadelphia, PA 74
Phips, Captain 132, 134
Plymouth 98, 106, 114, 127
Portsmouth 8, 15, 16
pre-revolutionary France 148–151
Princess Amelia 11

Quebec 110

Ranger 19, 70, 71, 72, 127, 129, 131–132
Robinson, Mr. 75, 151
Roman Catholic faith 76, 150
Romney 22
Rose 111, 130
Roxbury 104

Saint Kilda 113
Saint Kitts 98
Salem, MA 7

Saltonstall, Dudley 4
Sandy Hook, NY 152
Scarborough 23, 110
Seine River 93
Selkirk 68
Serapis 1, 6, 24–30, 32, 35–45, 47, 49, 63, 65, 68, 74–75
Shelburne, Lord 105
Slime Head 113
Speedwell 128
Spithead 53, 134
Staten Island, NY 152
Stormont, Lord 105
Strombolo 6
Sullivan, Lieutenant 62, 64, 75
Surprise 110, 118–119, 130

Texel, 44, 45, 49, 51, 54
Thames River 101, 108, 139
Thatcher, Mr. 151
Torbay 118

Tower of London 105–106

United States 61, 69, 92, 104, 109, 136, 147, 149
Ushant 82, 90

Vengeance 19, 21, 24, 29, 35–36, 39
Vergennes, Count 147
Versailles 143

Wales, Prince of 108
Wallace, James 111
Washington, George 74, 103, 152
Waterford 70
Westminster Abbey 107–108
Wickes, Lambert 4
Williams, Jonathan 98
wounded 124–125; *see also Eclipse*
Wren, Thomas 15

Yankee Doodle 16

www.ingramcontent.com/pod-product-compliance
Lightning Source LLC
Chambersburg PA
CBHW032047300426
44117CB00009B/1226